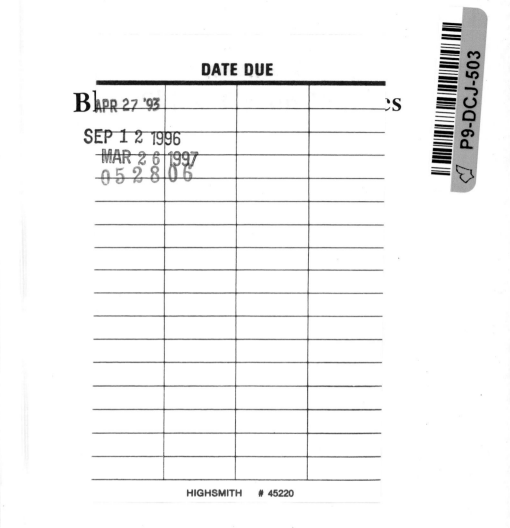

Blue Skies, Green Politics
The Clean Air Act of 1990

Gary C. Bryner
Brigham Young University

CQ
PRESS

A Division of Congressional Quarterly Inc.
Washington, D.C.

Printed in the United States of America

Cover design by Paula Anderson

Library of Congress Cataloging-in-Publication Data

Bryner, Gary C., 1951-
    Blue skies, green politics : the Clean Air Act of 1990 / Gary C. Bryner.
      p.   cm.
    Includes index.
    ISBN 0-87187-668-X
    1. Air--Pollution--Law and legislation--United States. 2. Environmental policy--United States. I. Title.
KF3812.Z9B78   1992
344.73'046342--dc20
[347.30446342]
                                    92-34505
                                        CIP

To Nicholas Stevens Bryner,
future scientist

Contents

Tables and Figures

Tables

Figures

Preface

⌊The passage of the Clean Air Act Amendments of 1990 was an impressive political achievement: it produced the comprehensive revision (after nearly a decade of deadlock) of one of the most important statutes ever enacted by Congress. It also serves as proof that divided government can work—that a legislative branch under the control of one political party can cooperate with an executive branch controlled by another party to produce major legislation.⌉

In *Blue Skies, Green Politics*, I attempt to give readers an opportunity to examine what Congress and the executive branch were trying to do in revising the Clean Air Act and to provide a framework that enables them to assess for themselves how well the two branches did their work. I hope that the information presented will encourage discussion about how to achieve cleaner air and how to ensure the effectiveness of public policies whose aim is to improve environmental quality. I encourage readers to seek their own answers to the questions posed here; my proposals are offered to stimulate their thinking.

One focus of this book is on the process of policy making. Passage of the 1990 amendments to the Clean Air Act provides a useful case study of how public policies are formulated. The central questions examined include how the issue of clean air came to be put on the national policy agenda; how the policy subsequently evolved; and how successfully Congress and the executive branch dealt with the political conflicts, policy disputes, and institutional limitations that caused the deadlock. Members of Congress not only had to confront regionally divisive issues but also had to sort out the competing demands of powerful interest groups, grapple with complicated scientific and technical issues, and balance public concerns about environmental quality and economic growth.

A second focus of the book is on the outcomes of the policy process. Here the questions examined are to what extent the goals of the statute are likely to be achieved and to what extent Congress provided the policy tools and incentives necessary to achieve them. This assessment also considers whether the goals themselves are appropriate and whether they reflect an adequate understanding of the nature of air pollution and of the political, economic, and legal contexts in which regulation takes place. The ultimate public policy questions are will the goal of cleaner air be realized under this new statutory framework and, if so, at what price. Much has been written about environmental law in general, and the Clean Air Act of 1970 and the 1977 amendments in particular. A review of some of these studies provides an opportunity to analyze whether Congress satisfied the criticisms of its earlier statutory handiwork in producing an improved model of clean air legislation in 1990.

A third focus of the book is on subsequent actions to implement the law. As is true of most major laws enacted by Congress, passage of the law is only the first chapter in the policy-making process. The debate then shifts to another forum, the federal and state regulatory agencies that are responsible for translating legislative mandates into effective administrative programs. In so doing, they will review most of the policy choices made by Congress and the executive branch. Given the complexity of the causes of air pollution, and the wide range of activities that must be regulated in order to control it, Congress will likely have to revisit the 1990 Clean Air Act, and the actions taken to implement it, sometime in the future. Changes in industrial technologies, the development of new pollution control capabilities, population growth and increases in pollution-causing transportation, conclusions drawn from new research on the health effects of air pollution, and changes in the global economy will extinguish any belief that Congress has finished its work.

Congress and the executive branch had been bitterly divided on the subject of environmental regulation during most of the 1980s. The law was made possible, in part, by an extraordinary set of negotiations between a group of senators and representatives of the executive branch in early 1990, when the bill had become stalled in the Senate. The new Clean Air Act raises, but clearly does not settle, a number of questions that are central to formulating regulatory policy and structuring administrative power, such as how much discretion should be given to agencies implementing regulatory statutes and how detailed and prescriptive statutes should be. Given the past ten years of conflict between Congress and the Environmental Protection Agency over how environmental laws are to be implemented, many members of Congress distrust executive branch officials and are seeking new ways to ensure that the goals of the laws they enact are more fully realized. Their experience with the new law illustrates the difficulties of trying to make certain that agencies faithfully adhere to congressional intent, yet are allowed sufficient flexibility to administer the law in an effective manner.

The Clean Air Act also raises fundamental questions about how responsibility for implementing regulatory legislation should be divided between the states and the federal government. Many people have argued that states should be given flexibility in deciding how to balance the improvement of environmental quality and the regulation of industrial, commercial, and individual activities. Since pollution levels are much higher in some areas, different standards and approaches may be required, depending on the seriousness of the problems they face. Others have argued that standards should apply uniformly throughout the United States; otherwise, some states might relax standards in an attempt to attract industries from other states.

Because the Clean Air Act of 1990, like other complex statutes, relies on a variety of policy instruments, it is also a useful vehicle for assessing the strengths and weaknesses of traditional approaches to regulation as well as alternative policy mechanisms, including the use of marketlike incentives. One of the most important provisions in the new law creates a marketlike system for reducing emissions of the pollutants responsible for acid rain. The 1990 Act is a complex combination of the traditional regulatory approach that imposes technology-based limits on emissions as well as market-based innovations that will help shape the future of environmental law.

The story of the passage of the Clean Air Act Amendments of 1990, including an explanation of what Congress and the Bush administration were trying to do in producing some 400 pages of statutory language, requires the reader to confront a mass of detailed, technical information. But the technicalities cannot be avoided if one is to grasp the essential elements of the Clean Air Act, to get a sense of how Congress deals with complicated policy issues, and to assess the response of Congress and the executive branch to the problem of air pollution.

The underlying goal of the Clean Air Act is to ensure that air pollution does not continue to harm public health. Air pollution causes the premature death of thousands of people each year and requires the hospitalization and medical treatment of many more. It indirectly contributes to poor health by weakening the human immune system, thus increasing susceptibility to disease. Perhaps most significantly, it is a risk that most people expose themselves to involuntarily. The economic benefits of some pollution-producing activities, such as industrial processes, are received largely by corporate owners and workers, whereas the adverse health effects are experienced by the entire community. Children and the elderly are especially susceptible to the hazards of air pollution and often lack the resources to seek community support to protect their interests. Viewed from this perspective, reducing air pollution becomes a moral imperative.

Clean air is also compatible with other policy goals such as a strong economy. Because environmental quality affects the health of workers and consumers, its improvement is a prerequisite for efficient economic activity. Moreover, since pollution from industrial activity is waste, reducing it can reduce the costs of production. Pollution from energy sources can be reduced in ways that also conserve those sources and thus save money. Pollution reduction is often achieved by modernization and quality control improvements that also increase industrial competitiveness. The problem is that the costs of instituting cleaner processes and technologies are immediate and often narrowly focused, at least initially, whereas the benefits are frequently delayed and dispersed geographically. Those who profit from the status quo will continue to lead the fight against change; they have considerable resources and incentives to block new approaches and inhibit new research. Nevertheless, increasingly stringent environmental regulations are inevitable. Other countries, such as Germany and Japan, have concluded that improving environmental quality represents great economic opportunities. The United States may no longer be the leader in environmental regulation because of industry resistance to change and government timidity in encouraging these changes.

Although it is difficult to dispute the argument that the benefits of the Clean Air Act (or any other policy initiative) should exceed the costs of complying with them, it is also difficult to assess the Clean Air Act from that perspective alone. It is not clear, for example, how many lives will be saved by improving air quality by specific increments, since a host of other factors are involved, from personal behavior to weather patterns. We do not know how to quantify the benefits of cancer cases prevented and respiratory attacks avoided. Similarly, the costs of compliance are difficult to assess, since industrial practices are dynamic; changes in production methods, reduced use of materials, and modernization of equipment may all ultimately reduce costs. Given the moral implications of imposing the risks of pollution on involuntary victims, however, the uncertainties about costs and benefits cannot justify inaction. We buy insurance against the possibility of bad things happening, and pollution controls are simply another form of insurance against unknown hazards. That reasoning does not eliminate the possibility of weighing costs and benefits, but allows them to be viewed more realistically. Cost-benefit analysis might help us allocate resources among competing public concerns. If we spent less money on air pollution controls, we could spend more money on safer highways or research to find more efficient drugs. But at present we have no mechanism for making such comprehensive risk comparisons; therefore, most policies cannot simply be assessed and analyzed on the basis of their distribution of costs and benefits.

The expectations created by the language of the Clean Air Act greatly exceed the resources provided to implement it, and over time, this inconsistency is likely to contribute to our cynicism about government. The EPA might not meet its deadlines for issuing regulations; states might not fully implement the programs assigned them; the investments necessary to achieve compliance will be greater than what businesses believe they can afford to spend; and we will probably not reach our air quality goals. Advocates of clean air may argue that we should aim high, so that if we fall short, we have nevertheless made considerable progress. That argument may make sense solely from the perspective of improving environmental quality. But the viability of democratic government and the capacity of the policy-making process must also be considered; the Clean Air Act continues a tradition of detailed statutes that seek to force the executive branch to take actions it might not otherwise take. Although the Clean Air Act proves that divided government can work, the tension and disagreement between Congress and the president concerning implementation of the law that surfaced soon after its passage is an ominous sign.

Blue Skies, Green Politics begins with a discussion of environmental problems in general and some of the challenges they pose for the policy-making process; Chapter 1 also presents a model of the policy-making process. Chapter 2 explores different ways in which the problem of air pollution can be defined and understood. Chapter 3 traces the evolution of clean air policy in Congress and the executive branch and provides a detailed account of the passage of the 1990 law. Chapter 4 examines some of the important issues central to the passage of the 1990 law, which have implications for the future of environmental law and regulation in the United States. The final chapter analyzes the prospects for successful implementation of the Clean Air Act Amendments and for achieving the goal of clean air.

Acknowledgments

I owe an enormous debt to many people who contributed to this book in many ways. I benefited greatly from the opportunity to interview a number of congressional staff members, executive branch officials, and representatives of environmental organizations and industry groups. Those interviews were largely held off the record and therefore have not been acknowledged. But they were absolutely indispensable, and I greatly appreciate the time these individuals took to answer questions and explain events. They include Richard Ayres, Greg Barnett, Bill Becker, John Blodgett, Rob Brenner, David Cantour, Jeff Clark, Trent Clark, Jack Clough, Len Coburn, Mira Courpas, Kathy Cudlipp, Terry Davies, David Doninger, Blake Early, Rick Erdheim, Bill Fay, Eddie Flaherty, Dirk Forrester, Bob Friedman, David Gardiner, Theresa Gorman, Bob Grady, Melanie Griffin, Heidi Halek, David Hawkins, Ed Heidig, Kate Kimball, Jessica Laverty, Skip Luken, Chris Neme, Jimmy Powell, Bill Roberts, William Rosenberg, Philip Schiliro, Zoe Schneidner, Russ Shay, Deborah Sheiman, Mike Shields, Dan Weiss, Greg Whetstone, Ron White, and Terry Yosie.

The Brookings Institution provided office space and support when I was studying the Clean Air Act in 1990 and 1991; I especially appreciate the help of Tom Mann and the staff members at Brookings during my stay there.

I attended a number of conferences and lectures and, in particular, benefited greatly from the opportunity to attend the Inside EPA Clean Air Conferences in 1990 and 1991, as well as the Clean Air Strategy Session organized by the Natural Resources Defense Council and the Natural Resources Council of Maine. Earlier versions of some chapters of this book were presented as papers at meetings of the American Political Science Association, the Association for Policy Analysis and Management, and the Association for Canadian Studies in the United States. I am most grateful to those who offered comments and criticisms or discussed with me their views on the Clean Air Act, particularly Bob Katzmann, Mike Kraft, Paul Light, Ted Lowi, Norm Vig, Kathy Wagner, Aaron Wildavsky, and Ned Woodhouse.

The Canadian Government Faculty Research Program; the College of

Family, Home, and Social Sciences; and the Political Science Department at Brigham Young University provided resources to help finance the research. I learned much about air pollution from members of the Utah County Clean Air Coalition, officials from Region 8 of the EPA, the Division of Environmental Quality of the State of Utah, and, in particular, from the research of C. Arden Pope III and Samuel Rushforth. Barry Balleck, John Dunn, Rex Facer, Paul Kube, David Passey, and Jon Tasso, students at Brigham Young, provided outstanding research help. Students in my public policy classes at the university helped me develop many of the ideas expressed here through their thoughtful questions about and discussions of environmental policy. Lisa Miller's word-processing skill was indispensable to the project. Jane Stevens Bryner helped in innumerable ways throughout this project.

Criticisms and suggestions by the reviewers whose comments were arranged by CQ Press greatly improved the manuscript, and I appreciate their candid assessments. The editors at Congressional Quarterly, Brenda Carter, Chris Karlsten, and Shana Wagger, have marvelously balanced helpful criticism of and supportive interest in the project. Their efforts and the painstaking editing of Lydia Jeanne Duncan have improved immensely what I first submitted to them.

Finally, I have learned a great deal from a wide range of scholars who have written about American politics and public policy, environmental regulation in general, and air pollution in particular. I have acknowledged their outstanding work in the endnotes, but those references do not adequately express my indebtedness to them and to their knowledge, creativity, and skill.

1 Challenges in Environmental Policy Making

Protecting the environment has become a major policy concern of government at all levels. Public opinion polls and other measures of public sentiment show strong support for more aggressive laws and regulations to attempt to solve pollution problems and to protect natural resources. According to recent polls, more than 70 percent of Americans believe that "protecting the environment is *so* important that requirements and standards cannot be too high, and continuing environmental improvements must be made *regardless* of cost" (italics in original).[1] Political candidates have used environmental issues as a springboard to electoral success. Environmentalism played a significant role in the 1988 presidential election as well as in a number of other political races.

Environmental protection has also become a major public health issue. Toxic waste dumps that contaminate drinking water, the release of hazardous chemicals into the air and water, damage to the stratospheric ozone layer that filters out harmful ultraviolet radiation, and a host of other problems threaten human health and natural resources. Air pollution is one of the most serious environmental problems in the United States and throughout the world. According to the Environmental Protection Agency's 1990 report of urban air quality trends, more than 100 million Americans live in areas where pollution exceeds federal air quality standards. According to one study, some forms of air pollution alone are responsible for more than 50,000 to 60,000 premature deaths in this country every year.[2]

The Clean Air Act[3] is one of the most important environmental laws ever enacted in the United States for it is the primary legislative means of addressing one of the nation's most serious environmental problems. The flagship of some two dozen environmental laws, it has raised widespread expectations for a remedy to the problem of air pollution. The act also has major economic consequences for virtually every sector of the economy. Given its importance, the Clean Air Act can improve our understanding of the policy-making process and shed light on the prospects for improving policy-making capabilities in environmental and other areas. This chapter examines some of the challenges confronting policy makers attempting to solve environmental problems.

Overview of Environmental Policy Making

Environmental regulation poses a number of particularly difficult challenges to policy makers. There is considerable uncertainty surrounding the causes and consequences of pollution; furthermore, long lead times are frequently required before the adverse health effects and other consequences of pollution are discovered. Policy making must therefore include learning from experience and making adjustments, which can be particularly risky because the effects of some environmental hazards are largely irreversible, in terms of loss of human life or ecological changes.

There is little agreement concerning how much needs to be known about the health and environmental effects of pollutants and how much risk should be accepted before regulatory action is taken. A central issue is how risks should be calculated. Some argue that intervention should ensure that all persons are protected, including those most susceptible to the effects of pollution; others insist that the risk posed to the community in general should be the basis of regulatory action. A second issue is how reduction of environmental risks should be balanced with other values such as individual and corporate freedom.

The distribution of the consequences of technological advances is another issue facing policy makers in a democracy. Many of the adverse environmental consequences of industrial activity will be felt by future generations, whereas the benefits are largely confined to the current generation. It is not clear how their interests, and specifically those of subgroups of the population that have limited economic and political resources, can be protected in a political system dominated by well-financed interest groups.

Environmental policy makers must consider both environmental and economic goals and concerns. The question they attempt to answer has often been posed in stark terms of whether priority should be given to the protection of human health and ecological systems, or to economic growth and competitiveness. Environmentalists argue that the benefits promised by regulation outweigh projected costs, that protection of human health must be provided regardless of cost, and that benefits are so difficult to estimate that any comparison of costs and benefits is unfair. Opponents are quick to argue that environmental regulations restrict the global competitiveness of U.S. industry and will simply drive jobs overseas.

Cost-benefit analysis has been widely heralded as the way to balance environmental protection and economic growth. But there is usually little agreement about what costs and benefits to include in the calculations. Should costs be limited to pollution control equipment, for example, or should they include the impact on individuals who lose their jobs when industries cannot afford to meet regulatory requirements? The benefits in terms of lives saved or illnesses prevented are similarly difficult to measure. Disagreements also focus on how to assess the distribution of costs and benefits across generations and whether the current monetary value of costs and benefits should be discounted in comparing their long-term value. Cost-benefit analysis also provides little help in determining the advantages and disadvantages for different industries subject to regulation.

Some of the progress that has been made in reducing air pollution has been a consequence of economic growth and modernization. In many cases, when new, more efficient equipment and machinery has been put in place, pollution has diminished. Regulation can easily cement into practice established control technologies, however. One of the central challenges to the makers of environmental policy is to encourage continual modernization and development of more efficient, less polluting processes and equipment.

Finally, all the lawmaking and administrative rule making in the world is of little use if laws and regulations are not enforced and complied with. Regulatory programs must therefore include effective incentives for compliance. Some believe that economic or marketlike incentives (such as taxes on emissions of pollutants) are the key to increasing compliance at lower cost; others prefer traditional regulatory approaches (standards are set by federal agencies and implemented by state officials). Incentives must extend to state and local regulatory officials, to encourage them to make the difficult choices that are required. Perhaps most important, regulatory programs should reduce and prevent pollution rather than simply transfer it from one medium to another. These issues are explored in more detail in subsequent chapters.

The Policy-making Process

Although observers and students of the policy-making process often disagree about how that process *ought* to take place, there is a fair amount of agreement concerning the way it *actually* does take place. Policy making is a dynamic process. Charles Lindblom has described it as a "complex analytic and political process to which there is no beginning or end, and the boundaries of which are uncertain." [4] It is also a continual process of identifying problems, formulating governmental responses or policies, organizing administrative mechanisms for carrying out the policies, and evaluating the extent to which policy objectives are achieved.

Most policy efforts are incremental rather than comprehensive; they are primarily a series of marginal adjustments of earlier efforts rather than dramatic departures from past practices. Although many scholars have defended such an approach as reasonable, given the limitations of policy analysis and the impossibility of formulating comprehensive solutions to most policy problems, it may produce policies that do not resolve such problems.

The process of making public policies is not particularly precise. Since it is often difficult to identify with precision the nature of the problems to be addressed or the policy response that would most likely lead to their resolution, a lot of action may be taken with little effect. Policies often help to move society away from some of the effects of a problem, yet do not really move it closer to a solution. Policy efforts may treat symptoms of problems without addressing root causes.

One of the most important characteristics of policy making is that different kinds of policies tend to be associated with different kinds of political relationships and processes. Theodore Lowi has persuasively argued that there are three primary types of policies—distributive, redistributive, and regulatory—and that each type of policy is associated with a particular political process.[5] (Lowi identifies a fourth kind of policy—constituent policy—that is less relevant for the discussion here.) All public policies, according to Lowi, are coercive because they seek to alter individual and societal conduct. There are different ways of controlling behavior, however, and they have different implications both for the way the policy-making process works and for the implementation of the policies that result. Complicated statutes like the Clean Air Act may incorporate all three kinds of policies.

Distributive policies include grants and subsidies that give protection to certain interests against competition and underwrite or directly provide benefits. Grants to states for pollution control equipment and programs are an example of distributive policies. The formulation and implementation of such policies are likely to be accompanied by political relationships in Congress and the executive branch that are disaggregated or individualized, that involve logrolling—the trading of votes or exchanges of support among legislators—and that are removed from public scrutiny. Legislation regarding implementation is likely to be quite specific and to allow little administrative discretion. The key decisions—who is to receive the benefits and how much they are to receive—are usually made by the legislators, who have a considerable interest in ensuring that recipients can clearly trace the origins of the benefits given them.

Redistributive policies are concerned with the economy and society. They include the actions of the Federal Reserve Board of Governors that affect credit and the supply of money, as well as the income tax and Social Security. Redistributive policies are ideological; they raise basic issues about the proper role of government in societal and economic matters. They usually capture the attention of both legislative and executive branches and are formulated in a more centralized manner than other policies. Some redistributive policies are only vaguely defined by law and require considerable administrative expertise and discretion in implementation; other policies are clearly defined by law and require only routine methods of administration.

Regulatory policies seek to alter individual behavior directly by imposing standards on regulated industries. Most of the provisions of the Clean Air Act fall in this category. Regulatory policies are much more likely to arouse controversy. Private interests may be significantly constrained or have compliance costs imposed upon them by regulatory actions. Powerful interest groups are likely to be organized around regulatory issues, and the interaction of these policy advocates plays an important role in determining the nature of the policy. Technical information is also likely to be important in decision making. Regulatory policies often involve complex, technical decisions or concern areas of effort where appropriate policy actions cannot easily be determined; much time will be spent discussing technical issues, and the role of experts in administrative agencies and interested groups will be paramount.

Although the policy-making process differs for different kinds of policies, some elements are present in all policy efforts. As outlined by Charles Jones and others, the policy process includes four major steps: initiation and definition, formulation and enactment, implementation, and impact and evaluation.[6] This model does not explain why policies take the shape they do, but it provides a useful way of examining the factors that determine the policy process and of organizing the ideas and concerns that have been central to the policy-making debate over how to regulate air pollution in the United States. It is also a convenient framework for examining the making of environmental policy. In the following section, a general discussion of each step in the policy-making process is followed by an analysis of the circumstances and variables that are specific to that step in the making of environmental policy.

How Environmental Policy Is Made

Initiation and Definition

The policy process begins when people identify social and economic problems that might be resolved by governmental efforts. After the problem is perceived and defined, interests are aggregated and organized in anticipation of presenting demands or proposals to government officials. (Government officials themselves, particularly administrative officials, are often involved early in this step of the process, as they seek to develop support for policies of interest to them.) Depending upon the strength of the political forces behind a proposal and government officials' perception of its importance, the proposal may become an element of the policy agenda.

[Handwritten margin note: Need to Find Root cause not Just symptoms]

[The way policy problems are identified and the assumptions and values that give shape to the definitions can have a number of important consequences for the administration of public policies. Misperception of the problem (attention directed toward symptoms rather than root causes, for example) may lead to a proposed policy response that is inadequate or lacks proper focus. The political support (or lack of it) generated during this initial stage of the process can have an important effect on policy development, implementation, and evaluation. Some problems may be ignored—and attention given to other, less serious problems—simply because they fail to attract strong political support.]

For more than two decades, environmental policy has been defined as a balancing of environmental quality and economic growth. Despite the broad language of some statutes that set absolute goals of clean air and water and no loss of endangered species, the cost of compliance with environmental regulations has usually determined to what extent the goals are met. In a typical regulatory action, the Environmental Protection Agency (EPA) estimates the level of harm posed by a chemical, chooses some acceptable level of harm such as an increased risk of cancer of one case in a million, establishes a standard to maintain that level of risk, and requires some kind of control technology to trap pollutants and reduce emissions to meet the standard. Before they go into effect, most major regulatory initiatives are challenged in court by regulated industries that believe the regulations are too stringent and environmental groups that find them too weak.

Policy makers must balance some level of risk to society with some level of expenditures for pollution control equipment. They fear the public outcry that will result if the risk is too great or the costs too high. But they are confronted with considerable economic and scientific uncertainties, even though they are bombarded with material from environmental and industry groups. Sorting out the competing and contradictory data is a daunting task.

Pollution and Public Health.   Although literally hundreds of articles have been published in medical and scientific journals concerning the adverse health effects of environmental pollutants, the study of the health and ecological effects of pollution is a relatively new science. [The synergistic effect resulting from the exposure to a number of different pollutants, for example, is not well understood. There is, however, compelling scientific research proving that pollution can cause sickness and death in humans, adversely affects crops and farm animals, corrodes statues and buildings, damages forests and lakes, reduces visibility, and causes unpleasant odors. Studies have demonstrated a strong association between death rates and poor air quality. Sulfates and fine particulates that contain toxic metals and carcinogens are some of the most hazardous forms of air pollution in the United States.[7]]

[Handwritten margin note: scientific research proves Air poll exists]

In some ways, the state of scientific understanding concerning the health effects of pollution is comparable with that on the health effects of smoking in the 1950s and 1960s. The evidence mounted during those decades proving the risks of tobacco use, but the studies were challenged as inaccurate by the tobacco industry. Many industry groups continue to challenge the idea that industrial emissions pose public health threats. Given the long latency period between exposure to some pollutants and the onset of disease, and the difficulties in tracing the source of pollutants that have done damage, many have demanded more research or delays before imposition of control measures.[8]

Most research on the health effects of pollution falls into one of three categories: epidemiological studies, direct or laboratory human exposure, and animal testing. Epidemiological studies attempt to derive statistical correlations of the relationships between observed levels of pollution and such health effects as personal discomfort, diminished lung capacity or damage, or death. The strong correlations these studies have identified have raised major concerns about the health effects of various pollutants and have led in some cases to the imposition of federal regulations. But differences between epidemiological studies often make comparisons difficult and the aggregation of findings problematic. And there is little information on the synergistic effect of exposure to several pollutants. Moreover, the standards of epidemiological studies are difficult to meet; they usually require a high level of statistical confidence in estimating risk. Aggressive regulatory programs are not usually launched until there are major disasters, "bodies in the streets," making them politically signifi-cant.[9]

Epidemiological studies are particularly useful in attempts to identify the long-term results from exposure to pollutants. But since these studies show only a statistical correlation and thus cannot *prove* that a particular pollutant causes specific health problems, they are often the target of criticism by industry officials. The response is a familiar one: despite study after study that associates tobacco use with cancer, cigarette companies still argue that the health effects are uncertain.

Direct testing of the effects of pollutants on volunteers in a controlled setting provides more direct evidence than epidemiological research of the adverse health effects associated with specific pollutants. These studies have found decreased lung functioning of healthy adults exposed to various levels of ozone, for example.[10] But such experiments usually fail to provide an adequate basis for regulation. Only healthy people are permitted to participate in these experiments, so little data is available concerning the effects on people with existing respiratory problems or on children or elderly persons. There is also an inadequate understanding of the relationship between acute symptoms and long-term risks. Critics of regulation have dismissed research on short-term effects, arguing that people can recover from short-term respiratory exposure to pollutants without suffering permanent damage. Some health researchers, however, believe that there is a connection between acute and chronic exposure. In the case of pollution and respiratory disease, for example, short-term exposure causing inflammation of lung tissue may cause the lungs to become more "leaky." This may result in increased levels of protein in the lung, trigger the creation of excess white blood cells, and eventually produce scarring of lung tissue and reduced lung capacity.[11]

Animal testing of chemicals is widely used because of the difficulties of conducting tests on humans. Since the physiology of some animals is quite similar to that of humans, these tests have become particularly important in determining whether certain substances should be considered carcinogens. There are also a number of difficulties with animal testing, however, including their expense (tests of one chemical can cost more than $1 million) and the pain and suffering they cause animals. The results of these tests are often controversial, since scientists disagree about how to extrapolate from the high doses given animals to produce results as rapidly as possible (humans are usually exposed to lower doses), and how to account for possible differences between animals and humans in the way cancer and other diseases develop and spread. There are also disagreements about which species and sex of animal to use for these tests, what exposure path should be used to introduce to the animal the chemical to be tested, and how many animals should be included in the test group. Laboratory tests of one chemical in isolation may not be a realistic test of environmental pollution, which exposes humans to a host of chemicals simultaneously. Such tests can, at best, only demonstrate associations between exposure to chemicals and disease; they cannot prove causality.[12]

Advocates of the public health view of environmental pollution argue that eliminating pollution is a moral imperative, since those who suffer the adverse effects of pollution are not always the same individuals as those who benefit from the economic activity of which pollution is a by-product. Air pollution regulation can be viewed as one of many public health measures aimed at protecting the majority from a threat posed by a group of individuals. Economists argue that polluting industries that fail to invest in pollution prevention equipment are "externalizing" or imposing their costs on others. But the problem is not economic inefficiency as much as the unfairness of subjecting innocent people to air pollution hazards.

Economic Competitiveness and the Costs of Regulation. Although the public health issue has been an important consideration in determining the objectives of environmental policy, economic issues have dominated decisions about implementation and enforcement. The costs of compliance with environmental regulation and the consequences for employment have been major concerns throughout the policy debate, even though the economic consequences of environmental controls are as ambiguous as the impact on health of specific sources of air pollution. There is little agreement about the impact of regulation on the competitive position of American industry in global markets, but evidence of the declining position of American industries in global markets is widespread. Industries that dominated the world market two decades ago have seen their share of that market shrink dramatically in recent years. U.S. firms that developed the technology for videocassette recorders and color televisions now only have less than 2 percent of the videocassette markets and 10 percent of the television markets. Japanese sales of semiconductor chips, another product developed by American scientists, have eclipsed sales by U.S. companies. If current relative rates of growth continue, Japan will replace the United States as the world's leading manufacturer of electronics before the mid-1990s.[13]

The competitiveness of U.S. firms in global markets has major implications for the standard of living Americans will enjoy in the future. World economic leadership also has great symbolic importance to Americans, for it helps determine U.S. influence in international affairs.[14] The state of the economy also affects the political prospects of candidates in presidential, congressional, and state elections. The success of policy makers and industry leaders in promoting American competitiveness will determine the extent to which resources will be available to pursue other important goals, such as alleviating poverty, promoting public health, protecting environmental quality, and preserving natural resources.[15]

There is, however, little information concerning the impact of pollution control costs on the competitiveness of American companies. In 1990, nearly $100 billion was spent by the public and private sectors to control pollution, and that figure is expected to rise to $150 billion by the end of the century, as shown in Figure 1-1 (p. 11). Nor is much information available concerning the cost of compliance with environmental regulations faced by industries in other nations. Some U.S. industries have moved to other countries, primarily the less developed ones, to escape stringent environmental regulations (as well as for other reasons), but America's major economic competitors appear to have regulatory requirements at least as stringent as those in the United States.[16] As shown in Table 1-1 (pp. 12-13), between 1972 and 1988, the majority of the expenditures for environmental quality were devoted to pollution abatement and control; only a fraction was spent on regulation and monitoring, and on research and development. Although spending for pollution control equipment is undoubtedly the most expensive component of the total, the relatively small amount allocated to these other purposes means that we have limited information about pollution trends and levels, the effects of pollutants on humans and ecosystems, and options for reducing emissions. One of the key debates in environmental policy is whether a greater investment in research and data collecting would result in more effective regulatory efforts. Industries, as one would expect, have the highest expenditures for pollution abatement and control, as shown in Table 1-1.

In 1984 and 1988, state and local governments spent about four times as much as was spent by the federal government for pollution control. Although the states have the primary responsibility for enforcing most environmental laws, they spent only about as much as the federal government did on regulation and monitoring in those years. One of the most important challenges confronting state and federal policy makers is to generate support for increased spending for research and monitoring so that air pollution problems can be better understood. Table 1-1 also demonstrates that spending to control air and water pollution were roughly equal, whereas expenditures for solid waste collection and disposal were about one-half of the amounts spent for the other two categories. Although expenditures for control of air and water pollution dominate now, projections for the end of the century indicate that spending for collection and disposal of solid waste will approach that for control of air and water pollution.

From the public health perspective, the costs that are most relevant are those of continued high levels of air pollution. From the perspective of economic competitiveness, however, the reduction in risk to public health is less important than the threat of lost jobs and factory shutdowns. But it is not at all clear that this balancing of costs and risks is satisfactory or inevitable. Once an acceptable level of pollution is reached, for example, there is little incentive for industry to reduce emissions further. The health hazard posed by pollution comes to be accepted by society as inevitable even though in other areas, such as air travel or disease prevention, we continue to strive for reduced risk.

Barry Commoner, who has been an outspoken critic of the EPA, and Gus Speth, president of the World Resources Institute, make the case for pollution prevention from a public health or ecological preservation perspective. Commoner argues that environmental goals are much more likely to be achieved if changes are required in industrial design. He points out that progress in remedying most environmental problems has been quite slow and much less successful than has been envisioned in virtually every environmental statute. The only real successes, Commoner argues, have come when basic changes have been made in the means or technology of production.[17] An alternative to attempting to trap pollution with control equipment is to try to prevent it, for example. Lead emissions fell by 86 percent between 1975 and 1985, primarily because lead was removed from most gasoline sold. Concentrations of polychlorinated

Figure 1-1 Total Expenditures for Pollution Control, Assuming Full Implementation of Laws, 1972-2000

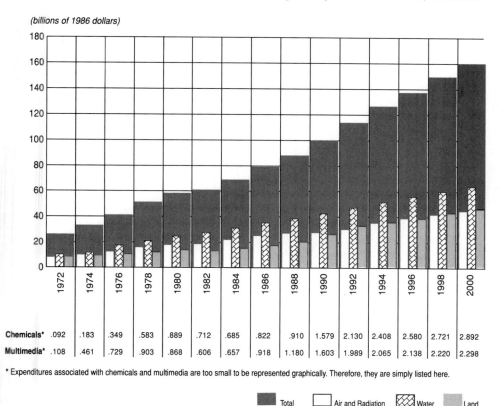

(billions of 1986 dollars)

	1972	1974	1976	1978	1980	1982	1984	1986	1988	1990	1992	1994	1996	1998	2000
Chemicals*	.092	.183	.349	.583	.889	.712	.685	.822	.910	1.579	2.130	2.408	2.580	2.721	2.892
Multimedia*	.108	.461	.729	.903	.868	.606	.657	.918	1.180	1.603	1.989	2.065	2.138	2.220	2.298

* Expenditures associated with chemicals and multimedia are too small to be represented graphically. Therefore, they are simply listed here.

■ Total   □ Air and Radiation   ▨ Water   ▪ Land

Source: Environmental Protection Agency, *Environmental Investments: The Cost of a Clean Environment* (Washington, D.C.: EPA, 1990), 3-1.
Note: Chemicals: hazardous chemicals that have economic value and are not simply waste products. Multimedia: more than one environmental medium (air, water, land).

biphenyl (PCB), in body fat declined by 75 percent a few years after its production was banned in 1979. The concentration of mercury in lake sediments decreased by 80 percent between 1970 and 1979 because of the discovery of substitutes for it in chlorine production.[18] (Nonpolluting substitutes are not available for all pollution sources, however.)

Gus Speth has also emphasized the importance of promoting "rapid and far-reaching technological change." Economic growth and environmental sustainability will occur only "if there is a transformation in technology; a shift, unprecedented in scope and pace, to technologies—high and low, soft and hard—that facilitates economic growth while sharply reducing the pressures on the natural environment." Environmental considerations

Table 1-1 Total Expenditures for Improving Environmental Quality, 1972-1988 (billions of current and constant [1982] dollars)

By Type of Activity

Year	Pollution abatement and control[a]		Regulation and monitoring		Research and development		Total	
	Current	Constant	Current	Constant	Current	Constant	Current	Constant
1972	16.7	40.3	0.4	0.8	0.8	1.9	18.1	43.0
1976	31.9	53.2	0.7	1.2	1.3	2.2	33.9	56.5
1980	50.5	58.4	1.3	1.5	1.8	2.1	53.5	62.1
1984	65.2	61.3	1.4	1.2	2.3	2.2	68.9	64.7
1988	81.5	70.0	1.7	1.3	2.8	2.3	85.9	73.7

By Type of Pollution

Year	Air		Water		Solid waste	
	Current	Constant	Current	Constant	Current	Constant
1972	5.6	14.6	8.5	19.7	3.3	7.1
1976	12.6	21.7	14.9	24.5	5.2	8.4
1980	21.9	24.7	21.3	24.7	8.8	10.7
1984	29.6	28.6	25.2	23.3	11.8	10.8
1988	31.9	29.3	32.2	27.5	18.8	14.6

By Sector[b]

Year	Pollution abatement and control					Regulation and monitoring		Research and development		
	Private/personal[c]	Business	Federal government	State government	Local government	Federal government	State/local government	Private	Federal government	State/local government
1972	3.26	31.50	0.35	2.85	7.07	0.40	0.38	1.26	0.47	0.21
1976	6.46	33.23	0.81	2.92	9.73	0.62	0.53	1.22	0.88	0.07
1980	7.16	37.89	0.58	3.29	9.50	0.93	0.61	1.31	0.70	0.08
1984	10.57	39.50	0.88	3.51	6.87	0.68	0.55	1.58	0.55	0.02
1988	11.01	45.54	1.13	4.45	7.87	0.68	0.66	1.74	0.55	0.02

Source: Council on Environmental Quality, *Environmental Quality: 21st Annual Report* (Washington, D.C.: CEO, 1990), Part 2, tables 9-11.

Notes: Excludes agricultural production except for feedlot operations. Interest costs are not included. Totals may not agree because of independent rounding.

[a] Spending for goods and services that U.S. residents use to produce cleaner air and water and to collect and dispose of solid waste.

[b] In billions of constant (1982) dollars.

[c] Spending to purchase and operate motor vehicle emission reduction devices.

must be "integrated into the basic design of our transportation, energy, and other systems." Regulation must ensure that the "major sectors of the U.S. economy—manufacturing, agriculture, transportation, housing, and energy—[are] redesigned in the years ahead so that they fulfill economic needs without destroying our national and global environments."[19]

Many companies have found that the public health or ecological preservation perspective also makes economic sense. Pollution is ultimately waste and reducing it saves money. This idea was codified in the Pollution Prevention Act of 1990, which encouraged companies to prevent waste generation and to recycle waste whenever "feasible."[20] In some cases, however, imposing controls or making changes in a manufacturing process may be more expensive than simply producing waste. Moreover, the materials might themselves be underpriced if the real cost of producing them is not reflected in their price. In other cases, companies may simply lack the information or technology to improve their operations or meet other investment priorities. The costs of dealing with pollution and the demands of consumers for "greener" products can also have a powerful effect on corporate decision making.[21] The costs of disposing of hazardous waste directly, and the liability costs imposed through litigation, are major expenses in some industries. Liability for cleaning up toxic waste sites can be ascribed to virtually any company that had any involvement with operations, including those that merely lent money. Responsibility can be retroactive and can be based on an ability to pay rather than on the amount of waste produced. There are tremendous opportunities for technological entrepreneurs who can develop cleaner sources of energy, more effective ways of recycling, and more environmentally friendly products. Industries that are ahead of their competitors in this regard can introduce new pollution control technologies according to their own schedule, gain further market advantages, and help shape the requirements that will likely be reflected in regulation, since regulatory requirements are often based on existing controls.[22]

Environmental quality is increasingly viewed as a precondition for a healthy, sustainable economy.[23] An engineer for a Swedish firm emphasized industry's inevitable interest in the environment this way: "We treat nature like we treated workers a hundred years ago. We included then no cost for the health and social security of workers in our calculations, and today we include no cost for the health and security of nature."[24] In some countries, environmental regulation may follow the pattern of social regulation. Although one can argue about its ultimate consequences for the economy, environmental regulation, like social welfare, will come to be seen as a prerequisite for all economic activity.

Chemical companies in the United States and Europe appear to be undergoing the most dramatic transformation in environmental consciousness, for they are allocating a large percentage of their spending to environmental protection. One of the most striking aspects of this change is the extent to which some companies have gone beyond minimum regulatory requirements. Both Monsanto and DuPont have voluntarily reduced emissions of hazardous air pollutants and have pledged to eliminate them entirely. Some companies have also embraced the idea of zero emissions as a parallel to product defects. These companies have found that environmental damage as well as product problems are more cheaply dealt with by attempting prevention than by installing equipment at the end of the pipe or, even worse, cleaning up pollution after emission.[25] By basing arguments for regulation on economic benefits—true costs, expanding market shares, money saved from reduced use of raw materials, long-run economic viability—it may be easier to attract industry support and overcome opposition. The economic case for pollution control is clear and persuasive, particularly from a long-run perspective. But the public health perspective is also a powerful one. Will it lose some of its moral force if it is reduced to an appeal for companies to act in ways that are in their self-interest?

Although many people continue to resist regulation as inconsistent with economic growth, it is becoming increasingly clear that environmental quality and economic health can be compatible policy goals. Attainment of environmental goals requires economic resources; healthy economies have many more resources to invest in achieving and preserving environmental quality than do faltering economies. Modernization of industrial processes can improve the quality of products as well as reduce air and water pollution. In the short run, regulation imposes costs that may be quite burdensome, but in the long run, regulation can contribute to modernization, increased efficiency, and global competitiveness. Companies that develop cleaner, more environmentally sensitive processes have access to lucrative worldwide markets. The regulatory requirements imposed on some industries create new markets and customers for producers of pollution control equipment. One of the greatest challenges in environmental policy making, and one of the clearest criteria by which the Clean Air Act and other statutes can be assessed, is the development of specific policy interventions that balance environmental protection with long-run economic viability.

Formulation and Enactment

The second step in the policy process includes formulating a program to respond to the demand for action, getting it on the policy agenda of the governing body that is to take action, enacting legislation to authorize implementation of the program, and appropriating sufficient funds for implementation. This requires the interaction of the legislature, the groups advocating the proposal, and the executive branch agency that will ultimately be responsible for implementing the policy. Proposals that are supported by interests with political clout and large financial resources for congressional campaign contributions and other efforts are much more likely to be acted upon and implemented than those that are not.

The coalition building and compromise that is central to the legislative process often results in laws that are imprecise and leave much room for interpretation by administrative officials. Difficult choices might be deferred to the agency implementing the policy, thus deflecting the political controversy from the legislative process to the administrative process. The political environment in which agencies operate is thus highly charged because agencies end up making basic policy decisions that are expected to satisfy the various interests affected. Even legislation that is quite specific usually gives agencies responsibilities that greatly exceed their resources, requiring that they set priorities and make basic policy choices.

An assessment of the Clean Air Act requires some reflection on the general process of translating policy demands into laws. Public policies are influenced by political factors; political motivations, calculations, and concerns usually overwhelm technical analyses in importance. The success of policy makers in accurately defining the nature and causes of problems and in developing and implementing effective solutions is a function of policy analysis as well as political acumen and luck.

Environmental law and regulation are at a critical point in their development in the United States. Considerable progress has been made in cleaning up some of the most egregious and visible forms of air and water pollution. There is in place a complex infrastructure of agencies, legislation, regulations, and enforcement mechanisms for protecting the environment. Government (federal, state, and local), regulated industry, the scientific community, and public interest groups have all invested significant resources in addressing the challenges of assessing environmental and health risks and enforcing laws and regulations.

The environmental and health hazards that remain are among the most difficult ones that must be addressed. Regulating these pollutants frequently means increasingly larger compliance costs for increasingly smaller increments of protection and hazard reduction. Some problems transcend national boundaries and require international cooperation on an unprecedented scale.

The current policy debate is dominated by basic questions such as how much authority, flexibility, and responsibility should be given to the EPA and other federal and state agencies and how environmental statutes might be restructured in a way that will permit more effective and potentially more comprehensive policy making. It is not at all clear that the regulatory system (environmental laws, EPA regulations, and state enforcement programs) now in place is capable of addressing these increasingly complex environmental problems.

There is also an important debate over the success of different statutory approaches in achieving the most effective implementation of environmental policies to attain policy goals. A common assumption is that the approach of all environmental laws resembles that of the Clean Air Act of 1970, the oldest major environmental law. A close examination, however, reveals that some statutes include clear and specific delegations of authority to administrative agencies, whereas others allow more agency flexibility.

Environmental statutes enacted in the late 1970s and early 1980s and designed in response to the congressional abdication of policy-making power that characterized regulatory statutes enacted during the New Deal have placed a variety of checks on agency actions. The paralyzing effect of these fetters may not have been anticipated by congressional advocates of the programs affected, but the efforts to ensure greater agency accountability also limit the ability of administrative agencies to accomplish the tasks delegated to them.[26]

[Most environmental statutes are extremely broad and ambitiously promise to reduce or eliminate virtually all environmental and health hazards, but they reflect little consideration of the costs of achieving that goal. Some statutes include very specific mandates for the implementing agencies, particularly the EPA. These statutes read much like agency regulations: they sometimes include emission standards, or impose deadlines for agency actions; some include "hammer" provisions, which go into effect if the agency does not issue a regulation by a certain deadline to deal with specified problems.]

Regulation and the Structure of Government. [In designing the American political system, the framers of the Constitution intended policy making to be inefficient, to check the power of policy makers, and to permit action only when there is widespread support among different constituencies and their representative institutions. Deliberative democracy, once defended as an ideal, is now frequently afflicted by institutional deadlock, causing elected officials to resign or retire in frustration. Many believe the institutional obstructions to coherent, unified, and effective policy making prevent the United States from responding to the challenges confronting it. Divided government—the legislative and executive branches dominated by leaders of different political parties, whose primary goal is the political defeat of the opposition—makes effective policy making extremely difficult at best, and often impossible.[27]

There is little agreement how policy making can best proceed in a system of divided government.[28] A tradition of bipartisanship in foreign policy gives some hope that as environmental pollution comes to be viewed universally as a major threat to U.S. interests, the divisiveness of political competition can be overcome.[29] Other examples of domestic policy making demonstrate the ability of Congress and the president to work together when major problems must be addressed.[30] Some partisans, however, urge confrontational, hardball politics that highlight differences. For presidents, the strategy is often to use their institutional prerogative and address the nation directly, sometimes coupling this with aggressive use of the veto power. Members of Congress can use their institutional prerogative to produce legislation that is extremely detailed and leaves a minimum of flexibility and discretion to the executive branch.[31]

The tension that is part of divided government and political competition, along with the separation of powers and competing institutional prerogatives, has implications for the kind of legislation that Congress enacts. Some scholars have long argued the importance of statutes that give implementing agencies unambiguous direction, preserve a commitment to the rule of law, and limit bureaucratic discretion. Others argue that the price of political compromise and policy complexity is the passage of statutes that blur distinctions and permit differing interpretations.[32] The tension between the two branches of government during the 1980s and early 1990s has focused debate on how specific statutes ought to be. Should they minimize administrative discretion, so that congressional will is more likely to prevail? Should they include deadlines for executive action and legislative hammer provisions? Or should laws give administrative officials the kind of discretion and freedom that will permit flexible and, it is hoped, efficient administration?[33] Such a debate has been taking place throughout government, but it has been particularly sharp in Congress with regard to environmental legislation, given the deep frustration many members had with the EPA during the early years of the Reagan administration, when the ranking agency officials defied their congressional overseers and rejected traditional interpretations of congressional intent concerning many environmental statutes.

Federalism. Environmental regulation is further complicated by the politics of federalism. At the state level, citizen groups have lobbied for legislation that is more protective of health and the environment, sponsored ballot initiatives when state legislatures have failed to take action, organized boycotts of products sold by companies that fail to protect the environment or that otherwise increase health risks, conducted research on environment-related health problems, and established communication networks for victims of environmental hazards and other concerned individuals. In most states, demands for improved environmental quality are seen as inconsistent with economic growth. Bidding wars among states to attract new industries may raise questions about how stringent state environmental regulations and enforcement measures should be. Environmental regulation officials and their allies in the state legislatures and the governor's office may compete with economic development agencies and their political proponents. Some states have largely settled this issue one way or the other; in others there is an ongoing battle.

Although most Americans surveyed in nationwide polls say that protecting the environment is so important that it should be done regardless of cost, there are also real fears that environmental regulation will result in layoffs and plant shutdowns. Tension frequently exists between workers and community residents, even though the workers themselves often have health problems believed to be related to pollution. Concentrations of pollutants in the workplace usually exceed those in the community, so the tradeoff for workers is greater.

State regulatory efforts have become a key issue in environmental regulation. Most of the responsibility for enforcing the Clean Air Act and EPA regulations issued pursuant to it rests with the states. Some industries have pushed for legal provisions that prohibit states from taking more stringent regulatory initiatives than are specified in the federal law and regulations. Others have sought provisions that permit states to opt out of certain federally mandated programs if warranted by local conditions. Proponents of strong federal legislation and regulations that are uniform nationwide argue that they are necessary to avoid state bidding wars for new industries. But many state officials resent federal intrusion in their regulatory activities, especially the threat of EPA involvement. Even though the EPA has been extremely reluctant to impose sanctions on the states, state air quality officials can use the threat of federal intervention to obtain concessions from industry.

states key to Fed Regulat

Implementation

Implementation, the third step in the policy process, is often a long, complicated procedure that includes interpreting congressional intent, balancing statutory and presidential priorities, creating administrative structures and processes, reviewing congressional debates on policy formulation as regulations are devised, and building political support for enforcement of regulatory requirements. This model of the policy process assumes a simple relationship between policy formulation and implementation that largely mirrors the separation of powers: Congress makes the policy choices and the executive branch and the states implement them. It reflects a widely held perception that major policy decisions are the responsibility of elected representatives. In reality, the line between making and implementing policies is blurred and there is much overlap; those who implement laws are often required to make policy choices.

One of the most important challenges in formulating environmental policy is to structure the law in such a way that it will be effectively implemented. Incentives, ranging from sanctions and other penalties to subsidies and technical assistance, can be used to induce compliance by regulated industries. The Reagan and Bush administrations and the EPA have emphasized the advantages of cooperation and consensus building rather than confrontation in implementing regulations. Government agencies do not have the resources to monitor every source, so the willingness of regulated industries to comply with regulations is important. Compliance might be enhanced if industry officials are allowed to participate in formulating standards, thus encouraging a sense of shared responsibility for making them work. But the fundamental nature of regulation cannot be disguised; it is designed to get industries to do things they otherwise would probably not do. There are clear incentives for industry to delay implementation of regulations, so an agency committed to consensus building and cooperation is faced with a real challenge.

Traditional Approaches to Regulation. The most common regulatory approach employed by the EPA and other agencies to implement and enforce statutes and regulations is often described as "command and control." The agency sets specific requirements with which sources of pollution must comply, and enforcement responsibilities are turned over to the states. One advantage of this combination of national standard setting and decentralized enforcement is that expertise and knowledge concerning basic requirements are concentrated in the federal agency, but local variations and needs can be accommodated.

The command and control approach has been widely criticized, however, for being excessively rigid and insensitive to geographical and technological differences and for being inefficient. Uniform standards are more expensive than they need be for some facilities, and there is no provision of incentives for polluters to develop more effective means of reducing emissions—rather, past polluters are rewarded. Aggressive enforcement by a state may encounter political opposition because it discourages investment in new facilities that are more efficient and less damaging to the environment.

One way of characterizing this debate over statutory strategies is to differentiate between goal-oriented and rule-oriented statutes.[34] Some statutes are expressions of broad goals that give general guidance and direction to regulatory agencies and require that they develop policy details, whereas others provide specific rules that agencies are to administer. Some strategies are more compatible with certain kinds of environmental problems. The formulation and enactment of environmental statutes must be guided by a careful consideration of the imperatives of implementation and enforcement. Agencies must be given enough flexibility to permit rational administration, yet not so much discretion that the rule of law is threatened and congressional intent jeopardized.

Marketlike Incentives. One way government regulations can be made more effective is to increase the incentives for compliance—that is, to provide positive inducements for reducing pollution rather than relying on fear of penalties. Market, or economic incentives have been increasingly heralded as the most effective mechanism for accomplishing environmental goals. Since the costs of controlling pollution vary so widely among firms, efficiency demands that "the degree by which individual sources have to reduce their pollution discharges should vary." [35] If sources of pollution are permitted to find the cheapest way of reducing emissions, the costs of pollution control will be minimized.

Incentives are also championed as being essential to "harnessing the 'base' motive of material self-interest to promote the common good." [36] It is simply not effective to condemn polluters as being immoral or selfish; what is needed are clear incentives to encourage them to change their behavior, to ensure that they take actions that are consonant with the public good. Regulatory policies that rely on economic incentives include

1. Taxes levied on emissions of pollutants or on inputs to activities producing pollutants
2. Fees that are part of pollution discharge permits or other regulatory requirements
3. Emission allowances that can be traded, banked or saved for future use, or sold by polluting companies as long as limits on total emissions are not exceeded
4. Tax concessions or direct subsidies for antipollution control investments
5. Deposits and refunds on products
6. Legal liability and associated fines for certain kinds of pollution[37]

One important market-oriented innovation developed by the EPA beginning in 1974 was an emissions trading program that allows companies to receive credit for reducing emissions in some areas that can be used for higher emissions elsewhere. The EPA views total emissions from each industry plant as encapsulated within a large "bubble," rather than attempting to regulate each smokestack. Regulatory officials establish maximum total allowable emissions and allow plant managers to determine emissions from individual sources. Sources can "bank" emissions for future credits or sell them to new sources that need to purchase offsets of existing emissions in order to operate.[38]

Another way in which economic incentives might be harnessed to improve environmental quality is a pollution tax. The regulatory agency first places a limit on the amount of each pollutant to be emitted. Permits to release a pollutant up to the level allowed by the regulatory agency are either auctioned to the highest bidder or sold at a fixed price, and companies are prohibited from emitting pollutants without a permit. The number of permits or amount of each emission can be reduced over time, thereby diminishing total emissions. The agency may also tax each unit of pollutant emitted; the tax can be higher for emissions that exceed levels provided for in the permit. The permit system ensures that air quality standards are met, and the tax provides an incentive for polluters to reduce their emissions further than is required. Revenue from the permits and tax can be used to fund the regulatory program, sponsor research on the health effects of air pollution, treat individuals suffering from respiratory diseases, and subsidize efforts to develop less polluting industrial processes.

A pollution tax or fee, if it is high enough, can encourage companies to reduce their emissions below permitted levels in whatever way is most efficient for them—closing down some operations, using cleaner fuels, investing in control technologies, or changing work practices. Under the traditional approach to regulation, companies gained no economic advantage from emitting less pollution than was legally permitted them; with the pollution tax, they save money every time they reduce emissions. Pollution taxes are considered a cost factor in production; they preserve the flexibility and autonomous decision making that are important to businesses, as well as minimize the need for coercion. Agency officials are also given important incentives to enforce the law if pollution tax revenues remain with the agency. Companies that are complying with the law support strong enforcement efforts aimed at ensuring that their competitors also pay the required taxes.

The 1986 Emergency Planning and Community Right-to-Know Act, a separate law that is technically Title III of the Comprehensive Environmental Response, Compensation, and Liability Act of 1980 (the "Superfund" law, which was aimed at the cleanup of hazardous wastes), is another good example of the way market forces can encourage companies to reduce emissions. The law requires companies to publicly disclose their emission of hazardous air pollutants, thus creating an incentive to reduce emissions to avoid generating public fears and criticism.

The use of economic incentives to reduce pollution may represent a middle ground that is important in public debate. Conservatives can champion an approach that tries to make markets work, is consistent with a market economy, and promotes autonomy for business decision makers. Liberals who favor environmental protection can get more of that for the same level of expenditure. Pollution taxes and emissions permit charges are a form of user fees that ensures that those who benefit from the use of a natural resource pay for those benefits.[39]

Market-oriented approaches are not the solution to every environmental problem in every economy. A combination of market incentives and other approaches such as technological control mandates and bans on certain activities will likely be required in comprehensive regulatory programs.

[margin note: market incentives better than bureaucratic methods]

But market incentives are believed by many to be the key to ensuring that environmental goals are achieved at lower costs than are possible using bureaucratic, centralized approaches.[40]

There are, however, considerable barriers to be overcome in relying on economic incentives. Critics argue that the environment is an endowment that is shared by everyone. Placing these values in a market would ultimately result in their unequal distribution and eventual devaluation.[41] Furthermore, such incentives fail to recognize the importance of preventing pollution. Barry Commoner, for example, emphasizes that technological changes are needed that reduce or eliminate emissions rather than focusing on treatment and disposal. For Commoner, the creation of a free market in pollution simply allows companies to buy permits when they choose not to install mechanisms to control or prevent pollution. Giving polluters a certain quantity of pollution they can emit

[margin note: Technology needs to be focus]

> is a perverse parody of the "free market." . . . Instead of goods—useful things that people want—being exchanged, "bads" that nobody wants are traded. It is a market that cannot operate unless it is provided with what it is supposed to exchange—pollutants. This is a proposal that not only fails to prevent pollution but actually *requires* it.[42]

Marketlike incentives may send the wrong signal that pollution is acceptable if the polluter is wealthy enough to pay for it. Moreover, regulators usually lack sufficient information about the economic status of individual firms to permit them to set pollution taxes at the optimal level. And industry groups, usually vigorous proponents of market incentives like emissions trading that do not cost them anything, quickly withdraw their support when pollution taxes or fees are proposed.

[margin note: Market incentives send wrong message]

The debate over marketlike approaches to regulation reinforces the importance of devising effective means of implementing policies. An analysis of policy implementation should focus on questions such as the extent to which the provisions of the act are likely to be implemented, the major challenges that will confront those who will be involved in implementing it, and whether federal and state officials have been given the tools they need to achieve the policy goals assigned them. Recent environmental statutes have been ambitious in their goals, yet specific in their mandates. Regulatory agencies such as the EPA are expected to fulfill the expectations that have been raised, yet have been given only limited discretion and resources to do so.

Impact and Evaluation

It is somewhat misleading to say that policy evaluation or analysis is the last step in the policymaking process; in fact, it occurs throughout the entire process. Congress and the executive branch oversee the implementation of the law or policy and regularly assess the effectiveness of its major provisions, including the clarity with which policy goals are expressed. They also consider the extent to which policy objectives have been achieved and reformulate policies as necessary. Administrators are expected to make a politically neutral professional judgment, but policy evaluation by legislators is a very political undertaking, pursued by politicians for a variety of purposes.

Central to the policy-making process is the ability of policy makers to assess the strengths and weaknesses of existing policies and alter them when necessary. Policy analysis in general rests on the expectation that the technical assessment of competing policy options will be separated from the political calculations of the policy makers, and that there will be an objective, nonpolitical assessment of policy options before the inevitable political calculations shape the decisions eventually made. Careful policy analysis should precede the application of narrow political pressure and ensure that policies producing the greatest net gains in social welfare will be pursued. In practice, of course, policy making is a very political exercise.

The reliance of most analytic techniques on measures of economic efficiency and utility may clash with other values such as distributive justice.[43] Reliance on analytic techniques may give the illusion of precision, certainty, and objectivity, when in fact decisions must be made on much more subjective grounds. Policy analysis may enhance the role of experts at the expense of elected officials, thus reducing the accountability of policy making to the people.[44] This model of rational policy analysis and policy making often falls short in providing guidance for policy making that takes place under conditions of uncertainty and where trial and error are inevitable.[45]

Assessing environmental policies is particularly challenging because policy making so often rests on limited knowledge and scientific and economic analyses that are still being widely debated.[46] Environmental laws give little guidance to federal and state agencies about how to measure and balance costs and benefits in making the ultimate political decisions. Furthermore, the executive and legislative branches of government frequently disagree about the direction environmental regulation should take. Recent presidents have been preoccupied with the health of the economy, whereas the Democratic majority in Congress has emphasized a broad range of domestic policies. For many congressional sponsors of environmental legislation, reducing hazards is the primary goal; costs are secondary. Officials in the executive branch have sought to achieve a balance between economic and environmental policies. The environmental hazards and plant shutdowns that are blamed on expensive regulations can have important electoral consequences. Tension also results from the competition between members of opposing political parties, who are bent on defeating each other. Moreover, there have also been judicial challenges to virtually every major regulation issued, delays in issuing regulations, and charges of minimal enforcement and compliance with laws and regulations. Although the debate has been carried on in the media, political campaigns, academic journals, and blue ribbon panels, it might be best understood by reviewing the debate in the federal government during the past decade over whether environmental regulation has been too stringent or not stringent enough and whether economic growth should be given priority over pollution reduction and protection of health.

Criticisms of Excessive Regulation. Environmental regulations, particularly those aimed at air pollution, have been widely criticized as being too stringent and unjustified when their expected costs are compared with the benefits they promise. These criticisms are rooted in analyses of the costs and benefits of regulation that were initiated by the Ford administration and continued under President Jimmy Carter. In 1981 President Ronald Reagan directed that the regulatory review process be centered in the Office of Management and Budget (OMB) and established the Presidential Task Force on Regulatory Relief.[47] The Bush administration continued these presidential initiatives and created in 1989 the Council on Competitiveness to oversee regulatory reform efforts.

Many OMB officials have been relentless critics of the EPA and other regulatory agencies and, by implication, Congress, for failing to provide adequate justification for clean air regulations and other regulatory initiatives.[48] They have argued that agencies should not take regulatory actions unless sufficient scientific evidence is available to justify them—that is, until scientific uncertainties and ambiguities are reduced or eliminated. In a recent compilation of regulatory actions proposed by several agencies, the OMB summarized its indictment of regulatory agencies: "risk-assessment practices continue to rely on conservative models and assumptions that effectively intermingle important policy judgments within the scientific assessment of risk." As a result, senior agency officials are forced to make regulatory decisions "based on risk assessments in which scientific findings cannot be readily differentiated from embedded policy judgments." Not only does this "make it difficult to discern serious hazards from trivial ones, and distort the ordering of the Government's regulatory priorities," but it may even "increase health and safety risks" by regulating less serious problems and ignoring more serious ones.[49]

The OMB officials also charge that agencies employ unreasonably conservative or cautious assumptions in assessing risks; they adopt upper bounds of estimates rather than the most likely projections, treat benign tumors as malignant, use the most sensitive species and sex in laboratory tests and in determining acceptable exposure levels, and apply the most cautious models in extrapolating from animals to humans and from low to

Agencies argue with each other

high exposure levels. Although such conservative approaches individually may not be particularly unreasonable, the cumulative effect is to produce assessments of risks that have "extremely conservative biases" and "do not provide decisionmakers with the information they need to formulate an efficient and cost-effective regulatory strategy." According to the OMB, a reliance on conservative or worst-case assumptions and analyses may overstate risks by several orders of magnitude. Assessments usually include "margin of safety" factors and upper-bound estimates that really represent policy choices rather than scientific assessments. Although it may make sense to use such approaches initially as screening devices to exclude risks that are shown to be insignificant even in the worst-case scenarios, the OMB complains that agency officials continue to rely on these biased estimates and thus greatly overstate the benefits that would result from regulatory intervention. Given the uncertainties surrounding animal bioassays, agency officials have considerable discretion in determining how results are used. These officials often rely on tests using the most sensitive animals available and expose the animals to such high doses that some response is inevitable. Models used to extrapolate human risks from animal tests, according to the OMB, are from nine to thirty times more likely to produce false positives (the test erroneously appears to demonstrate an effect) than false negatives (the test mistakenly indicates no effect). Models used to extrapolate low doses from high doses require the use of the upper limit of a 95 percent confidence level (so that there is only a 5 percent chance that the real risk exceeds the estimate), rather than an unbiased estimate. The OMB cites differences in modeling that produce estimates of the risk from dioxin, for example, that vary by a figure as high as 5,000.[50]

Risk assessments serve as the basis for calculating the costs and benefits of regulatory options. The OMB has criticized the EPA and other agencies for failing to provide adequate analyses of the benefits and costs of regulations they want to impose. The OMB and other agencies have differed over the calculation of both costs and benefits. Benefits are particularly difficult to determine, as they often rely on minimal information concerning the levels of exposure to the regulated substance and the nature of the exposure-response relationship. But the calculation of costs also requires choices that are not strictly technical. Costs may be limited to direct expenditures for compliance or may include allowances for the projected impact on prices and competitiveness and on unemployment, and for other possible consequences of increased expenditures by the regulated industries. Basic assumptions and beliefs concerning the appropriateness and value of regulations cannot help but color the way in which actual dollar values are assigned in the cost-benefit analysis. Agencies have failed to rely on market-based measures such as the "willingness to pay" that are, for the OMB, the only real means of "comparing alternative sources of value to individuals . . . and allocating goods and services to the highest-valued use." [51]

Cost-benefit analysis is generally understood to require the quantification of all costs and benefits and the calculation of their dollar values in a numerical ratio. These calculations are, of course, extremely controversial when estimating the value of human life or protection of ecosystems. Therefore, calculations of their cost effectiveness means comparing alternative regulatory strategies or different regulations without requiring explicit value calculations. A cost-effective standard requires that the goal be achieved at the lowest cost or that the most good be achieved with the resources available. Cost-benefit analysis, however, requires that the policy goal be justified by showing that the projected benefits exceed the anticipated costs. Agencies may select a regulatory option with the highest cost-effective ratio, and may compare the cost effectiveness of different regulations in deciding whether to pursue them. Problems with this approach remain, and OMB officials have criticized the EPA (and other agencies) because the cost effectiveness of regulations varies greatly. [52]

The OMB and the regulatory agencies have also differed over the selection of discount rates for computing the effects of regulations over time. In many areas of regulatory activity, benefits and costs develop on different time schedules, but their net present values are determined so that alternative regulatory actions can be compared. The net present value is dependent upon the discount rate selected; the higher the rate used, the greater the incentive to defer the effective date of regulations. In general, OMB officials appear to prefer a higher rate than do agencies, thus making it difficult to justify new regulations. Agencies have been hesitant to discount costs and benefits, and that biases decisions in favor of regulatory interventions. [53]

Recent reports of the president's Council of Economic Advisers (CEA) have also been part of the debate over the costs and benefits of regulation. Markets and the legal system of liability, CEA officials argue, provide sufficient incentives for safety in most cases. Markets "accommodate individual preferences for avoiding risk and produce information that helps people make informed choices." Since many of the most significant risks to health, such as smoking, are a result of individual choice, "government regulation can never replace the need for responsible individual action." [54] The costs of regulation are particularly serious, including "restricting freedom of individual choice" and "retarding innovation, investment, and economic growth." Regulations with the "highest expected net gains should be undertaken first." All statutes and regulations of the federal government should be consistent in their minimization of risk so that the most cost-effective strategy can be pursued. Congress is at fault here because "statutory language sometimes impedes the realization of consistency by setting goals that do not take into account costs." [55]

Many economists also argue that we cannot afford the inefficiency inherent in traditional regulatory schemes and criticize regulation that insulates some companies from competitive forces. They also reject national standards as being inefficient. The diversity of the American economy means that pollution problems are more serious in some areas than in others; therefore, such standards will only perpetuate arbitrariness, inequity, and waste.[56]

Bruce Ackerman and William Hassler, in their criticism of the 1977 Clean Air Act, charged that imposing technological controls on all new stationary sources was making policy "in an ecological vacuum—without a sober effort to define the costs and benefits of designing one or another technology into the plants of the future." [57] Robert Crandall has contended that votes on environmental issues demonstrate that members of Congress representing declining industrial areas see regulation as a way to protect their constituents by imposing costs on new facilities locating in the sunbelt. Standards imposed on stationary sources "do not generate pollution reduction at the lowest possible cost." [58] For Lester Lave and Gilbert Omenn, "regulation of air pollution imposes costs and causes economic efficiencies and social disruption. Society desires pristine air, but is not willing to sacrifice much of the standard of living to achieve it." [59] Paul Portney has reviewed studies assessing the costs and benefits of the clean air regulation and has concluded that although there is great uncertainty, and wide variation in the estimates of costs and benefits, there is little disagreement that it is possible to "substantially reduce the costs of meeting the nation's current air quality goals. . . . By reallocating control effort away from high-cost and toward low-cost sources," he has asserted, "the total cost of pollution control can be reduced while emissions of air pollutants remain constant, or even decline." [60] Bruce Yandle has bemoaned the "rent-seeking" behavior of polluters who use regulation to gain artificial economic advantage (or "rents") by pushing for new source standards that are "set very high, while allowing existing polluters to operate older plants that continue to pollute the environment." [61]

Environmental Politics and Regulatory "Unreasonableness." Environmental policy has been blamed for the inefficiency or "unreasonableness" of environmental regulation. Critics argue that environmentalists have made wildly exaggerated claims to arouse fears, as part of their strategy of attacking corporate power to enhance their own political influence and gain passage of strict laws.[62] They are effective at getting commitments from politicians to champion basic positions, but their political base cannot easily direct the details of administration. They have captured the agenda-setting power, and neither Congress nor the executive branch has been willing to challenge their claims and advocate a more realistic set of expectations and objectives. Environmentalists have convinced the public that the costs of regulation can easily be financed by industry's deep pockets. They, and their allies in Congress, the bureaucracy, the courts, and the media, are willing to impose tremendous regulatory burdens for marginal, hypothetical benefits. Presidents have been unwilling to push for real statutory reform of environmental laws to ensure that they establish mechanisms for balanced policy making; they have only tinkered with short-run administrative changes.[63]

Critics also argue that Congress has passed, and EPA officials have been unwilling to challenge, statutes that provide unrealistic criteria for policy making and raise unreasonable expectations that greatly exceed what the EPA and the states have actually accomplished. Both legislators and bureaucrats have failed to educate the public about the nature and inevitability of health hazards, the complexity of risk assessment, the costs of trying to eliminate risks, and other trade-offs. They have also failed to structure debate over environmental quality so that the policy choices are clearer to the public; been insensitive to the impact of the regulations on state and local governments; and been unable and unwilling to integrate environmental health problems with broader concerns, such as the quality of life in urban areas, that affect people directly and immediately.[64]

Many critics also believe that federal courts should bear some responsibility for pressuring the EPA to issue more stringent regulations, since they forced the EPA and other agencies to take more aggressive action in the 1960s and 1970s. In his study of the 1977 Clean Air Act, Shep Melnick found that judges "commonly criticized administrators for being too timid in their wielding of public authority rather than encroaching on private property." They insisted that agencies interpret their "nondiscretionary duties" broadly. Rather than restraining administrative power, activist judges "pushed agencies to be more aggressive in protecting citizens' 'fundamental personal interests in life, health, and liberty.' " [65] Activist courts required agencies to provide more documentation for their actions. Rather than deferring to agency expertise, courts took a "hard look" at or made a "searching and careful review" of agency decision making.[66] One impact of the heightened judicial scrutiny (some 80 percent of major EPA rules are contested in court) has been that agencies have exaggerated the health risks that will be reduced in order to have a strong case when the regulation is challenged in court.

Failure to Regulate Aggressively Enough. The federal government has been criticized for not going far enough to regulate environmental risks in the past two decades. Regulators have generally been unwilling to impose regulations that would close down factories and cause widespread job loss. Even though a large number of chemicals have been identified as causing cancer in animals, making them candidates for risk assessment to determine whether they pose hazards to humans, the EPA has taken few regulatory actions other than those forced on it by statutory deadlines.

Environmental, health, and safety regulations have been of particular interest to the White House, because of their high compliance costs. But it is not at all clear that there is too much government intervention in these areas and that the number of regulations should be dramatically reduced. Environmental and health hazards are continually reported in books, journals, and newspapers and on television programs. [According to a 1987 review by the Office of Technology Assessment, the EPA has analyzed only a small number of the chemicals within its regulatory jurisdiction. Under the 1992 Clean Water Act, it has established toxic effluent standards for six categories of pollutants, and it has agreed to prepare standards for sixty-five more categories. Of the twenty-nine nonbinding water quality criteria documents the agency has prepared for the states, only seven have been adopted, and only one has been adopted by more than one-fourth of the states. As authorized by the 1974 Safe Drinking Water Act, the EPA has issued maximum contaminant levels for nine chemicals. Many of the drinking water standards that are in effect are based on 1962 guidelines of the Public Health Service.[67] Environmental statutes recently enacted by Congress provide clear evidence of congressional dissatisfaction with the scope and pace of EPA regulation setting. In its 1986 reauthorization of the Safe Drinking Water Act, for example, Congress set deadlines for the EPA to regulate eighty-three chemicals.]

[Almost all the authors of a collection of essays on the topic "Protecting the Earth: Are Our Institutions Up to It?," published in a 1989 issue of *EPA Journal*, criticized the EPA and other agencies for not adequately protecting the environment. Gladwin Hill, former environmental correspondent for the *New York Times*, observed that despite some progress, we are "still in a reactive mode, avoiding collective action until it is forced upon us.[68] Arthur Koines, an official in the EPA Office of Policy Analysis, argued that the "system for providing environmental protection is on overload, and it isn't going to improve on its own. Our episodic efforts as a society to respond to environmental threats have led to institutions lacking in unified direction and efficient organization."[69] EPA Administrator William K. Reilly emphasized that regulatory efforts should focus on pollution prevention so that emissions are not simply transferred from one medium to another and so that improved environmental quality will be economically advantageous to industry.[70]

Walter Rosenbaum, in his study of environmental politics and policy, laments the "continuing failure of environmental institutions and policies to achieve many essential goals. Regulatory failure . . . is especially serious in the management of toxic and hazardous substances, in solid waste management, and in air and water pollution abatement." One of the key causes of this failure is the EPA's "lack of a large and dependable research and development (R&D) budget through which it can generate information and schedule future research appropriately for its statutory responsibilities and institutional needs." [71]

Causes of Limited Regulatory Activity. One reason for the limited progress in accomplishing environmental goals is that the EPA has been constrained by recent administrations concerned about controlling inflation and increasing the competitiveness of American firms in international markets. The executive branch, particularly since 1984, has insisted that reducing environmental and health risks is only one of several competing social goals. Michael Kraft and Norman Vig analyze the impact of appointments in the early 1980s of officials who were hostile to the agency's mission, and of the reduction, in constant dollars, of nearly one-third in the EPA's pollution control budget and 25 percent in outlays for research between 1981 and 1984.[72] This significantly limited the EPA's operational capacity. Later Reagan and Bush appointments have done much to restore agency morale and capability, but the EPA's budget has had only nominal increases in recent years.[73]

There is a history of tension between the White House and advocates of more regulation. The Reagan administration restrained the growth of regulation by insisting on OMB review of all proposed and final regulations. The regulatory review process has concentrated mainly on the EPA; one-third of all regulations submitted by the agency to the OMB have been changed or eventually withdrawn. But earlier administrations also pressured the EPA and other agencies to limit regulations.[74]

The regulatory review process has clearly been oriented toward relief rather than reform, toward reducing costs rather than improving regulations. The form developed by the OMB to monitor compliance with the regulating review process, outlined in Executive Order 12291 of February 17, 1981, included four categories of costs but no provision for calculating benefits.[75] The agenda of many senior EPA and OMB officials, when the process was instituted, was simply to reduce research, rule making, and enforcement rather than reshaping policy. Analysis was seen not as a tool for improved policy making, but as a means of limiting agency action. Susan Tolchin and Martin Tolchin have observed that the review process gave business interests an opportunity to block regulatory initiatives they disagreed with. The primary concern was to "alleviate the burdens of excessive regulation." The Reagan administration's regulatory "reform" effort was an "exercise in national self-deception because of the singularity of its dominant goal: short-term relief for business." [76]

A second reason for the limited regulatory activity is the length and complexity of the EPA's rule-making process. Virtually every regulation of consequence is challenged in court. Extremely stringent regulations that can withstand rigorous review by federal courts are expensive and time-

(handwritten margin notes:) EPA is limited by outside sources. / Past failures not EPA fault, it's the Executive Branch / Judicial process complicates env. policy

consuming, for the agency must invest considerable resources in developing regulations and defending them in litigation. The resources required in such regulatory proceedings are tied up for years and thus not available to respond to other problems. Given limited agency budgets (in part due to the unwillingness of administrations to expand agency activity), few major regulatory initiatives can be undertaken. The agreements reached are often only tentative steps for which the parties involved anticipate ultimate judicial determination; major regulations intended by Congress to be agreed upon within a few months take from three to ten years to promulgate. Although the EPA has begun to experiment with alternative processes, such as regulatory negotiations (the agency convenes a series of meetings with interested parties to develop the provisions of a regulation), rule making will probably continue to be a politically contentious and difficult undertaking.[77]

Third, regulations require that the level of risk approach zero, but the costs of achieving this goal tend to increase much faster, so that marginal benefits are decreasing while marginal costs are increasing, often exponentially. Reducing health risks to zero may be compatible with the other policy goals that governments must pursue (when safe products can be substituted or other technological processes are available), but in many cases, trade-offs are inescapable. If the goal of reducing health risks outweighs other policy concerns, then a conservative approach may be noncontroversial. If, however, the costs that regulatory agencies can impose are limited, it will likely collide with other policy concerns.

Failure to Regulate the Most Serious Risks. The EPA itself has provided the most detailed criticism of its regulatory agenda in reports prepared by an agency task force and by the agency's Science Advisory Board. A 1990 Science Advisory Board report also indirectly criticized Congress and environmental laws in general.[78] The board called the EPA a largely "reactive" agency, insufficiently oriented toward "opportunities for the greatest risk reduction." It pointed out that not all risks can be reduced, but not all problems are equally serious, and the agency has failed to set priorities for reducing the most important problems. The board also called on the EPA to pursue a much broader agenda than it has in the past, and to take responsibility for "protecting the environment, not just for implementing environmental law" by addressing "the most serious risks, whether or not Agency action is required specifically by law."[79] The EPA needs to ensure "a more rigorous, scientifically defensible comparison and merging of environmental risks and alternative strategies for reducing them." Interestingly, the board does not criticize the agency for excessive conservativism, as previously discussed.[80] According to the report, the agency has failed to employ a broad range of policy tools to reduce environmental risks. It has usually imposed "end-of-pipe controls that often cause environmental problems of their own" rather than "preventing pollution at the source—through the redesign of production processes, [and] the substitution of less toxic production materials," for example.[81] Agency officials have failed to ensure that "environmental considerations are a part of the policy framework at other Federal agencies whose activities [in such areas as energy production, agriculture, taxation, transportation, and foreign relations] affect environmental quality directly or indirectly." The EPA "must work to ensure that environmental considerations are incorporated into policy discussions across the Federal government."[82]

Fragmentation in the Regulation of Environmental Problems. Many of the criticisms of the Science Advisory Board really pertain to statutory problems that affect the EPA. The agency was not created by statute, but was part of a reorganization plan that consolidated a variety of programs that were spread throughout the executive branch. The EPA is currently responsible for implementing more than a dozen major environmental statutes, including the Clean Air Acts of 1970, 1977, and 1990, the Clean Water Act of 1972 (also known as the Federal Water Pollution Control Act), the Toxic Substances Control Act of 1976, the Federal Insecticide, Fungicide, and Rodenticide Act of 1972, the Resource Conservation and Recovery Act of 1984, and the Comprehensive Environmental Response, Compensation, and Liability Act of 1980 (also known as the Superfund law). There is little interaction between the program offices, each responsible for administering laws concerning a particular environmental medium, and little incentive for such interaction, which is necessary for more comprehensive environmental policy making. This fragmentation limits the flexibility of federal, state, and local governments to alter their resource allocation or coordinate their efforts in response to changing environmental threats.

More interaction is needed because the elements of the environment are interconnected. Regulations requiring treatment and removal of toxic substances in one environmental medium may merely result in their transfer to another environmental medium (e.g., what is filtered from the air may be deposited on the land or water). Such an approach might not reduce risk; it subjects industry to competing and contradictory regulatory requirements and needless expense, consuming resources that can be employed elsewhere.

The political pressures and incentives that have led Congress to launch expansive regulatory programs have not prompted it to ensure their aggressive implementation. Industry groups participate very effectively in the administrative process, where the discourse is technical, detailed, and largely out of public view, and as a result, industry concerns often prevail.

The EPA's budget and resources are overwhelmed by the areas of responsibility Congress and the White House continue to place under the agency's jurisdiction, by changes in technology, and by increases in industrial activity. Hazardous wastes accumulate and new chemicals and pesticides are introduced; yet the agency's budget and work force have decreased. In 1980 the EPA's budget was $5.9 billion and the agency had a work force of 13,078; in 1984, despite new legislation that gave the agency additional responsibilities, the budget was less than $4.1 billion and the work force had decreased to 9,998. By 1991 the agency's budget was $4.0 billion and the agency had 11,342 employees.[83]

EPA Needs More Funding + can't handle load (handwritten margin note)

The Outlook for Environmental Policy Making

Environmental policy making has taken place amid the contention of warring interest groups, partisan politics, and wrangling between the president and Congress. It has also been hindered by scientific uncertainty and lack of data. The debate over whether environmental laws have been too strict or not strict enough and whether regulatory efforts have been misdirected continues. Innumerable analyses are available to Congress and the executive branch concerning ways to address environmental problems and the shortcomings of existing regulatory efforts. Members of Congress have many factors to consider in formulating environmental laws.

Laws should be Flexible (handwritten margin note)

Policy makers should allow those responsible for implementing a law the flexibility to make the adjustments necessary to solve evolving problems and to learn from trial and error. Congress and the executive branch should also be willing to learn from experience when they review and revise laws, preferably on a regular basis. Policy evaluation requires clear goals and standards against which policy implementation efforts can be measured. But that kind of clarity is often lacking, and when it exists, the regulatory tasks may overwhelm available resources.

Laws + goals need to be consistant. (handwritten margin note)

Perhaps most important, policy makers should ask whether environmental laws are consistent with government's ability to achieve the goals they establish. These laws continually heighten public expectations, yet the government continually falls short in its attempts to meet them. Each law passed by Congress, particularly major statutes like the Clean Air Act, has a cumulative impact on future efforts to devise effective solutions to environmental problems. Government's unwillingness or inability to succeed may ultimately erode the public's faith.

The Clean Air Act of 1990 is placed in its political and historical contexts in Chapter 3. The challenges involved in regulating air pollution deserve additional exploration, however, and they are the subject of Chapter 2.

Notes

1. Robert Cameron Mitchell, "Public Opinion and the Green Lobby: Poised for the 1990s?" in Norman J. Vig and Michael E. Kraft, eds., *Environmental*

Policy in the 1990s (Washington, D.C.: CQ Press, 1990), 85. See also Riley E. Dunlap, "Public Opinion in the 1980s: Clear Consensus, Ambiguous Commitment," *Environment* 33, no. 8 (October 1991): 32.

2. U.S. Congress, Office of Technology Assessment, *Acid Rain and Transported Air Pollutants: Implications for Public Policy* (Washington, D.C.: Government Printing Office, 1984), 13.

3. The Clean Air Act was enacted in 1970; major amendments were added in 1977 and 1990. This book is primarily concerned with the act as amended in 1990.

4. Charles E. Lindblom, *The Policy-Making Process* (Englewood Cliffs, N.J.: Prentice-Hall, 1968), 4.

5. See, generally, Theodore Lowi, "Four Systems of Policy, Politics, and Choice," *Public Administration Review*, July-August 1972, 298-310.

6. This section is largely based on Charles O. Jones, *An Introduction to the Study of Public Policy* (Monterey, Calif.: Brooks/Cole, 1984). See also B. Guy Peters, *American Public Policy: Promise and Performance*, 3d ed. (Chatham, N.J.: Chatham House, 1991); and James Anderson, *Public Policy-Making* (New York: Praeger, 1975).

7. U.S. Congress, Office of Technology Assessment, *Acid Rain and Transported Air Pollutants*, 13.

8. For a review of the debate concerning the ecological and health risks of pollution, see the Conservation Foundation, *State of the Environment: A View toward the Nineties* (Washington, D.C.: Conservation Foundation, 1987); Lester Lave, *The Strategy of Social Regulation* (Washington, D.C.: Brookings Institution, 1981); National Research Council, *Risk Assessment in the Federal Government: Managing the Process* (Washington, D.C.: National Academy Press, 1983); Edith Effron, *The Apocalyptics: Cancer and the Big Lie* (New York: Simon & Schuster, 1984); and H. W. Lewis, *Technological Risk* (New York: Norton, 1990).

9. Office of Management and Budget, *Regulatory Program of the United States Government, April 1, 1990-March 31, 1991* (Washington, D.C.: Government Printing Office, 1990), 13-26.

10. U.S. Congress, Office of Technology Assessment, *Catching Our Breath: Next Steps for Reducing Urban Ozone* (Washington, D.C.: Government Printing Office, 1989), 39-78.

11. Becky Bascom, "Clean Air Strategy Session" (lecture delivered at a conference sponsored by the Natural Resources Council of Maine and the Natural Resources Defense Council, Washington D.C., May 28, 1991).

12. For a discussion of animal testing, see Lester B. Lave, "Methods of Risk Assessment" in Lave, ed., *Quantitative Risk Assessment in Regulation* (Washington, D.C.: Brookings Institution, 1982), 37-48. For a skeptical view, see Elizabeth Whelan, *Toxic Terror* (Ottawa, Ill.: Jameson, 1985).

13. Department of Commerce, *The Competitive Status of the U.S. Electronics Sector* (Washington, D.C.: Government Printing Office, April 1990), 7-10.

14. John A. Young, "Technology and Competitiveness: A Key to the Economic Future of the United States," *Science*, July 15, 1988, 314.

15. See Gary C. Bryner, ed., *Science, Technology, and Politics: Policy Analysis in Congress* (Boulder, Colo.: Westview Press, 1992), chap. 10.

16. This issue is explored in David Vogel, *National Styles of Regulation: Environmental Policy in Great Britain and the United States* (Ithaca, N.Y.: Cornell University Press, 1987).

17. Barry Commoner, "Let's Get Serious about Pollution Prevention," *EPA Journal*, July-August 1989, 15.
18. Barry Commoner, "Failure of the Environmental Effort," *Environmental Law Reporter* 18 (June 1988): 10195-10199.
19. Gus Speth, "EPA and the World Clean-up Puzzle," *EPA Journal*, July-August 1989, 26.
20. For a discussion of the law, see Council on Environmental Quality, *Environmental Quality* (Washington, D.C.: Government Printing Office, 1992), 151-158.
21. "The Environment: An Enemy, and Yet a Friend," *The Economist*, September 8, 1990, 3-26.
22. Ibid., 9.
23. "Growth vs. Environment," *Business Week*, May 11, 1992, 66-78.
24. Quoted in "The Environment: An Enemy, and Yet a Friend," 4.
25. Some examples of industries that seek a much more aggressive policy to reduce regulation are given in Bruce Smart, *Beyond Compliance: A New Industry View of the Environment* (Washington, D.C.: World Resources Institute, 1992).
26. For a further discussion of this issue, see Gary C. Bryner, *Bureaucratic Discretion: Law and Policy in Federal Regulatory Agencies* (New York: Pergammon, 1987).
27. See, generally, Burke Marshall, ed., *A Workable Government? The Constitution after 200 Years* (New York: Norton, 1987); Donald L. Robinson, *Reforming American Government: The Bicentennial Papers of the Committee on the Constitutional System* (Boulder, Colo.: Westview Press, 1985); Robert E. Hunter, Wayne L. Berman, and John F. Kennedy, *Making Government Work: From White House to Congress* (Boulder, Colo.: Westview Press, 1986); James MacGregor Burns, *The Power to Lead: The Crisis of the American Presidency* (New York: Simon & Schuster, 1984); and James L. Sundquist, *Constitutional Reform and Effective Government* (Washington, D.C.: Brookings Institution, 1986).
28. See James L. Sundquist, "Needed: A Political Theory for the New Era of Coalition Government in the United States," *Political Science Quarterly* 103 (Winter 1988): 614; and John E. Chubb and Paul E. Peterson, eds., *Can the Government Govern?* (Washington, D.C.: Brookings Institution, 1989).
29. For a review of the making of foreign policy, see Thomas E. Mann, ed., *A Question of Balance: The President, The Congress, and Foreign Policy* (Washington, D.C.: Brookings Institution, 1990).
30. One example is given in Paul Light, *Artful Work: The Politics of Social Security Reform* (New York: Random House, 1985).
31. For a helpful discussion of the politics of divided government, see Thomas E. Mann, "Breaking the Political Impasse," in Henry J. Aaron, ed., *Setting National Priorities: Policy for the Nineties* (Washington, D.C.: Brookings Institution, 1990), 293-317.
32. For more on this debate, see Theodore J. Lowi, *The End of Liberalism* (New York: Norton, 1979); Richard A. Harris and Sidney M. Milkis, *The Politics of Regulatory Change: A Tale of Two Agencies* (New York: Oxford University Press, 1989); Cass R. Sunstein, *After the Rights Revolution: Reconceiving the Regulatory State* (Cambridge, Mass.: Harvard University Press, 1990); and Gary C. Bryner, *Bureaucratic Discretion*.
33. See, generally, Lawrence Dodd and Richard Schott, *Congress and the*

Administrative State (New York: Wiley, 1979); Energy and Environment Study Institute, "Statutory Deadlines in Environmental Legislation: Necessary but Need Improvement" (Washington, D.C.: EESI, 1985); National Academy of Public Administration, *Congressional Oversight of Regulatory Agencies: The Need to Strike a Balance and Focus on Performance* (Washington, D.C.: NAPA, 1988).

34. See David Schoenbrod, "Goals Statutes or Rules Statutes: The Case of the Clean Air Act," *UCLA Law Review* 30 (1983): 740-828.

35. Allen V. Kneese and Charles L. Schultze, *Pollution, Prices, and Public Policy* (Washington, D.C.: Brookings Institution, 1975), 16.

36. Charles L. Schultze, *The Public Use of Private Interest* (Washington, D.C.: Brookings Institution, 1977), 18.

37. Offices of Sen. Timothy Wirth and Sen. John Heinz, "*Project '88.*"

38. See Richard A. Liroff, *Reforming Air Pollution Regulation: The Toil and Trouble of EPA's Bubble* (Washington, D.C.: Conservation Foundation, 1986).

39. Many countries have imposed emissions fees for the release of pollutants into lakes and streams. Germany has made wider use of effluent taxes and fees than has the United States, particularly for water pollution. In 1976 the Bundestag enacted a law that set annual charges for the emission of five pollutants; receipts are given to the *Lander* (states) to offset the costs of administering the program and to finance pollution abatement projects. France has also begun to include economic incentives in its environmental statutes. In 1964 the government created six regional river basin authorities, funded from a tax levied on industrial water users and polluters. The tax level is tied to discharge levels, thus creating incentives to reduce pollution. Tax receipts are made available to finance projects to reduce pollution. In 1986, the French government imposed a tax on emissions of sulfur oxide from combustion facilities of about $18 per ton emitted. Tax receipts are transferred to a clean air mutual fund that can be used to finance pollution control equipment in manufacturing plants. Although there has been general support and even praise in France for this initiative, critics have argued that because of business opposition to high tax levels, the tax is too low. *International Environmental Reporter*, February 2, 1986, 53-55.

40. Robert N. Stavins, "Harnessing Market Forces to Protect the Environment," *Environment* 31 (January-February, 1989): 5-35.

41. Steven Kelman, *What Price Incentives?* (Boston: Auburn House, 1981).

42. Barry Commoner, *Making Peace with the Planet* (New York: Pantheon, 1990), 188.

43. See, for example, Robert Nozick, *Anarchy, State, and Utopia* (New York: Free Press, 1974); John Rawls, *A Theory of Justice* (Cambridge, Mass.: Harvard University Press, 1971).

44. See M. E. Hawkesworth, *Theoretical Issues in Policy Analysis* (Albany, N.Y.: SUNY Press, 1988); Giovanni Sartori, *Democratic Theory* (Detroit, Mich.: Wayne State University Press, 1962).

45. For an elaboration of these issues, see Bryner, *Science, Technology, and Politics*.

46. Kathryn Wagner, "Congress, the Environment, and Technology Assessment," in ibid.

47. For a review of these efforts, see National Academy of Public Administration, *Presidential Management of Rulemaking in Regulatory Agencies* (Washington, D.C.: NAPA, 1987).

48. Office of Management and Budget, *Regulatory Program of the United States Government*, 33, 35.
49. Ibid., 14.
50. Office of Management and Budget, *Regulatory Program of the United States Government, April 1, 1985-March 30, 1986* (Washington, D.C.: Government Printing Office, 1986), xxii-xxvi.
51. OMB, *Regulatory Program*, 36-37.
52. Ibid., xxi.
53. Ibid., 40.
54. Council of Economic Advisers, *Economic Report of the President*, 1987, 207.
55. Ibid.,183. Other offices in the executive branch, such as the Council on Environmental Quality, have lined up more closely with the EPA. In 1984 the Office of Science and Technology Policy issued a "framework" for assessing cancer risks that included a review of scientific knowledge concerning cancer and a set of thirty-one principles that agencies could rely on in risk assessment; it generally paralleled the EPA's approach.
56. Kneese and Schultze, *Pollution, Prices, and Public Policy*.
57. Bruce Ackerman and William Hassler, *Clean Coal/Dirty Air* (New Haven, Conn.: Yale University Press, 1981), 12.
58. Robert W. Crandall, *Controlling Industrial Pollution: The Economics and Politics of Clean Air* (Washington, D.C.: Brookings Institution, 1983), 110-130.
59. Lester B. Lave and Gilbert S. Omenn, *Clearing the Air: Reforming the Clean Air Act* (Washington, D.C.: Brookings Institution, 1981).
60. Paul R. Portney, "Air Pollution Policy," in Portney, ed., *Public Policies for Environmental Protection* (Washington, D.C.: Resources for the Future, 1990), 87.
61. Bruce Yandle, *The Political Limits of Environmental Regulation* (New York: Quorum, 1989), 104.
62. Harris and Milkis argue that the "ideas behind environmentalism were especially attractive to reformers who sympathized with the radicalism of the 1960s, because these ideas offered a powerful indictment of the capitalistic foundation of American society." Environmentalists have been joined by others who seek to bring about a "radical reorientation of American values" by attacking capitalism as leading to "ecological ruin." Harris and Milkis, *Politics of Regulatory Change*, 233.
63. George Eads and Michael Fix, *Relief or Reform: Reagan's Regulatory Dilemma* (Washington, D.C.: Urban Institute Press, 1984).
64. Marc K. Landy, Marc J. Roberts, and Stephen R. Thomas, *The Environmental Protection Agency: Asking the Wrong Questions* (New York: Oxford University Press, 1990), 279-281.
65. R. Shep Melnick, *Regulation and the Courts* (Washington, D.C.: Brookings Institution, 1981), 3, 11-12.
66. Ibid, 11.
67. Office of Technology Assessment, *Identifying and Regulating Carcinogens* (Washington, D.C.: Government Printing Office, 1987).
68. Gladwin Hill, "A Management Job for the Human Race," *EPA Journal*, July-August 1989, 3.
69. Arthur Koines, "Under the Environmental Regulation Layer Cake," *EPA Journal*, July-August 1989, 19.
70. William K. Reilly, "The Greening of EPA," *EPA Journal*, July-August 1989, 8-10.

71. Walter Rosenbaum, *Environmental Politics and Policy*, 2d ed. (Washington, D.C.: CQ Press, 1991), 301, 304.
72. Michael E. Kraft and Norman J. Vig, "Environmental Policy from the Seventies to the Nineties: Continuity and Change," in Kraft and Vig, eds., *Environmental Policy in the 1990s* (Washington, D.C.: CQ Press, 1990), 3-32; and Vig and Kraft, "Conclusion: Toward a New Environmental Agenda," ibid., 369-389.
73. Norman J. Vig, "Presidential Leadership: From the Reagan to the Bush Administration," ibid., 33-58.
74. National Academy of Public Administration, *Presidential Management of Rulemaking*.
75. Harris and Milkis, *Politics of Regulatory Change*, 257.
76. Susan J. Tolchin and Martin Tolchin, *Dismantling America: The Rush to Deregulate* (Boston: Houghton Mifflin, 1983), 58, 266.
77. See, generally, Gail Bingham, *Resolving Environmental Disputes: A Decade of Experience* (Washington, D.C.: Conservation Foundation, 1986).
78. Environmental Protection Agency, Science Advisory Board, *Reducing Risk: Setting Priorities and Strategies for Environmental Protection* (Washington, D.C.: EPA, September 1990).
79. Ibid., 16.
80. Ibid., 17.
81. Ibid., 22.
82. Ibid., 23.
83. Environmental Protection Agency, Office of the Comptroller, "Budget Justifications of Appropriation Estimates for Committee on Appropriations" (Washington, D.C.: Government Printing Office, selected years); Office of Management and Budget, *Budget of the United States Government, Fiscal Year 1992* (Washington, D.C.: Government Printing Office, 1991), iv-158, 1007. Some of the budget decline is due to changes in grant programs.

2   The Problem of Air Pollution

A key step in the policy-making process, outlined in Chapter 1, is to define the problem to be remedied. If there is not an adequate understanding of the problem, subsequent policy efforts may be misguided. The different kinds of air pollution pose distinct policy-making problems. Air pollution occurs when gases and particles are combined or altered in such a way that they degrade the air and form substances that are harmful to humans, animals, and other living things. There may be as many as 7,000 air pollutants; no place on earth is really free of them. Some pollution is a result of natural processes such as forest fires and volcanoes, or is caused by windblown dust. Other kinds result from human intervention and include emissions from automobiles, wood-burning stoves, heating units, and industrial sources such as power plants and ore reduction. More than half the air pollution in the United States comes from motor vehicle exhaust. The Glossary at the end of the book provides additional information on air pollution.

The air we breathe is a mixture of nitrogen (78.084 percent), oxygen (20.948 percent), argon (0.934 percent), carbon dioxide (0.032 percent), and traces of neon, helium, krypton, hydrogen, xenon, methane, and nitrous oxide. With the exception of carbon dioxide, the concentration of these chemicals remains constant. Nitrogen, oxygen, and carbon dioxide are essential to plant and animal life. Nitrogen is a precursor of nitrate oxygen, a component of proteins, nucleic acids, and chlorophyll, which are essential to all living things. Oxygen in the atmosphere is a basic element of the biochemical reactions that are necessary for all higher forms of life to exist. The other chemicals are inert and do not play a major role in the atmosphere. These gases are held by gravity in the troposphere, seven to ten miles above the earth's surface, just below the stratosphere.[1]

A number of atmospheric gases (such as sulfur dioxide and nitrogen dioxide) vary in concentration. Water vapor is the most variable, ranging from 0 to 4 percent by volume in the lower troposphere. A greenhouse gas, it forms clouds that help radiate sunlight back into space and that constitute a source of water. Carbon dioxide is a key raw material for photosynthesis and food production. It also absorbs heat radiated from the earth's surface and, along with greenhouse gases such as water vapor, helps to warm the atmosphere. Oxygen is transformed into ozone, which forms a stratospheric layer that protects life on earth from dangerous ultraviolet light. Ozone also occurs at low altitudes. Biological and geological processes produce ammonia, methane, hydrogen sulfide, carbon monoxide, sulfur dioxide, and traces of other gases.[2]

 [Air pollution has been defined as a group of chemical compounds that "are in the wrong place or in the wrong concentrations at the wrong time. As long as a chemical is transported away or degraded rapidly relative to its rate of production, there is no pollution problem. Pollutants that enter the atmosphere through natural or artificial emissions may be degraded not only in the atmosphere but also by natural processes in the hydrocycle and geochemical cycles."]³

Two of the best-known forms of air pollution are smog and haze. In London and other European cities, fog from the North Sea and smoke from coal-burning stoves and factories form grey air or smog. In Los Angeles, another kind of smog is formed when automobile exhaust and other gases are trapped by the surrounding mountains and warmed by sunshine. The gases undergo a photochemical reaction, producing brown air or photochemical smog. Smog in other cities is usually a combination of automobile exhaust and smoke from the burning of fuels. Haze is much like smog, but the term usually refers to wide-scale, low-level pollution that obstructs visibility. It has become an increasingly serious problem in national parks and other rural areas as well as a chronic urban problem.[4]

The heart of air pollution regulation in the United States has been the requirement, in the Clean Air Act, that the EPA establish national ambient air quality standards, or NAAQS (acceptable levels of concentration in the ambient, or outside, air), for six major pollutants—carbon monoxide, ozone, particulate matter, sulfur dioxide, nitrogen dioxide, and lead. Emission standards were to be established at the level required to provide "an ample margin of safety to protect the public health."[5] (The standard for lead was added in 1977. A standard for hydrocarbons was issued under the 1970 law but was deleted in 1978 as unnecessary, since hydrocarbon emissions are a major component of ozone and are regulated under that standard.) The pollutants differ considerably in terms of their sources, levels, health impacts, and the control measures that have been developed to reduce their concentration in the air. Ozone has been the most pervasive and difficult to regulate; levels of carbon monoxide and particulate matter in the ambient air exceeded the national standards in many of the nation's urban areas in the early 1990s. Table 2-1 shows the environmental and health effects of traditional or ambient air pollutants regulated by the Clean Air Act.

The second regulatory effort focuses on a second category, the toxic or hazardous air pollutants. Air toxics vary significantly in the threats they

Table 2-1   Effects of Ambient Air Pollutants Regulated by the Clean
Air Act

Pollutant	Effects
Ozone	Respiratory tract problems such as difficulty in breathing, reduced lung function, possible premature aging of lung tissue, and asthma; eye irritation, nasal congestion, and reduced resistance to infection; damage to trees and crops
Particulate matter	Eye and throat irritation, bronchitis, lung damage, impaired visibility, cancer
Carbon monoxide	Impairment of blood's ability to carry oxygen; damage to cardiovascular, nervous, and pulmonary systems
Sulfur dioxide	Respiratory tract problems, including diminished lung capacity and permanent damage to lung tissue; primary component of "killer fogs"; precursor of acid rain, which damages trees, vegetation, and aquatic life
Nitrogen dioxide	Respiratory illnesses and lung damage, damage to immune system; precursor of acid rain
Lead	Brain damage and retardation, especially in children.

Source: Adapted from Environmental Protection Agency, *Environmental Progress and Challenges: EPA's Update* (Washington, D.C.: EPA, 1988), 13.

pose to human health. Many of them are carcinogens; others cause neurological damage or destroy organ tissue. Little information is available concerning the health effects of most chemicals, and we have little understanding of the relationship between exposure to pollutants and contraction of disease. Different population groups exhibit significant differences in sensitivity to chemicals and pollutants, and not much is known about the synergistic or interactive effect of exposure to a variety of potentially harmful substances. The variety of substances involved, the large number and diversity of sources, and the cost of regulatory controls have made regulation particularly challenging. These are chemicals for which no ambient air quality standard was applicable and that were determined by the EPA to "reasonably be anticipated to result in an increase in mortality or an increase in serious irreversible, or incapacitating reversible illness." By the time the act was amended in 1990, the EPA had only issued seven such standards (for asbestos, benzene, vinyl chloride, beryllium, mercury, radionuclides, and arsenic) and had merely proposed a standard for coke oven emissions, which were also classified as a hazardous air pollutant (see subsequent discussion). The major sources and health effects of these pollutants are shown in Table 2-2.

Table 2-2   Health Effects and Major Sources of Hazardous or Toxic Air
Pollutants Regulated by 1990 Amendments

Pollutant	Health effects	Major sources
Asbestos	A variety of lung diseases, especially lung cancer	Vehicle brakes, buildings
Benzene	Leukemia	Gas, solvents
Vinyl chloride	Lung and liver cancer	Chemical manufacturing
Beryllium	Primarily lung disease; also damage to liver, spleen, kidneys, and lymph glands	Foundries, incinerators
Mercury	Damage to the brain, kidneys, and bowels	Chemical manufacturing
Radionuclides	Cancer	Nuclear power, fossil fuel combustion
Arsenic	Cancer	Incinerators, coal

Source: Adapted from Environmental Protection Agency, *Environmental Progress and
Challenges: EPA's Update* (Washington, D.C.: EPA, 1988), 13.

Two global air pollution issues emerged in the late 1970s and 1980s that
have been added to the clean air agenda: acid rain and depletion of the
stratospheric ozone layer. Acid rain threatens the health of trees and other
plant and aquatic life, and also poses a serious threat to human health.
Similarly, destruction of the ozone layer threatens aquatic life and triggers
skin cancer and cataracts in humans. This chapter outlines some of the
issues concerning these different kinds of air pollution and the regulatory
challenges they pose.

Traditional or Ambient Air Pollutants

In 1988 the EPA estimated that 112 million people lived in areas where
at least one national ambient air quality standard was violated. That figure
was 84 million people in 1989 and 74.4 million people in 1990.[6] Although
there has been some improvement, this trend may be only temporary.
Such figures, regularly reported in the press, are somewhat misleading,
since nonattainment of air quality standards is measured over several
years. They reflect one of the challenges of meeting the standards.
Meteorological conditions affect ambient air quality; the hot, dry summer

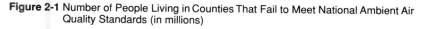

Figure 2-1 Number of People Living in Counties That Fail to Meet National Ambient Air Quality Standards (in millions)

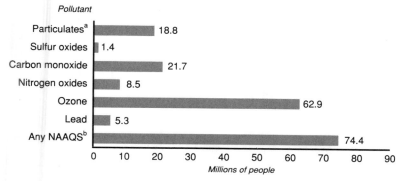

Source: Based on 1987 county population data, and on 1990 air quality data from Environmental Protection Agency, National Air Quality and Emissions Trends Report, 1990 (Washington, D.C.: EPA, 1991), 1-3.
[a]Before 1987, total suspended particulates were regulated; after that year, only particles less than 10 micrometers in diameter (PM_{10}) were regulated, but both forms of particulates continued to be monitored.
[b]Millions of people living in counties where any air quality standards are violated.

of 1988, particularly in the East, stimulated the formation of ozone. Pollution levels are also a function of changes in technology (as industrial and commercial facilities modernize and become more efficient, their emissions usually decrease); the implementation and enforcement of environmental laws and regulations by state and federal officials; and compliance efforts by regulated industries. Figure 2-1 shows the number of people living in counties where ambient air quality does not meet national standards.

Trends in Emissions of Traditional Pollutants

Carbon monoxide (CO) emissions in the United States peaked about 1970 and have fallen noticeably since then, largely as a result of automobile emission controls. Residential coal and wood burning significantly increased the carbon monoxide levels until about 1970. Coal has largely been replaced as a household fuel, but residential wood burning has increased since the late 1970s as wood-burning fireplaces have grown in popularity. Emissions of volatile organic compounds (VOCs), the primary constituent of ozone pollution, also peaked around 1970, but showed little decline throughout the 1980s. Emissions of total suspended particulates (TSP) peaked around 1950, declined steadily until 1980 (primarily as a result of increased use of cleaner fuels and controls placed on fuel burning), and have remained relatively stable since then. Monitoring of fine particulates began only in about 1985. Nitrogen oxide (NO_x) emissions

Figure 2-2 Emissions of Six Major Pollutants, 1970 and 1990

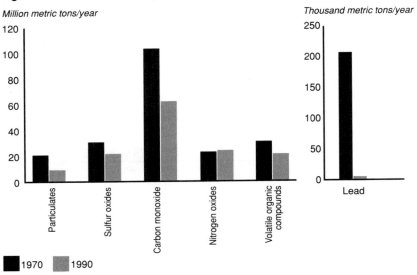

Source: Environmental Protection Agency, *National Air Quality and Emissions Trends Report, 1990* (Washington, D.C.: EPA, 1991), 1-2.

have held constant since the late 1970s. The most dramatic change has been the reduction in lead emissions as a result of the phasing out of leaded gasoline. Such technological changes hold tremendous promise for reducing pollution. Regulatory strategies that attempt to prevent pollution are generally much more effective than those that seek to control it, by installation of equipment on smokestacks and auto tailpipes, for example. Figure 2-2 compares the emissions of these six pollutants in 1970 and 1990.

Although there have been some major acute air pollution disasters, chronic exposure to pollutants has had a much greater impact on human health and ecological systems. Some pollutants harm humans as well as plants and animals. Oxides of sulfur and nitrogen, for example, damage lung tissue; they are transformed in the atmosphere to sulfate and nitrate particles, which fall to earth in dry form or as rain, making soils and water more acidic and killing some species. Carbon dioxide does not cause human health problems, but is classified as a pollutant because of concerns that its increasing concentration in the atmosphere is contributing to global climatic change.

Air pollution-related diseases include asphyxiation, pulmonary irritation, systemic toxicity, and cancer. Those with chronic respiratory problems such as emphysema, asthma, and bronchitis suffer increased damage to lung tissue that is already extremely sensitive. Air pollution can also damage other parts of the body. Some pollutants are absorbed into the bloodstream and are carried to sensitive organs. Two of the most general consequences of air pollutants for body tissues are formation of scar tissue and the accumulation of fluid, particularly in the lungs. Human respiratory tract defenses—nasal hairs, ciliated cells lining the upper airways, coughs and sneezes, and the sense of smell—are often overwhelmed by air pollutants. High levels of pollutants can weaken the immune systems of individuals who might otherwise be healthy and make them more susceptible to colds, infections, and other diseases that are seemingly unrelated to air pollution.[7]

Researchers have compared the incidence of bronchitis, chronic cough, and other respiratory diseases among children living with mothers who smoke at least one pack of cigarettes a day and children living in cities with high pollution levels. Children living in such cities are up to three times more likely to suffer from respiratory problems than children whose mothers smoke, thus demonstrating the seriousness of the health threat posed by community air pollution.[8] In controlled experiments, human subjects who breathe acid compounds and other particulates for short periods of time at levels commonly found in urban areas experience decreased lung capacity and other respiratory problems. Hospitalization of children for respiratory problems during periods of high levels of particulate pollution occurs at a rate three times that observed when such levels are below the national standard. People suffering from coronary heart disease suffer chest pains, reduced flow of oxygen to the blood, and decreased physical strength when exposed to levels of carbon monoxide that are lower than those found in many cities.[9]

Regulating Ambient Air Pollutants

Measuring the impact of regulations on air quality is fraught with difficulties. The reduction in emissions achieved by pollution controls might be offset by changes in meteorological conditions that result in increased levels of ambient air pollutants. Concentrations of ambient air pollutants may decrease as a result of a downturn in economic activity that causes the closing of polluting factories, and increase during periods of economic growth. Emissions and ambient air quality are also affected by changes in the relative cost of different forms of energy.[10]

The rate of emissions, the size of the airshed (or air quality region) into which they are emitted, and the circumstances under which they are emitted—including such variables as wind, rain, temperature, and geography—all significantly determine the impact of pollutants. The formation of temperature inversions in mountain valleys (a layer of warm air traps a layer of cold air beneath it, blocking the normal convection of air upward as the surface of the earth is heated), for example, limits the vertical

Table 2-3   Major Source Categories and Subcategories for Air
Pollutants

Transportation	Solid Waste Disposal
Highway vehicles (gasoline and diesel-powered)	Incineration
Aircraft	Open burning
Railroads	Fugitive Dust PM_{10} Sources
Vessels	Paved roads
Off-highway vehicles and machinery	Unpaved roads
Stationary Source Fuel Combustion	Agricultural tilling
Electric utilities	Construction activity
Industrial boilers	Mining and quarrying
Commercial and institutional boilers and furnaces	Wind erosion
Residential furnaces and space heaters	Industrial Processes
Miscellaneous	Chemical manufacturing
Forest fires	Petroleum refining
Other burning (agricultural burning, coal refuse burning, and structure fires)	Primary and secondary metals
	Iron and steel mills
	Mineral products
Miscellaneous organic solvents evaporation	Food production and agriculture
	Industrial organic solvent use
	Petroleum product production and marketing

Source: Environmental Protection Agency, *National Air Pollutant Emission Estimates 1940-1990* (Washington, D.C.: EPA, 1991), 4.

movement of polluted air. The mountains limit horizontal movement, and emissions of pollutants from stationary and mobile sources can build to unhealthy levels. Table 2-3 gives the major source categories and subcategories for air pollutants.

Emissions from stationary and mobile sources have generally decreased over the past few decades and ambient air quality has improved in many areas. But it is not clear how much of this progress can be attributed to the Clean Air Act, or why more progress has not been made, or how the act should be reformed or improved. Those engaged in the debate over the Clean Air Act during the past decade have taken two basic positions: The Clean Air Act should be strengthened to ensure that it protects human health and environmental quality and updated so that it regulates new risks; and the Clean Air Act should be reformed so that the costs of complying with its provisions are reduced.

In a 1991 study, the EPA attempted to estimate the effect of controls imposed under the Clean Air Act of 1970 by projecting emissions based on levels of control existing at the time of its enactment and comparing

Figure 2-3   Actual 1988 Emissions as a Percentage of Projected 1988 Emissions
Using 1970 as a Control

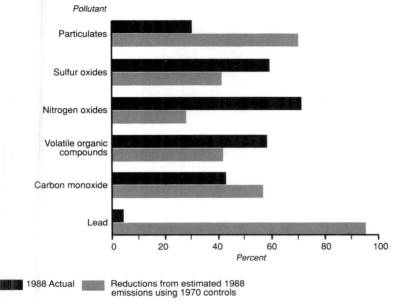

Pollutant

Source: Environmental Protection Agency, *Economic Investments: The Cost of a Clean Environment* (Washington, D.C.: EPA, 1991), 5-3.

them with actual 1988 emissions. The results of this study are shown in Figure 2-3. Emissions of lead, particulates, and carbon monoxide appear to have been most affected by control efforts resulting from the 1970 act. Installation of auto tailpipes was clearly effective in reducing lead and carbon monoxide emissions. Reductions in particulate emissions might be more a function of industrial modernization than of regulatory efforts, but the relative impact of different factors is difficult to determine. Although the EPA concluded that the Clean Air Act has resulted in the reduction of pollution, its goal—protecting public health with an adequate margin of safety—is far from being achieved.

Carbon Monoxide. Carbon monoxide is a colorless, odorless, invisible gas that is produced primarily by the incomplete combustion of organic (carbon-containing) material. Although carbon monoxide is generally viewed as being the ambient pollutant that is least potentially hazardous to the health of the population as a whole, there is increasing evidence that it does represent a serious health risk. Carbon monoxide reduces attention span, problem-solving ability, sensory ability, and visual acuity.[11] These effects usually disappear after a few hours, but CO has been implicated in

Figure 2-4 Emissions of Carbon Monoxide, 1940-1990

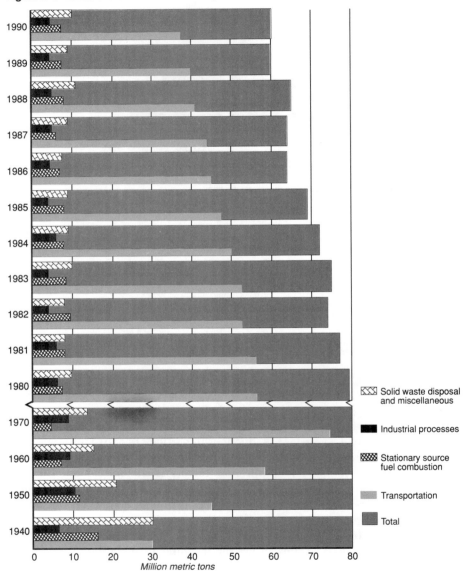

Source: Environmental Protection Agency, *National Air Pollutant Emission Estimates, 1940-1990* (Washington, D.C.: EPA, 1991), 12.
Note: See Table 2-3, which gives major source categories and subcategories for air pollutants.

accidents resulting from decreased attention and sensory ability. There is also some evidence that it causes or contributes to the severity of respiratory diseases such as asthma and bronchitis and reduces respiratory function.[12]

The most serious health threat from exposure to carbon monoxide, especially in urban areas, is the reduction in the capacity of blood to deliver oxygen throughout the body. Animal studies have shown that CO can damage the central nervous system of offspring that had chronic prenatal exposure to the pollutant.[13] Acute high doses can cause asphyxiation, heart and brain damage, and impaired perception. Chronic exposure to carbon monoxide can cause an increased density of red blood cells, leading to increased resistance of veins and arteries to blood flow, weakness, fatigue, and headache.[14] Such exposure has also been associated with heart and arterial disease and with angina.[15] At very high concentrations it is lethal.[16]

Both natural processes and human activity produce carbon monoxide, but there is little agreement over the magnitude of the relative contribution of the two sources.[17] Natural sources include volcanoes, forest fires, and electrical storms; CO is also found in marsh and mine gases and in the surface layers of the ocean. Human activity is the source of automobile exhaust, smoke from residential fireplaces and cigarettes, and fumes from industrial processes. Concentrations of CO range from 1 to 30 parts per million (ppm) in urban air to 20,000 to 60,000 ppm in cigarette smoke and 30,000 to 80,000 ppm in exhaust from older motor vehicles.[18] Industrial emissions of carbon monoxide have decreased somewhat since 1970, largely because reductions in emissions from a few high-polluting processes have exceeded increases in other areas of industrial output. Air pollution controls installed since 1970 have reduced emissions from solid waste disposal. Forest fires produced significant levels of CO in the 1940s, but as fire prevention efforts have improved, this source of carbon monoxide emissions has also decreased.[19] Mobile vehicles are the primary source of CO emissions. Residential wood burning, the second largest source, accounts for about 10 percent of such emissions. Figure 2-4 shows the trend in carbon monoxide emissions from 1940 to 1990.

Ozone. Ozone, a colorless gas with a pungent odor, is a naturally occurring constituent of the atmosphere. Its peak concentration is in the upper atmosphere (stratosphere). Ozone is a form of oxygen and composed of three atoms of oxygen, making it highly reactive and causing it to combine with virtually every substance with which it comes in contact. (The problem of depletion of the stratospheric ozone layer is discussed later in this chapter.) Ozone is produced by human activity when sunlight triggers chemical reactions between pollutants (such as volatile organic compounds and nitrogen oxides) and the gases that occur naturally in the atmosphere.

At low altitudes, ozone is a noxious pollutant. In the stratosphere, however, ozone provides a protective layer that absorbs most of the ultraviolet rays from the sun, thereby shielding life on earth from their harmful effects. Such radiation can, if it reaches the earth, damage biological molecules, including DNA, and bring about increases in the incidence of skin cancer and cataracts. Without the protection that the stratospheric ozone layer provides, life as we know it would probably not exist at all. In contrast, low-level ozone can break down body tissue and cells, particularly lung tissue, and is highly toxic when inhaled, causing or contributing to several pulmonary diseases including emphysema, bronchitis, pulmonary edema, and asthma, as well as premature aging of lung tissue. Ozone also irritates mucous membranes of the nose and throat and impairs lung-clearance mechanisms.[20] It has been shown to reduce the body's resistance to disease and to decrease the ability to engage in physical activity. Acute high-level exposure can cause stress on the heart; chronic exposure can result in heart failure.[21] Ozone can also harm trees and crops and damage fragile aquatic ecosystems.

There is considerable debate among scientists and physicians over whether the national ambient air quality standard for ozone is low enough to protect human health. In the fall of 1991, the American Lung Association sued the EPA for its failure to review the ozone standard in the face of new evidence concerning the adverse health effects of exposure at levels below the standard. A congressional Office of Technology Assessment report indicated that meeting the ozone standard would likely eliminate "several hundred million episodes of such respiratory symptoms as coughing, chest pain and shortness of breath," and "8-50 million days of restricted activity . . . days when someone feels ill enough to limit the day's activities, if not necessarily to stay in bed or home from work." No estimates were given, however, of the benefits of reducing the chronic effects of exposure to ozone.[22]

Ozone belongs to a broad group of pollutants, photochemical oxidants, that pose similar risks to human health and ecological systems. Volatile organic compounds are the primary constituent of ozone. Hydrocarbons are a particularly important subset of VOCs that contribute to its formation. Several hydrocarbons such as benzene are also known carcinogens.[23] Part of the challenge in meeting the ozone standard has been that small stationary sources and motor vehicles are the largest sources of VOC emissions. In 1985, for example, motor vehicles produced 11.0 million tons of VOCs, small stationary sources (such as dry cleaners and paint shops) released 10.6 million tons; large stationary sources (such as chemical manufacturing plants and oil refineries) released only 2.1 million tons, and other means of transportation such as air and rail produced 1.4 million tons.[24] Before passage of the 1990 amendments, emissions from small sources had generally not been regulated. Ozone levels are usually highest in the summer when the weather is warmest, sunlight is most intense, and traffic levels are highest.[25] Peak ozone readings are highly correlated with maximum daily temperatures and with the number of days where temperatures exceed 90° Fahrenheit. High temperatures increase the evaporation of VOCs and also stimulate the chemical reactions that produce urban ozone. Figure 2-5 shows the trend in emissions of volatile organic compounds from 1940 to 1990. Total emissions decreased slightly between 1979 and 1988 despite a 33 percent increase in vehicle miles traveled during that period.[26]

Ozone has been one of the most difficult pollutants to regulate. Every major urban area in the United States except Minneapolis-St. Paul (94 metropolitan areas—virtually every major eastern and midwestern city) has failed to meet the ozone air quality standard. More people live in areas that fail to meet the air quality standard for ozone (63 million in 1990) than live in areas failing to meet the standard for any other pollutant. Despite the formulation and implementation of state cleanup plans and the imposition of increasingly stringent control requirements, air quality levels have not appreciably improved. Gains in the use of cleaner technologies and processes have been offset by growth in the number of sources. The summers of 1986-1990 were five of the eight warmest summers ever recorded in the United States, and if this trend continues, meeting the ozone air quality standard will remain an elusive goal.

Particulate Matter. Particulate matter (PM_{10}) is a broad category of pollutants that includes a variety of chemicals and particles, ranging from dust to particles of heavy metals (such as chromium and nickel) and radioactive particles. Primary particulates include dust, dirt, soot, smoke, and liquid droplets that are emitted directly into the air by factories, power plants, and wood-burning stoves, as well as naturally occurring windblown dust. Secondary particulates are formed when gases such as sulfur dioxide and volatile organic compounds are transformed in the atmosphere into tiny particles. Until 1987, the national ambient air quality standard for particulates regulated levels of total suspended particulates. On July 1, 1987, the EPA promulgated a national ambient air quality standard for particulate matter that has an aerodynamic diameter of 10 micrometers or less. (A micrometer, or micron, is approximately 1/25,000th of an inch; 10 micrometers is about one-tenth the diameter of a human hair.)

Researchers studying the health effects of pollution conducted throughout the 1970s and 1980s concluded that fine particulates with a diameter of 10 micrometers or less pose a much greater risk to human health than larger particles.[27] Larger particles are usually filtered out by the body's defense mechanism in the nasal-pharynx region; fine particles are much

Figure 2-5 Emissions of Volatile Organic Compounds, 1940-1990

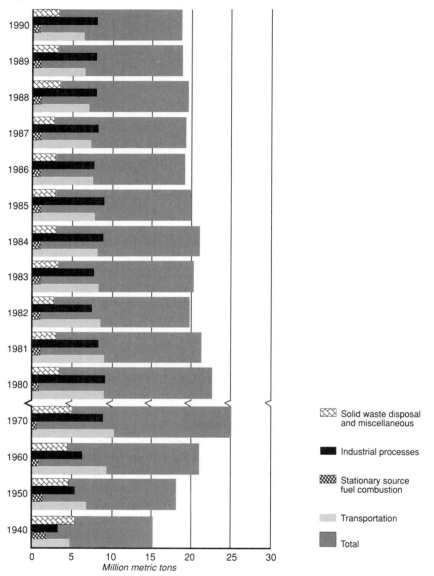

Million metric tons

Solid waste disposal and miscellaneous

Industrial processes

Stationary source fuel combustion

Transportation

Total

Source: Environmental Protection Agency, *National Air Pollutant Emission Estimates, 1940-1990* (Washington, D.C.: EPA, 1991), 11.
Note: See Table 2-3, which gives major source categories and subcategories for air pollutants.

more difficult for the body to filter out. They bypass the defense mechanisms and travel deep into the lungs. Some small particles, 0.05 micrometers in diameter or less, may remain in the lungs at the deepest or alveoli level for the life of the individual. Particulates of heavy metals and those of arsenic and asbestos, sulfates, nitrates, hydrocarbons, and other chemicals, as well as radioactive particles, diesel exhaust particles, and particles in smoke are dangerous when they are inhaled and become imbedded in lung tissue. Deep penetration of the lungs is especially dangerous if high concentrations of other pollutants (especially sulfur oxides and nitrogen oxides) are also inhaled. Particulates are a major cause of or contributor to respiratory diseases, and many are known carcinogens. In one study, hospital admissions for pneumonia, bronchitis, and asthma were found to be statistically correlated with high levels of particulate matter in the lungs. Such admissions were two to three times more numerous in the wintertime, when levels of pollution were high, than in periods when pollution levels were low. These relationships were clearly demonstrated, even after adjustment for temperature inversions and other factors.[28] Another study demonstrated adverse health effects of particulate matter at levels well below the national ambient air quality standard.[29] Animal experiments have shown similar damage to respiratory systems as a result of exposure to particulate pollution. Animals exposed to bacterial infections and air pollutants are likely to die sooner than animals having the same infections that were not exposed to pollutants. Pollen grains and fungal spores may also be 10 micrometers or less in diameter and can cause significant human health problems, especially allergic reactions.

Major industrial sources of PM_{10} are steel mills, smelters, power plants, cotton gins, and cement plants. Diesel engines, road dust, demolition, construction, and wood-burning stoves and fireplaces also produce fine particulates.[30] Figure 2-6 (p. 57) shows the trend in emissions of total suspended particulates from 1940 to 1990. Progress in reducing such emissions was made between 1950 and 1970, even before the Clean Air Act was passed, despite tremendous economic growth, as industries and power plants became more efficient. Residential burning of coal decreased substantially after 1940; there was also some reduction in the industrial use of coal as a fuel between 1940 and 1990. The use of coal in generating electricity more than doubled between 1970 and 1990, but TSP emissions actually decreased during that period as control equipment was installed. Industrial emissions decreased by about 75 percent from 1970 to 1990. Emissions of TSP from mobile sources decreased from 1940 to 1960 as coal-burning railroad locomotives were phased out, but they actually increased from 1960 to 1988 because the number of miles traveled grew. Emissions from stationary source fuel combustion, industrial processes, and incineration of solid waste also decreased after clean air legislation was enacted in 1970.[31]

According to EPA estimates made in 1987, residents of 72 counties in 20 states live in areas where the PM_{10} standard is violated. Another 110 counties may be in violation of the standards if current trends continue.

Sulfur Dioxide.   Sulfur dioxide (SO_2) is an invisible gas with a pungent odor. The major source of SO_2 is the combustion of sulfur-containing fuels, primarily coal and fuel oil. Until the 1950s, railroad engines that burned coal were a major source of emissions. Two-thirds of current sulfur dioxide emissions come from electric power plants. Other sources include refineries, pulp and paper mills, smelters, steel and paper plants, oil shale and synfuels facilities, and residential coal-burning furnaces and fireplaces; it is also emitted in the production of oil and gas.[32] Figure 2-7 (p. 58) shows the trend in emissions of sulfur oxides from 1940 to 1990. Sulfur compounds in the air have been implicated in increased mortality in several studies.[33] Sulfur dioxide is generally not the most harmful of the sulfur compounds in the atmosphere, even though it is the form that is most often monitored and is still a serious environmental problem.[34] Sulfur dioxide may also be transformed into sulfates and sulfuric acid, which are part of PM_{10}. Killer fogs in various parts of the world have been associated with high levels of sulfur oxides. Sulfur dioxide can thicken tracheal mucous layers and, in very high concentrations, can damage the lining of the trachea. It can also inhibit clearance of inhaled particles and cause bronchial constriction. Acute exposure to high levels of sulfur dioxides can cause edema (accumulation of fluid in tissue), bronchial spasms, shortness of breath, irritation of the respiratory tract, impaired pulmonary function and lung clearance, and increased susceptibility to disease. Sulfur dioxide can trigger asthma attacks and has been shown to cause or exacerbate emphysema.[35] One study found that schoolchildren who were exposed to high levels of sulfur dioxide for five to ten years suffered permanent effects.[36] Chronic exposure to sulfur dioxide can exert stress on the heart.[37]

Concentrations of sulfur dioxide have decreased by more than 25 percent since 1970, primarily as a result of the use of coal and other fuels with a lower sulfur content, installation of flue gas desulfurization equipment or "scrubbers" at power plants and factories, and other changes in industrial processes. Sulfuric acid manufacturing plants built since 1972 have been required to meet more stringent regulations issued by the EPA, resulting in lower emissions. Increased use of western, low-sulfur coal has also helped reduce SO_2 levels.[38] In order to disperse sulfur dioxide concentrations, many power plants and factories installed tall stacks in the 1970s. The pollutant was dispersed locally, but it was transformed to sulfates and fell to the earth hundreds of miles away as acid rain (see pp. 68-71). Only one major urban area, Pittsburgh, currently exceeds the NAAQS. The standard is exceeded in counties in about sixteen states, primarily in the Midwest, because of the existence of large power plants.[39]

Figure 2-6   Emissions of Total Suspended Particulates[a], 1940-1990

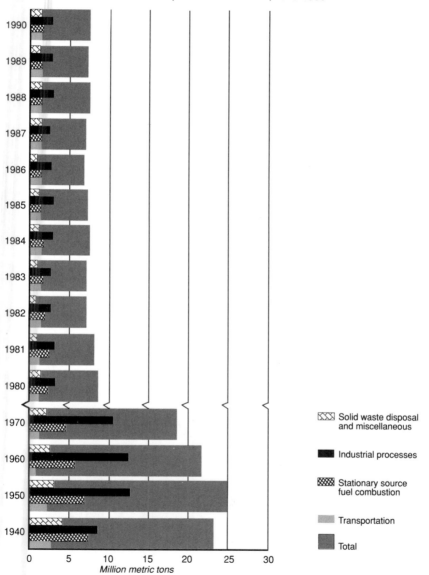

Source: Environmental Protection Agency, *National Air Pollutant Emission Estimates, 1940-1990* (Washington, D.C.: EPA, 1991), 7.

Note: See Table 2-3, which gives major source categories and subcategories for air pollutants.

[a]Although the EPA and the states continue to monitor total suspended particulate emissions, the national ambient air quality standard applies only to PM_{10}.

Figure 2-7   Emissions of Sulfur Oxides, 1940-1990

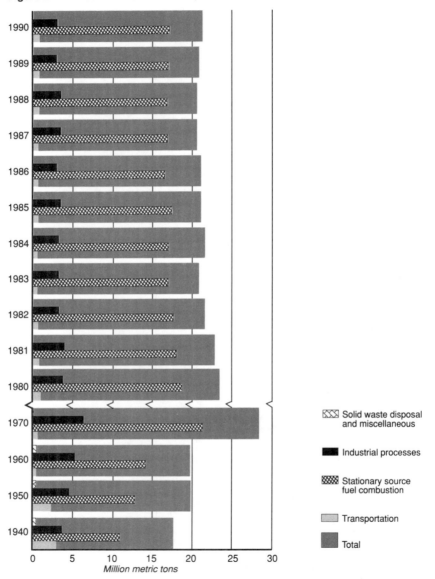

Source: Environmental Protection Agency, *National Air Pollutant Emission Estimates, 1940-1990*
(Washington, D.C.: EPA, 1991), 9.
Note: See Table 2-3, which gives major source categories and subcategories for air pollutants.

Nitrogen Dioxide. [Nitrogen dioxide (NO_2) is a yellowish, brownish red gas with a pungent odor. It forms in the atmosphere when nitrogen oxides are oxidized or gain oxygen. Nitrogen dioxide forms when fuel is burned at high temperatures; the formation of nitric acid, nitrates, and other pollutants in the atmosphere from nitrogen oxides seems to be the greatest concern. Nitrogen dioxide is a major component of ozone and acid rain.[40] Major emission sources are motor vehicles, power plants, and industrial boilers.]

[In low concentrations, nitrogen dioxide can impair the sense of smell, damage cell membranes and tissue, irritate and damage the pulmonary system, and aggravate respiratory diseases such as asthma, bronchitis, and emphysema. In high concentrations, it causes pulmonary edema and death. Relatively little is known about the long-term effects of nitrogen dioxide at current ambient air quality levels. Some studies indicate that some effects of nitrogen dioxide are reversible and that a tolerance may develop with repeated exposure.[41] One study found that schoolchildren in Chattanooga suffered from reduced respiratory function and increased incidence of bronchitis when exposed to nitrogen dioxide.[42] Exposure to the pollutant appears to lower the body's resistance to infection. Like carbon monoxide, it inhibits the ability of blood to carry oxygen to the body. Some studies have shown that NO_2 concentrations are associated with increases in mortality and heart disease.[43]]

[Emissions of nitrogen oxides increased rapidly from 1940 to 1970, peaked about 1980, and remained fairly constant throughout the 1980s, as shown in Figure 2-8. Controls on emissions of motor vehicles and coal-fired electric power plants have moderated the increase in emissions of nitrogen oxides despite the growth in transportation and industrial activity. Los Angeles is the only area where the national ambient air quality standard was exceeded in the 1980s.]

Lead.   The primary sources of lead emissions have been motor vehicles. For many years, this toxic metal was added to gasoline as an antiknock compound. Cars using lead-free gasoline were introduced in 1975, however, and the amount of lead in leaded gas has also been reduced. As a result, lead emissions have been cut dramatically; they decreased 93 percent between 1979 and 1988, as shown in Figure 2-9 (p. 61). Lead poses a major health risk at high levels. It decreases red blood cell production, affects the central nervous system thus causing loss of sensation, and has retarded the mental development of young children. High levels of lead emission are still a problem, primarily in areas where lead smelters are located. Only four areas of the United States exceeded the national ambient air quality standard in 1988.[44]

Figure 2-8   Emissions of Nitrogen Oxides, 1940-1990

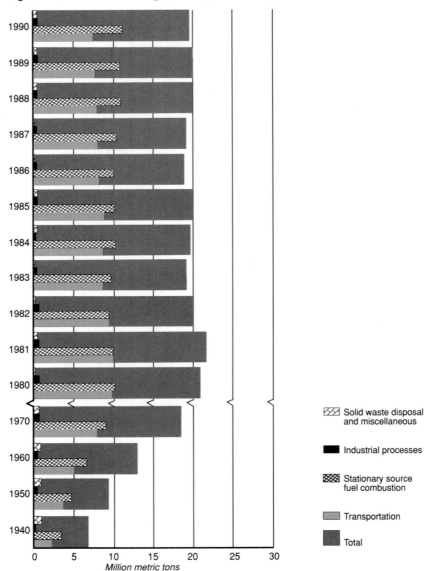

Source: Environmental Protection Agency, *National Air Pollutant Emission Estimates, 1940-1990*
(Washington, D.C.: EPA, 1991), 10.
Note: See Table 2-3, which gives major source categories and subcategories for air pollutants.

Figure 2-9  Emissions of Lead, 1970-1990

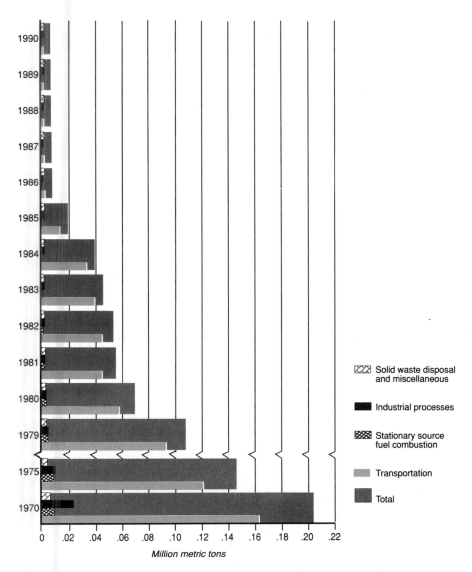

Source: Environmental Protection Agency, *National Air Pollutant Emission Estimates, 1940-1990* (Washington, D.C.: EPA, 1991), 13.
Note: See Table 2-3, which gives major source categories and subcategories for air pollutants.

Table 2-4   Ten U.S. Manufacturing Sites Releasing Most Toxic
Chemicals, 1989

Site	Company	Pounds released (millions)
Alvin, Texas	Monsanto	206.5
Westwego, Louisiana	American Cyanamid	192.4
Tooele, Utah	Magnesium Corporation of America	119.1
Wichita, Kansas	Vulcan	92.3
Beaumont, Texas	DuPont	88.1
Port Lavace, Texas	British Petroleum	65.5
New Johnsonville, Tennessee	DuPont	57.4
Chicago, Illinois	Inland Steel	57.3
Lima, Ohio	British Petroleum	56.7
Wichita, Kansas	Atochem	54.5

Source: John Holusha, "The Nation's Polluters—Who Emits What," *New York Times,*
October 13, 1991, F10.

Toxic or Hazardous Air Pollutants

The 1986 Emergency Planning and Community Right-to-Know Act,
also known as Title III of the Superfund law, aimed at cleaning up toxic
waste sites, requires manufacturers of some 300 different chemicals to
report annually to the EPA and to the states in which they operate the
amounts of these substances they release directly to the air, water, or
land. Facilities with ten or more employees that manufacture or process
more than 25,000 pounds of the reportable chemicals, or that use more
than 10,000 pounds of them, are required to file reports. The annual
publication of the EPA's *Toxics Release Inventory* based on the data, as
well as major accidental releases of chemicals (such as the toxic leak
from a Union Carbide Company chemical plant in Bhopal, India, in 1984
that killed thousands of people), generated widespread concern about air
toxics in the mid-1980s and increased support for strengthening the
Clean Air Act's provisions. Table 2-4 lists the ten worst manufacturing
sites in the United States in terms of the total amount of toxic chemicals
released.

Most of the information concerning the environmental and health
hazards posed by air toxics comes from laboratory tests with animals;
conclusions based on it are, at best, only tentative, however, since it is not
clear to what extent results can be extrapolated from animals to humans
and from high experimental doses to low actual exposure levels. Epidemiological data on which regulatory action might be based are often

Figure 2-10 Release and Transfer of Toxic Chemicals, 1987-1989

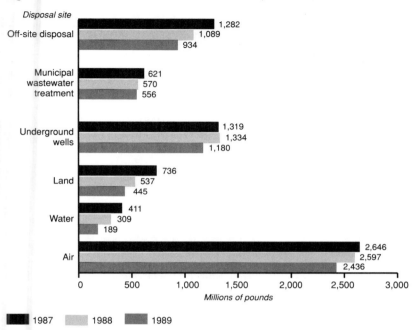

Source: Environmental Protection Agency, The Toxics-Release Inventory, Aggregate Data, 1991, 1.
Note: Chemicals were either disposed of off-site or released directly into the air, water, or publicly owned facilities for treatment of waste water; deposited on land; or injected into underground wells.

incomplete or inconclusive, because of conditions in the environment in which the exposure occurs. According to one estimate, only partial or minimal toxicity information is available regarding about 15 percent of the 13,000 chemicals that are produced in large quantities in the United States (more than a million pounds a year). Another 22,000 chemicals are estimated to be released in unknown quantities, and little or no information is available on their toxicity.[45]

In 1989, the EPA reported in its inventory that more than 5.7 billion pounds of toxic chemicals were released to the air, water or land, or injected underground. From 1987 (when the first inventory was compiled and published) to 1989, reported releases decreased by 1.3 billion pounds, even though more companies were reporting in 1989 and there was an increase in industrial production. These figures are rough estimates, since monitoring of toxic releases is still in its infancy; there is no enforcement mechanism to ensure accurate or complete reporting, for example. Consequently, the inventory may significantly understate the amount of air toxics released each year. Figure 2-10 shows the results of the first three

Table 2-5   Fifteen Toxic Chemicals Released into the Air in Largest Amounts, 1989

Chemical	Pounds released (millions)
Toluene	255.4
Ammonia	244.5
Methanol	199.7
Acetone	199.2
1,1,1-Trichlorethane	168.6
Methyl ethyl ketone	127.6
Xylene (mixed isomers)	147.5
Chlorine	132.3
Dichloromethane	109.3
Carbon disulfide	99.8
Freon 113	63.2
Hydrochloric acid	60.7
Trichlorethylene	44.3
Glycol ethers	47.7
Ethylene	41.4

Source: Environmental Protection Agency, *Toxics Release Inventory, Aggregate Data,* 1991.

years of the inventory. In 1989, approximately 2.4 billion pounds of toxic chemicals were released into the air, approximately 1.2 billion pounds were injected into underground wells, 445 million pounds were deposited on land, and 189 million pounds were released into bodies of water, for a total of approximately 4.2 billion pounds. An additional 934 million pounds were transported to other locations for disposal and 556 million pounds were sent to municipal wastewater treatment plants.

More toxic chemicals are released into the air than into any other medium. Table 2-5 lists the fifteen toxic chemicals that were released into the air in the largest amounts in 1989. Table 2-6 inventories toxic air emissions by industry. Many of the air toxics that are found in the greatest quantity (such as ammonia, a colorless gas with a strong odor; toluene, a liquid hydrocarbon similar to but less toxic than benzene; methanol, an alcohol made from wood or methane; and acetone, an organic compound) are used in liquid form as solvents. The vast majority of air toxics are released by chemical manufacturers, followed by producers of primary metals, and by the paper, plastics, and metal fabrication industries. These pollutants pose serious health hazards, especially in high concentrations. Most of them can irritate the nose, throat, mouth, eyes, and lungs. Toluene can also cause dizziness and headaches; damage bone marrow, liver, and kidneys; and damage the developing fetus. Ammonia and chlorine can burn the skin and eyes, sometimes causing permanent damage, and can

Table 2-6   Total Air Emissions of Toxic Chemicals by Industry, 1989

Industry	Pounds released (millions)
Chemicals	776.5
Primary metals	256.7
Transportation	219.4
Paper	216.2
Plastics	186.2
Fabrication of metals	141.1
Electrical	102.7
Petroleum	70.5
Furniture	61.8
Machinery	59.8
Printing	57.2
Instruments	52.9
Lumber	38.1
Textiles	37.3
Miscellaneous manufacturing	27.1
Stone/clay	24.7
Food	23.1
Tobacco	13.9
Leather	12.8
Apparel	4.5
Total	2,382.5

Source: Environmental Protection Agency, *Toxics Release Inventory, Aggregate Data,* 1991.

cause pulmonary edema. Acetone is flammable; it can irritate the eyes, nose, and throat and burn the skin. But these four are not generally considered to be the most serious air toxics.

The sources of air toxics are diverse and widely dispersed making regulation particularly difficult. Table 2-7 shows the distribution of the major sources of toxic air pollutants in the United States in 1988. About two-thirds of all industrial emissions come from point sources (major facilities such as power plants); the other one-third is released from nonpoint (area, or fugitive sources—small facilities such as bakeries and dry cleaners) that are widely dispersed and more difficult to monitor and regulate. The *Toxics Release Inventory* reports only emissions from relatively large industrial sources. The total amount of emissions in 1989 was more than double the estimated 5.7 billion pounds, since motor vehicle emissions account for more than half of all air pollution in the United States. Regulation of tailpipe exhaust, as discussed in Chapter 4, helps to reduce such emissions. Shifting to alternative fuels and reformulated gasoline may also help, although in the case of some of these fuels, one set of air toxics is merely substituted for another.

Table 2-7   Major Sources of Toxic Air Pollutants and Percentages Emitted, 1988

Source	Percent of total emissions
Area	
Motor vehicles	56
Treatment, storage, and disposal works	5
Secondary formaldehyde, nonpoint	5
Wood-burning smoke	4
Asbestos, demolition	4
Gasoline marketing	3
Solvent use/degreasing	1
Other/unspecified	2
Total	80
Point	
Electroplating	6
Cooling towers in power plants	3
Chemical users/producers	2
Secondary formaldehyde, point	2
Iron and steel production	1
Coal and oil combustion (nonresidential)	1
Other/unspecified	6
Total°	20

Source: Environmental Protection Agency figures, reported in George Hager, "The 'White House Effect' Opens A Long-Locked Political Door," *Congressional Quarterly Weekly Report,* January 20, 1990, 143.

° Percentages do not add to total because of rounding.

The EPA's regulation of air toxics under the Clean Air Act of 1970 was widely viewed as a failure. The agency was either unable or unwilling to define safe levels of exposure for these substances, and issued emission standards for only a handful of substances. In contrast, the Occupational Safety and Health Administration had regulated some 500 workplace toxic chemicals and the states had regulated more than 700 air toxics.[46] The clear failure of regulation efforts under the existing law, combined with widespread public fear of the health threat posed by air toxics (generated largely by the publicity given to chemical accidents), kept pressure on Congress to pass new legislation regulating emissions. In addition, the chemical industry, traditionally opposed to regulation, was now more willing to support some kind of legislation because of the growing public relations problem; some companies had already committed themselves to massive reductions in emissions.

Figure 2-11   Emission of Sulfur Oxides and Nitrogen Oxides from Electric
Utility Coal Combustion

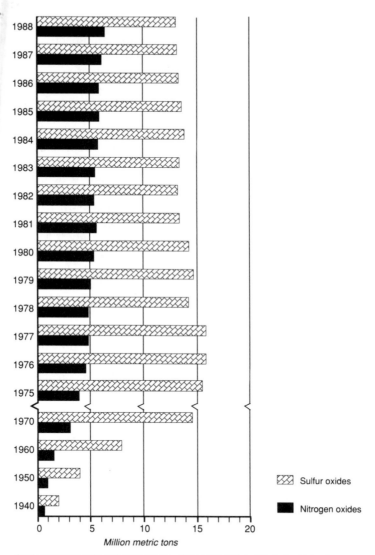

Source: Environmental Protection Agency, *National Air Pollutant Emission Estimates,
1940-1990* (Washington, D.C.: EPA, 1991), 57.

Acid Rain

Acid deposition (or, more commonly, acid rain) is a by-product of the burning of fossil fuels, which produces sulfur dioxide (SO_2) and nitrogen oxides (NO_x). These gases are transformed in the atmosphere into sulfuric acid and nitric acid. The acids usually remain in the atmosphere for weeks and may travel hundreds of miles before settling on or near the earth as dry particles or precipitation. Acidic particles and gases can also be formed at ground level and are absorbed directly by plants or oxidized into sulfates and nitrates and absorbed by the soil.

Most of the concern surrounding acid rain has focused on its danger to forests and aquatic resources. Studies conducted throughout the 1980s indicated that acid rain is a threat to watersheds, lakes, and streams in New England, forests and coastal plains in the mid-Atlantic region, and forests in northern Florida. Ozone and acid rain pollution are believed to harm red spruce and pine trees in the eastern and southeastern United States. The precipitation in many of the eastern states and Canadian provinces is thirty to forty times more acidic than it was in the 1980s.[47] The Office of Technology Assessment concluded that acidic aerosols (fine droplets composed of sulfur, nitrogen, and chlorine compounds and other chemicals) may be responsible for as many as 50,000 deaths in the United States each year and pose a serious threat to individuals with respiratory problems.[48]

The acidity of a substance is indicated by its pH factor, measured on a logarithmic scale. A change of one unit on the scale represents a tenfold increase or decrease in acidity. As shown in the scale at the bottom of Figure 2-12 (p. 70), battery acid has a pH rating of 1, lemon juice has a pH rating of approximately 2, and milk and pure water have a rating of 7, the neutral point. Natural sources cause rainfall that is otherwise unpolluted to have a pH factor of 5.5 to 7.0. Rain rated below a pH factor of 5.6 is generally considered to be sufficiently acidic to have negative environmental consequences.

Sources

The primary source of acid rain is sulfur oxides. Approximately 20 million tons of SO_x are emitted each year in the United States: 75 percent from electric utility power plants that burn fossil fuels, about 20 percent from industrial sources, and 5 percent from transportation sources. Fifty power plants, primarily older facilities not subject to the regulations for new sources issued under the Clean Air Act, are responsible for one-half of all SO_x emissions.[49] Figure 2-11 (p. 67) shows emissions of sulfur and nitrogen oxides by coal-fired power plants from 1940 to 1988. They have decreased by about 20 percent since 1977, even though the consumption of coal has increased significantly. Utility companies have been spending about $10 billion a year on air pollution controls.

Nitrogen oxides are the second major source of acid rain. In the United States, approximately 43 percent of NO_x emissions are from motor vehicles, 33 percent are from utilities, 15 percent are from other industrial combustion, and about 9 percent are from all other sources. These emissions are diverse and widely dispersed, and therefore are difficult to regulate. Both SO_x and NO_x emissions increased significantly until 1970. SO_x emissions peaked in 1976 and 1977 and have decreased since then.[50] NO_x total emissions have not been affected by reductions in utility emissions in recent years because they have been offset by increased motor vehicle travel and the use of oil and natural gas to fuel industrial combustion.[51]

Geographical Differences

Some areas are more susceptible to acid rain damage than others. The western and midwestern regions of the United States and Canada, for example, have a natural alkaline geological foundation, composed of limestone, that neutralizes acid rain. The granite foundation of eastern Canada and the northeastern states does not provide that natural buffer. According to some estimates, one-half of all the acid rain that falls on Canada comes from its southern neighbor; Canadian industries are responsible for 15 percent to 25 percent of the acid rain in the northeastern United States.[52] This dispersion of pollutants is largely a factor of prevailing wind patterns. Moreover, as a result of the health concerns voiced by residents of urban areas adjacent to industrial facilities, many of the coal-burning power plants built in the Midwest in the 1950s, 1960s, and early 1970s were equipped with tall smokestacks to disperse air pollution; it eventually traveled to the northeastern states and to Canada.[53] More than 90 percent of Canada's population is located within 150 miles of the U.S. border, and major sections of Canada's economy, including the fishing, forestry, and tourism industries, have been affected by acid rain.[54] Figure 2-12 shows acid rain concentrations in the United States and Canada.

A second critical regional difference, in the United States, is that coal has varying levels of sulfur content. Indiana, Illinois, Ohio, West Virginia, and Pennsylvania produce coal with a high sulfur level, and resist efforts to deal with the problem of acid rain by switching fuels. Kentucky and West Virginia have both low- and high-sulfur coal, whereas the considerable reserves in the western states consist primarily of low-sulfur coal. The most cost-effective means of reducing sulfur emissions is to burn low-sulfur coal, but members of Congress from midwestern states have warned that such a change would economically devastate some communities whose main industry is the production of high-sulfur coal.

Figure 2-12 Acid Rain Concentrations in the United States and Canada, as Measured by pH Values, 1985

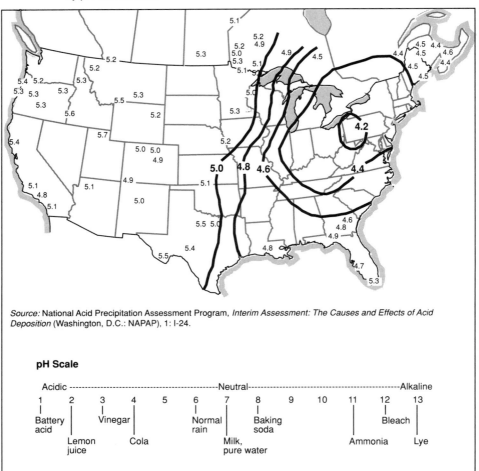

Source: National Acid Precipitation Assessment Program, *Interim Assessment: The Causes and Effects of Acid Deposition* (Washington, D.C.: NAPAP), 1: I-24.

pH Scale

Acidic					Neutral						Alkaline
1	2	3	4	5	6	7	8	9	10	11	12	13
Battery acid		Vinegar			Normal rain		Baking soda				Bleach	
	Lemon juice		Cola			Milk, pure water				Ammonia		Lye

The northeastern United States has relied on oil-fired facilities and nuclear power plants. Both the northeast and Canada rely on hydroelectric power. Midwestern critics of proposals to control acid rain have argued that Canadians have tried to sell more electricity to their neighbors to the south.[55] Environmental laws and regulations, in general, have been more stringent in the Northeast than in the Midwest.

Fossil fuel combustion not only contributes to acid rain but is also the major source of carbon dioxide, a greenhouse gas implicated as a primary cause in theories of global climatic change. NO_x emissions from automobiles are part of the larger problem of ozone that plagues most large cities in the United States. Regulations limiting motor vehicle emissions will help reduce acid rain, and that, in turn, will contribute to progress in resolving these other environmental problems.

The Stratospheric Ozone Layer

The depletion of the stratospheric ozone layer is one of the air pollution problems that, like acid rain, are global in scope and impact, and are the subject of international agreements and treaties as well as national legislation. Significant decreases in ozone levels have been discovered throughout the stratosphere, particularly at the North and South poles.[56] Some scientists have estimated that for every 1 percent decline in atmospheric ozone, there is a 2 percent increase in the amount of ultraviolet radiation that reaches the earth's surface. The Environmental Protection Agency calculates that a 1 percent decline in atmospheric ozone could result in a 5 percent increase in cases of nonmalignant skin cancer and a 2 percent increase in cases of malignant skin cancer (melanoma), which claims over 5,000 American lives each year. The EPA has warned that if ozone destruction continues unchecked, there will be more than 155 million additional cases of skin cancer and more than 3.2 million additional cancer deaths in the next century.

Causes of Stratospheric Ozone Depletion

In the 1960s, scientists found some evidence that ozone was being destroyed in the atmosphere. This destruction was generally attributable to solar ultraviolet radiation, which, during periods of high intensity, was believed to bombard ozone molecules and break them down. When this radiation lessened, the ozone was allowed to regenerate itself. In 1971, researchers became concerned that the proposed fleet of supersonic transport (SST) aircraft would damage the ozone layer because emissions of water vapor and nitrogen oxides from the SSTs had been shown to attack ozone. The SST fleet never came to fruition, but rising levels of nitrous oxides (N_2O), as a result of increased combustion and increased use of nitrogen-rich fertilizers, led to similar concerns in the early 1970s that the ozone layer was being destroyed.

In 1974, Mario J. Molina and F. Sherwood Rowland, scientists at the University of California at Irvine, proposed that the increasing use of compounds known as chlorofluorocarbons (CFCs) posed a new threat to the ozone layer that overshadowed all previous concerns. These compounds (which, as the name suggests, consist of chlorine, fluorine, and carbon) were discovered in the early 1930s when the struggling refrigerator industry was searching for a reliable, nontoxic, and nonflammable coolant. A chemist in the Frigidaire Division of General Motors astounded the scientific community when, at a meeting of the American Chemical Society, he inhaled vapors from a beaker of clear liquid, then turned to a burning candle and exhaled the gas, extinguishing the flame.

Chlorofluorocarbons constitute one of the most reliable groups of chemicals developed in the past half century and have a variety of industrial and commercial applications; for example, they are used as coolants for air conditioners and refrigerators, propellants for aerosol sprays, blowing agents to produce foam and insulation, and cleansers for computer microchips and other electronic parts. Their usefulness is a function of their chemical properties: CFCs are highly stable and unreactive and are therefore nontoxic.

Ironically, it is these characteristics of CFCs that make them so dangerous to ozone in the stratosphere. Since they are not broken down at the earth's surface, the intact CFC molecules rise slowly into the upper atmosphere. At levels above 25 kilometers, which is roughly where ozone is at its highest concentration, CFC molecules are bombarded by intense ultraviolet light, which breaks the normally stable CFC molecules into more reactive forms, such as chlorine atoms.

Chlorine is believed to be at the root of ozone depletion. Ozone (O_3) is created when an intact oxygen molecule (O_2) is struck by ultraviolet light. An ultraviolet photon splits the molecule into two highly reactive oxygen atoms (O). These atoms quickly combine with intact oxygen molecules to form ozone. This gas then readily absorbs ultraviolet light and is disassociated into its component parts (O_2 and O); the freed oxygen atom subsequently joins with another oxygen molecule to re-form ozone. This ozone is continually broken apart and re-formed until it collides with a free atom of oxygen, thereby forming two stable oxygen molecules. Ozone will thus reach a steady state in which its rate of formation is equal to its rate of removal, if constant conditions are maintained.

Chlorine, however, upsets this balance and reduces the amount of ozone by hastening the formation of stable oxygen molecules (O_2). When a chlorine atom (Cl) collides with an ozone molecule (O_3), the chlorine "steals" the third oxygen atom of ozone, resulting in the formation of a chlorine monoxide radical (ClO) and an oxygen molecule. Radicals, which are molecules that have an odd number of electrons, are quite reactive. When the chlorine monoxide radical meets a free oxygen atom, the oxygen atom in the chlorine monoxide becomes highly attracted to the free oxygen atom and breaks away to form a new oxygen molecule. This frees the chlorine atom to begin ozone destruction anew. Consequently, each chlorine atom can destroy as many as 100,000 ozone molecules before it is inactivated or returned to the troposphere by precipitation or other processes.

The concern, then, is that the release of millions of tons of CFCs into the atmosphere will cause an accumulation in the stratosphere capable of causing destruction to the ozone layer. The problem is especially acute because CFCs can remain in the atmosphere for decades. (Two of the major varieties of CFC, CFC-11 and CFC-12, have atmospheric lifetimes of approximately 75 and 100 years, respectively.) Even if the release of CFCs into the atmosphere were halted today, the destruction of ozone would continue well into the next century.

Some researchers suggest that CFCs may not be the only source of stratospheric ozone depletion.[57] One theory is that particles of the stratospheric clouds that form over the Antarctic region in the winter, when the absence of sunlight frequently results in temperatures below $-80°$ C, might stimulate the conversion of chlorine reservoirs into active chlorine: "It is possible that these particles trap and slowly modify the major chlorine reservoirs, preparing chlorine monoxide to make a rapid escape when the sun begins to shine." [58]

International Agreements to Protect the Stratospheric Ozone Layer

The research conducted by scientists in the mid-1970s led to the first international agreement to protect the ozone layer. International initiatives concerning ozone began in March 1977, when the secretariat of the United Nations Environment Program convened a meeting of experts who had been designated by governments and by intergovernmental and nongovernmental organizations. As a result of that meeting, an initiative entitled "A World Plan of Action on the Ozone Layer" was adopted and an international Coordinating Committee on the Ozone Layer was established.[59] In 1978, the United States, Canada, and several Scandinavian countries agreed to restrict or ban nonessential aerosol uses of CFCs. By 1983, regulatory action and voluntary industry restrictions in several CFC-producing countries had resulted in a reduction in CFC production of 21 percent below the peak level of 1974.[60]

In May 1981, a working group was established under the United Nations to draw up a framework for a general convention on the protection of the ozone layer. Despite the group's failure to agree on a specific provision for CFCs, its draft convention was adopted in 1985 as the Vienna Convention for the Protection of the Ozone Layer and was signed by twenty nations. The convention consists of twenty-one treaty articles and two technical annexes, or additions. The major provisions of the agreement emphasize the general responsibility of states for preventing environmental harm caused by human interference with the ozone layer; specify the duties of states with regard to intergovernmental cooperation, including monitoring, information exchange, and the harmonization of national measures; and create new international institutions (including a subsequent conference of the parties to the convention and a secretariat) to implement the agreement and to develop more specific rules in the form of protocols, technical annexes, and financial and procedural provisions.[61]

The Vienna Conference was only the beginning of international efforts to protect the ozone layer. New concerns arose over the seemingly accelerated rate at which the ozone layer was being depleted. In late 1985, a British research team published a report stating that springtime amounts of ozone over Antarctica had decreased by more than 40 percent between 1977 and 1984. Other research groups confirmed the conclusions of the British report and showed that the region of depletion was wider than the continent of Antarctica and spanned much of the lower stratosphere. In effect, they suggested the existence of a "hole" in the earth's protective layer of ozone. This theory prompted a search for the cause of the ozone loss. Most researchers returned to an explanation that had been proposed in the mid-1970s: that human-made chemicals, specifically CFCs, were depleting the ozone layer. Laboratory studies had previously showed that chlorine destroys ozone, and the millions of tons of CFCs that had been released into the atmosphere for decades were sufficient to produce the kind of damage that had been identified.

In 1986, delegates from fifty-four nations met in Geneva, Switzerland, to discuss limitations on the production and use of CFCs. The result of that meeting was the Montreal Protocol on Substances That Deplete the Ozone Layers, which was signed on September 16, 1987, by thirty-one nations. It limited the production of five CFC compounds (11, 12, 113, 114, and 115) and three forms of halon—a chemical used most commonly in fire extinguishers that, although used in smaller quantities than CFCs, is more effective in destroying ozone. The agreement also provided a graduated reduction schedule that would bring a 50 percent decline in CFC usage by 1999 for the industrialized nations and a smaller reduction for the developing countries.[62]

The Montreal Protocol called for an assessment of efforts to curb CFC production beginning in 1990. Barely a month after it was signed, however, a National Aeronautics and Space Administration expedition brought back definitive proof of a hole in the ozone layer, which demonstrated the inadequacy of the protocol's provisions and renewed calls for a total ban of CFCs. Findings released in 1988 by the Global Ozone Trends Panel, an international group of more than 100 scientists, showed that ozone depletion was occurring at two to three times the rate predicted by computer models. This meant, according to the scientists, that the world had already suffered more ozone depletion than was thought would occur by the year 2050 if nations observed the reduction schedule of the Montreal Protocol.[63] In June 1990, eighty-six nations agreed to go beyond the terms of the protocol and eliminate CFCs by the year 2000.[64] Significantly, the Western industrialized countries and Japan agreed to help the third world nations achieve such a reduction.[65]

Regulating air pollution is a complex policy task, given the wide variety in the kinds and sources of pollutants. The Clean Air Act of 1990 has many of the shortcomings of the 1970 law but also extends it to several major new areas. Chapter 3 traces the evolution of the law since 1970.

Notes

1. Thad Godish, *Air Quality* (Chelsea, Mich.: Lewis, 1991), 1-4.
2. Ibid.
3. Edward A. Keller, *Environmental Geology* (Columbus, Ohio: Merrill, 1987), 496.
4. Godish, *Air Quality*, 25-26.
5. Clean Air Act, sec. 112, 42 U.S.C. sec. 7412 (1990).
6. Environmental Protection Agency, *National Air Quality and Emissions Trends Report, 1990* (Washington, D.C.: EPA, 1991), 1-3.
7. See, generally, Charles E. Kupchella and Margaret C. Hyland, *Environmental Science: Living within the System of Nature* (Boston: Allyn & Bacon, 1989).
8. D. W. Dockery, J. H. Ware, B. G. Ferris, Jr., F. E. Speiser, N. R. Cook, and S. M. Herman, "Changes in Pulmonary Function in Children Associated with Air Pollution Episodes," *Journal of the Air Pollution Control Association* 32 (1982): 937-942; and C. Arden Pope III and Douglas W. Dockery, "Acute Health Effects of PM_{10} Pollution on Symptomatic and Asymptomatic Children," *American Review of Respiratory Disease* 145 (1992): 1123-1128.
9. For a review of a number of studies, see James S. Cannon, *The Health Costs of Air Pollution: A Survey of Studies Published 1978-1983* (Washington, D.C.: American Lung Association, 1985).
10. For further discussion, see Paul Portney, "Air Pollution Policy," in Paul Portney, ed., *Public Policies for Environmental Protection* (Washington, D.C.: Resources for the Future, 1990), 49- 52.
11. C. H. Conolly, *Air Pollution and Public Health* (New York: Dryden Press, 1973); and Alan J. Krupnick, Winston Harrington, and Bart Ostro, "Ambient Ozone and Acute Health Effects: Evidence from Daily Data" (Washington, D.C.: Resources for the Future, 1989), discussion paper QE 89-01.
12. S. M. Ayres, Robert Evans, David Licht, Jane Griesbach, Felicity Reimold, Edward F. Ferrand, and Antoinette Criscitiello, "Health Effects of Exposure to High Concentrations of Automotive Emissions," *Archives of Environmental Health* 27 (1973): 168-178.
13. L. D. Fechter and Zoltan Annau, "Toxicity of Mild Prenatal Carbon Monoxide Exposure," *Science* 197 (1977): 680-682.
14. Kupchella and Hyland, *Environmental Science*.
15. Paul Astrup, Knud Kjeldsen, and John Wanstrup, "Effects of Carbon Monoxide Exposure on the Arterial Walls," in *Biological Effects of Carbon Monoxide*, Annuals of the New York Academy of Science 174 (1970): 294-300; and Michael T. Kleinman, Dennis M. Davidson, Richard B. Vandagriff, Vincent J. Caiozzo, and James L. Whittenberger, "Effects of Short-term Exposure to Carbon Monoxide in Subjects with Coronary Artery Disease,"

Archives of Environmental Health 44 (1989): 361-369.

16. L. R. Babcock and N. L. Nagada, "Cost Effectiveness of Emission Control," *Journal of the Air Pollution Control Association* 23 (1973): 173-179.

17. D. J. Spedding, *Air Pollution* (Oxford: Clarendon Press, 1974), 58-62.

18. Utah County Clean Air Coalition, "Health Effects of Carbon Monoxide," 1991; World Health Organization, *Environmental Health Criteria 13: Carbon Monoxide* (Geneva: WHO, 1979).

19. Environmental Protection Agency, *National Air Pollutant Emission Estimates, 1940-1988* (Washington, D.C.: EPA, 1990), 4, 5, 60.

20. C. T. Stewart, *Air Pollution, Human Health, and Public Policy* (Lexington, Mass.: D.C. Heath, 1979); Kupchella and Hyland, *Environmental Science*.

21. D. L. Coffin and Herbert E. Stokinger, "Biological Effects of Air Pollutants," in Arthur C. Stern, ed., *Air Pollution*, 3d ed. (New York: Academic Press, 1977); Theodore D. Sterling, Seymour V. Pollack, and J. Weinkam, "Measuring the Effect of Air Pollution on Urban Morbidity," *Archives of Environmental Health* 18 (1969): 485-494.

22. U.S. Congress, Office of Technology Assessment, *Catching Our Breath: Next Steps for Reducing Urban Ozone* (Washington, D.C.: Government Printing Office, 1988), 8-9.

23. Godish, *Air Quality*, 41-48.

24. U.S. Congress, Office of Technology Assessment, *Catching Our Breath*, 13.

25. Environmental Protection Agency, *Environmental Progress and Challenges: EPA's Update* (Washington, D.C.: EPA, 1988), 18-19; Environmental Protection Agency, *National Air Quality and Emissions Trends Report, 1988* (Washington, D.C.: 1990), 65.

26. Environmental Protection Agency, *National Air Quality and Emissions Trends Report, 1988*, 65-73.

27. David F. S. Natusch and John R. Wallace, "Urban Aerosol Toxicity: The Influence of Particle Size," *Science* 186 (1974): 695-699.

28. C. Arden Pope III, "Respiratory Disease Associated with Community Air Pollution and a Steel Mill, Utah Valley," *American Journal of Public Health*, May 1989, 623-628.

29. C. Arden Pope III, Joel Schwartz, and Michael Ransom, "Daily Mortality and PM_{10} Pollution in Utah Valley," *Archives of Environmental Health* 47 (May-June, 1992): 211-217.

30. Environmental Protection Agency, *Environmental Progress and Challenges*, 21.

31. Environmental Protection Agency, *National Air Pollutant Emission Estimates, 1940-1988*, 3, 51-52.

32. Environmental Protection Agency, *Environmental Progress and Challenges*, 26-27.

33. For example, Lester B. Lave and E. P. Seskin, *Air Pollution and Human Health* (Baltimore: Johns Hopkins University Press, 1977). Other studies, however, have not shown this association. See, for example, R. B. Engdhal, "A Critical Review of Regulations for the Control of Sulfur Oxide Emissions," *Journal of the Air Pollution Control Association* 23 (1973): 364-375.

34. The national ambient air quality standards are for SO_2 and NO_2, but the EPA monitors emissions of SO_2 and NO_2. Emissions data thus include all oxides, but monitoring is limited to SO_2 and NO_2.

35. S. Ishikawa, D. H. Bowen, V. Fisher, and J. P. Wyatt, "The 'Emphysema Profile' of Two Midwestern Cities in North America," *Archives of Environ-*

mental Health 18 (1969): 660-666.

36. Carl M. Shy, Victor Hasselblad, Robert M. Burton, Cornelius J. Nelson, and Arlan A. Cohen, "Air Pollution Effects on Ventilatory Function of U.S. School Children," *Archives of Environmental Health* 27 (1973): 124-128; William H. Durham, "Air Pollution and Student Health," *Archives of Environmental Health* 28 (1974): 241-254.
37. Kupchella and Hyland, *Environmental Science.*
38. Environmental Protection Agency, *National Air Pollutant Emission Estimates, 1940-1988,* 55-56.
39. Environmental Protection Agency, *National Air Quality and Emissions Trends Report, 1988,* 26.
40. Environmental Protection Agency, *National Air Quality and Emissions Trends Report, 1989* (Washington, D.C.: EPA, 1991), 3-20.
41. For example, W. D. Wagner, Burris R. Duncan, Paul G. Wright, and Herbert E. Stokinger, "Environmental Study of Threshold Limit of NO_2," *Archives of Environmental Health* 10 (1965): 455-456.
42. Carl M. Shy, John C. Creason, Martin E. Pearlman, Kathryn E. McClain, Ferris B. Benson, and Marion M. Young, "The Chattanooga School Children Study: Effects of Community Exposure to Nitrogen Dioxide," *Journal of the Air Pollution Control Association* 20 (1970): 539-545.
43. See Lave and Seskin, *Air Pollution and Human Health;* Kupchella and Hyland, *Environmental Science,* for example.
44. Environmental Protection Agency, *National Air Quality and Emissions Trends Report, 1988,* 12, 97.
45. Conservation Foundation, *State of the Environment: An Assessment at Mid-Decade* (Washington, D.C.: Conservation Foundation, 1984), 64. For a fuller discussion of these and related issues, see National Research Council, *Risk Assessment in the Federal Government: Managing the Process* (Washington, D.C.: Government Printing Office, 1983).
46. David Durenberger, "Air Toxics: The Problem," *EPA Journal* (January-February 1991), 30-31.
47. Cecie Starr and Ralph Taggart, *Biology,* 5th ed. (Belmont, Calif.: Wadsworth, 1989), 795.
48. U.S. Congress, Office of Technology Assessment, *Acid Rain and Transported Air Pollutants: Implications for Public Policy* (Washington, D.C.: Government Printing Office, 1984).
49. Environmental Protection Agency, *National Air Quality and Emissions Trade Report, 1990* (Washington, D.C.: EPA, 1991), 3-13.
50. Ibid., 3-22.
51. Philip Shabecoff, "An Emergence of Political Will on Acid Rain," *New York Times,* February 19, 1989, A1.
52. John Carroll, *Acid Rain: An Issue in Canadian-American Relations* (Washington, D.C.: National Planning Association, 1982).
53. Section 123 of the Clean Air Act of 1970 was amended in 1977 to prohibit companies from relying on dispersal of pollutants by means of tall smokestacks to meet national ambient air quality standards rather than adhering to emission limits.
54. Tom McMillan, "Why Canadians Worry about Acid Rain," *EPA Journal,* June-July 1986, 8-10.
55. Sydney G. Harris, "Canadian Positions, Proposals, and the Diplomatic Dilemma: Acid Rain and Emerging International Norms," *Toledo Law Review*

17 (Fall 1985): 130-131.

56. See, generally, Cynthia Pollock Shea, *Protecting Life on Earth: Steps to Save the Ozone Layer*, Worldwatch Paper 87 (Washington, D.C.: Worldwatch Institute, 1988).

57. Mark R. Schoeberl, a scientist at the Goddard Space Center, contends that chlorine has little or nothing to do with the ozone "hole" and theorizes that "unusual atmospheric winds create the hole simply by shoving the ozone around." Photographs taken by Goddard's Nimbus 7 satellite that show an increase of ozone at lower latitudes when the hole appears at higher latitudes support this theory, for they suggest that the ozone is simply pushed from one region to the next. Ellen Ruppel Shell, "Watch This Space," *Omni* 9 (August 1987): 80.

58. Richard S. Stolarski, "The Antarctic Ozone Hole," *Scientific American* 258 (January 1988): 35.

59. Ibid., 40.

60. Peter H. Sand, "The Vienna Convention Is Adopted," *Environment* 27 (June 1985): 20.

61. Ibid.

62. Mike Mills, "Ozone Pact OK'd, But Some Say It's Not Enough," *Congressional Quarterly Weekly Report*, March 19, 1988, 706.

63. David D. Doniger, "Global Emergency," *Environmental Forum*, July-August 1988, 17.

64. The Soviet Union's representative told the meeting that his country would abide by the Montreal Protocol but that it would not support a drive led by the United States and the European Community for a total ban on CFCs by the turn of the century.

65. For a discussion of the history of the Montreal Protocol and of its provisions, see Richard E. Benedick, *Ozone Diplomacy* (Cambridge, Mass.: Harvard University Press, 1991).

3   From the Clean Air Act of 1970 to the 1990 Amendments

The passage of the Clean Air Act Amendments of 1990 was a remarkable political event and a landmark achievement in the making of environmental policy. The stage was set in 1989 for a fundamental change in the politics of clean air in Congress and a break in the legislators' decade-long deadlock. The summer of 1988 had been the hottest on record, intensifying fears of global warming and reminding Americans that they were not giving sufficient attention to protecting the environment. Environmental awareness was heightened in March 1989 by the Exxon *Valdez* Alaskan oil spill. The fact that many urban areas continued to fail to meet cleanup goals gave renewed impetus to demands that Congress update the 1970 law, even though the EPA had decided not to impose sanctions as long as Congress was considering clean air legislation.[1]

The debate over the Clean Air Act brought together two powerful forces—an alliance of environmental groups and a coalition of major U.S. industries—in a classic test of political power. Their resources and strategies differed in important ways. Environmentalists were able to frame most of the issues as clear choices for or against clean air. Industry representatives enjoyed ready access to many members of Congress and were able to shape many details of the bills they considered. Both groups were able to evoke powerful images—of job loss and economic devastation, ecological damage and human health risks.

The politics of clean air is not just a conflict between environmentalists and proponents of industry. Just as divisive have been the regional conflicts. Northeasterners blame air pollution from the Midwest for the damage done to their forests and lakes. Midwestern coal miners compete with westerners to gain enactment of legal provisions that encourage the use of their resources. (A shift away from the high-sulfur coal found largely in the eastern states increases demand for the low-sulfur coal abundant in western states.) Heavily polluted communities such as Los Angeles require the most stringent controls possible, whereas other areas resist pollution controls that they may not need and cannot afford. "Clean" states, in regions such as the sunbelt, where industrial and utility facilities are relatively new or where investments have already been made in pollution control equipment, resist proposals that they share in the cleanup costs, claiming they should be borne by the midwestern and northeastern states, where emissions are greatest. These states, which have extensive but aging industrial infrastructure, are supportive of regulatory restrictions on new pollution sources, whose effect is to impede industrial investment in clean states.[2]

The legislative process is influenced to a large degree by the legislators' personalities, personal motivations and priorities, and interpersonal and negotiating skills. The history of the clean air bill would probably have been different if the congressional leaders had been different. An important event in the evolution of the clean air bill was the replacement in 1989 of Senate Majority Leader Robert Byrd (D-W. Va.), champion of his state's high-sulfur coal miners and midwestern utility companies, by Sen. George Mitchell (D-Maine), a major proponent of acid rain regulations. Byrd had blocked clean air bills from reaching the Senate floor for several years, so Mitchell's leadership aroused hopes that the bill could finally be brought to a vote. (Byrd continued to be a major force as chairman of the Senate Appropriations Committee.) Mitchell had a long-standing commitment to the legislation, dating from his service as chairman of the Senate Committee on Environment and Public Work's Subcommittee on Environmental Protection in 1987-1988. The debate over the bill was a major test of Mitchell's leadership ability and that of Speaker Thomas Foley. Foley, although not known as an advocate of clean air legislation, seemed determined that disputes among Democrats in Congress would not be blamed for the demise of such a major piece of legislation. Rep. John Dingell (D-Mich.), chairman of the House Energy and Commerce Committee and a tireless champion of the auto industry, carefully controlled Democratic appointments to his committee throughout the 1980s to protect his constituents in Detroit from new regulatory requirements. The constituency of Rep. Henry Waxman (D-Calif.), chairman of that committee's Subcommittee on Health and the Environment, which had initial jurisdiction over the bill, included Los Angeles, a city with serious air pollution problems. Waxman also led the efforts to extend the life of the Clean Air Act in the early 1980s. The hearings of his subcommittee and those of the Senate Committee on Environment and Public Works were a major source of ideas for the 1989 bills.

It is useful to put the 1990 Clean Air Act in historical context by briefly reviewing its evolution beginning in 1970 and examining how it was affected by developments in the 1980s. The issues surrounding clean air policy have been debated in Congress for two decades, and many of them are still matters of controversy. The conflict that developed in the early 1980s between members of the Reagan administration and congressional Democrats over how the Clean Air Act and other environmental laws were to be implemented and enforced created an atmosphere of distrust that continued for the remainder of the decade.

The Clean Air Act of 1970

Early Efforts to Control Pollution

The first clean air laws in the United States were enacted by cities. Chicago and Cincinnati passed ordinances in the 1880s to limit smoke emissions. By the 1940s, the health effects of pollution had become a concern of public health officials. In Los Angeles, state and local officials and industry leaders launched a research program to study the health effects of air pollution. Heavy fogs in Donora, Pennsylvania, in 1948 (and also in London in 1952) resulted in thousands of deaths. In 1962, Oregon became the first state to establish a comprehensive air pollution program.[3] The federal government's involvement in improving air quality began in 1955, when the Public Health Service was authorized to conduct research on air pollution.[4] The first Clean Air Act was a very modest response to the initial concern in the nation about air pollution. It increased the funds earmarked for research and established a legal process by which municipalities, states, and the federal government could take regulatory action against sources of pollution.[5] Much of the attention was focused on motor vehicle emissions of carbon monoxide, hydrocarbon, and nitrogen oxides, which were blamed for 60 percent of all air pollution. Stationary sources, especially those emitting sulfur oxides and particulates, were responsible for the remaining 40 percent. In 1965, Congress authorized the secretary of the Department of Health, Education, and Welfare (HEW) to establish standards for emissions of hydrocarbons and carbon monoxide by new motor vehicles. The regulations were issued in 1966 and took effect in the 1968 model year.[6]

Between 1955 and 1970, the federal government became increasingly involved in helping to fund state efforts to regulate air pollution. Congress was reluctant to give any real regulatory power to federal officials, however, even though the states were doing relatively little and many air pollution problems transcended state boundaries.[7] A major expansion of regulatory authority was achieved with passage of the Air Quality Act of 1967. Under the act, the federal government was to establish metropolitan air quality regions throughout the United States. States were authorized to establish air quality standards and to develop plans to achieve them. If they failed to do so, HEW was authorized to issue and enforce federal standards. By 1970, no state had put in place a complete set of standards for any pollutant and the federal government had designated less than one-third of the metropolitan air quality regions that had been projected.[8]

Public Controversy and Governmental Debate

In his State of the Union Address in January 1970, Richard Nixon called for "comprehensive new regulations" to protect the environment.[9] The Nixon administration also proposed legislation to strengthen the 1967 Clean Air Act. Part of its motivation was a concern that regulation in some states but not in others put regulated industries at a competitive disadvantage. In its version of the bill, the administration proposed that HEW be authorized to establish national ambient air quality standards for pollutants it determined were health risks. Authority would remain with the states to develop implementation plans to ensure that federal health standards were met. The proposals contributed to a wave of public concern over the environment in 1970 that led to the first Earth Day in April, widespread demands for increased protection of air quality (including the demand that Congress proclaim "the right of each individual to an unpolluted environment"[10]), demonstrations that included ceremonial burial of new cars because their emissions endangered public health, and creation of the Environmental Protection Agency by a presidential reorganization plan.[11]

Much of the controversy surrounding the bill centered on whether standards for new vehicle emissions would be set by the EPA (the Nixon administration's position) or written into the law, as proposed by both the House and Senate. The auto industry launched a major lobbying effort to allow the EPA to set emission standards.

The auto industry also fought hard against inclusion of stringent tailpipe emission standards in the law, arguing that the proposed standards could not be met with existing technology. The industry's defenders in Congress, particularly Sen. Robert P. Griffin (R-Mich.), charged that Congress was "hold[ing] a gun at the head of the American automobile industry in a very dangerous game of economic roulette." Deadlines for meeting the tailpipe emission standards were the most contentious issue throughout the debate in Congress.[12]

On June 3 the House Interstate and Foreign Commerce Committee reported a bill that was quite similar to the administration's version, introduced in February. The House passed the bill on June 10 after efforts to make it more stringent were defeated. Several House members had pressed for a number of amendments to require stricter auto emission and fuel efficiency standards, charging that the committee had "ben[t] over backward to accommodate the auto and oil industries."[13]

The Senate Environment and Public Works Committee's bill, reported out in September, was much more aggressive than the House or administration versions. It authorized more money for research and grants, mandated stricter penalties for violations, required a 90 percent reduction in auto emissions by 1975 (with provisions for a one-year extension if needed), gave the EPA broad discretion to regulate use of fuels, and permitted citizen suits against polluters and the EPA. The House-Senate conference accepted some of the Senate's provisions, such as the 1975 deadline, stricter enforcement penalties, and EPA regulation of fuel emissions. Other provisions, such as funding levels, warranties for pollution control equipment, and testing standards, were compromises between the House and Senate bills.[14]

The clean air bill was passed in December 1970.[15] Although Nixon championed the legislation as a cooperative, bipartisan effort, his administration eventually came to see that the issue of clean air could be used to political advantage. The leading proponent of clean air legislation in Congress, Sen. Edmund S. Muskie (D-Maine), was not invited to the presidential signing ceremony, apparently because he was rumored to be a candidate for the Democratic party's 1972 presidential nomination.[16]

Main Provisions of the Act

The Clean Air Act of 1970 was an ambitious attempt by Congress to protect every American from the health risks of polluted air. Its stated aim was "to protect and enhance the quality of the Nation's air resources so as to promote the public health and welfare and the productive capacity of its population."[17] To achieve the goal of cleaning up the nation's air within five years, it established national ambient air quality standards and gave the states responsibility for developing and enforcing implementation plans to meet those standards. Stationary pollution sources were to come into compliance with state implementation plans by 1975, with one extension of two years permitted. The act made federal funds available to states for the development of implementation plans and increased funding for research on the health effects of airborne pollutants. Such plans were to be submitted to the EPA within nine months of the issuance of the standards. The EPA was to ensure that each plan included emission limitations and monitoring requirements for pollution from stationary sources, a program for the regulation of new sources of pollution, inspection and testing of motor vehicles for emissions, and provision of adequate state resources to implement and enforce the plan. If the states failed to submit acceptable plans, the EPA was authorized to amend them or formulate a federal plan to achieve national ambient air quality standards. State implementation plans were to achieve compliance with the federal standards within three years of their approval, but a three-year extension could also be granted by the EPA. Motor vehicle emissions of carbon monoxide and hydrocarbons were to be reduced by 90 percent from 1970 levels beginning with the 1975 model year. Emissions of nitrogen oxides were to be cut by 90 percent from a 1971 baseline level by

1976. Emission standards were to be met for five years or 50,000 miles, whichever was less. Anyone removing pollution control devices was subject to a $10,000 fine. The EPA was authorized to test new vehicles for compliance with the mandated emission reductions, to set standards for pollution control equipment warranties, and to regulate use of fuel additives that endangered public health.[18]

The 1970 law provided both enforcement powers and penalties. The EPA was authorized to seek injunctions to halt emissions that endangered public health. Citizens could initiate suits against the EPA for failure to take nondiscretionary actions, and against polluters who violated federal standards. Enforcement actions against polluters who knowingly violated provisions of state implementation plans could result in fines of up to $25,000 a day for each violation and up to one year in prison.

The Nixon administration helped to generate political support for reauthorizing and strengthening clean air legislation. Part of its motivation was a concern that regulation in some states but not in others put regulated industries at a competitive disadvantage. Industry representatives also lobbied for one set of federal standards rather than a variety of state provisions. They prevailed on Congress to prohibit the states (except California, since it had already developed stringent auto emission and fuel standards) from imposing more aggressive regulation than provided in the Clean Air Act of 1970.

The Clean Air Act of 1977

The Clean Air Act of 1970 was amended in 1971, 1973, 1974, and 1976, primarily to provide waivers for the motor vehicle emission standards.[19] Congress decided to take action in 1976 to amend the Clean Air Act for a number of reasons. The 1975 deadline for achieving national ambient air quality standards and enforcing state implementation plans had passed with thousands of sources still not in compliance. The deadlines for meeting auto tailpipe emission standards had been extended three times, twice by the EPA and once by Congress, and were to apply to the 1978 model year. But auto industry representatives argued that they needed an additional five years to find ways of meeting the emission standards, particularly that for nitrogen oxides, without adversely affecting fuel economy. Under the 1970 act, metropolitan air quality regions with high levels of pollution were to have in place by 1977 transportation control measures that would include an extremely unpopular program of gas rationing. Finally, research findings were published in the mid-1970s concerning damage to the stratospheric ozone layer that some scientists believed had resulted from the release of fluorocarbons used as refrigerants and aerosol propellants.[20]

One of the most controversial issues in clean air policy, the prevention of deterioration of relatively clean air (commonly referred to as prevention of significant deterioration), arose as a result of interpretations of the 1970 act by the judicial and executive branches. In 1974 the EPA issued regulations that divided metropolitan clean air regions into three categories. The air in class I areas, such as national parks, would be protected against any deterioration. The law specified what increments of additional pollution would be permitted in class II areas; and pollution would be permitted in class III areas until national ambient air quality standards were met. The regulations were challenged in federal court and the EPA put them on hold in anticipation of congressional reauthorization of the Clean Air Act. The Ford administration, the oil industry, electric utility and paper companies, real estate and construction interests, and other business groups all opposed the deterioration prevention provisions.

Nevertheless, both the House and Senate passed Clean Air Act Amendments in 1976 that extended deadlines for meeting auto emission limits, national ambient air quality standards, and guidelines for protecting areas with relatively clean air. The auto industry aggressively opposed the legislation, but it was a filibuster by western senators that killed the bill. Led by Sen. Jake Garn (R-Utah), they argued that the bill would limit economic growth and energy exploration. When Congress adjourned in October of 1976, the filibuster still had not been broken.[21]

Advocates of more stringent provisions were in no hurry to bargain. Auto industry officials warned that the 1978 model cars, scheduled for production beginning in August 1977, would not meet the existing tailpipe emission standards. They threatened to close down assembly lines rather than subject their companies to a fine of up to $10,000 for every car failing to meet the standards. Realizing the possible economic consequences of plant shutdowns, President Carter urged Congress to pass the amendments before the August congressional recess. Congress amended the Clean Air Act in the summer of 1977. Motor vehicle emission standards continued to be the most difficult issue to resolve. The amendments gave the auto industry two more years to meet tailpipe emission standards, but more stringent standards were mandated for 1980 and subsequent years. The EPA was given discretion to waive the stricter standards if the technology to achieve them was not available.

Congress resolved the other contentious issue, deterioration of air quality in areas with relatively clean air, by accepting the three area categories defined by the EPA. A compromise was struck that established maximum allowable increases of particulates and sulfur dioxide for each category. Variances were permitted for up to eighteen days a year in the cleanest (class I) areas. Nonattainment areas were given until the end of 1982 to meet national ambient air quality standards. Cities with severe ozone and carbon monoxide problems were given an extension to 1987. All areas were required to demonstrate "regular, consistent emission reductions" until compliance was achieved. Penalties for noncompliance by stationary sources were increased in an attempt to make the cost of noncompliance exceed the expenditure required to come into compliance. Civil penalties of up to $25,000 a day were authorized for violations of the act; criminal sanctions were to be imposed on those who knowingly violated the act. States were also required to collect permit fees from major stationary sources. In a key compromise, new fossil-fuel-burning power plants were required to utilize "the best technological system of continuous emission reduction," understood to mean "scrubbers." Scrubbing of the sulfur dioxide emissions was required even if companies used low-sulfur coal, thus removing much of the incentive to replace high-sulfur coal with low sulfur and protecting the high-sulfur coal industry.[22]

The Clean Air Act in the Reagan Era

Some progress in cleaning the air was achieved during the 1970s, particularly in reducing levels of particulates, sulfur dioxide, and carbon monoxide. But ozone and nitrogen dioxide levels remained high and most environmentalists believed that the EPA had not implemented the Clean Air Act as vigorously as it should have, for many sources of pollution were not being effectively regulated. Industry group representatives and Reagan administration officials, in contrast, argued that the law was too stringent and burdensome. Authorization for the Clean Air Act terminated in 1981, and Congress funded its implementation throughout the 1980s by passing appropriations resolutions. Political maneuvering to amend the act lasted for a decade.

In March 1981, the National Commission on Air Quality, created in the 1977 amendments to the Clean Air Act,[23] recommended that the attainment deadlines be extended, that tailpipe emission standards be lowered, and that the prevention of significant deterioration program be significantly weakened.[24] The Reagan administration's draft reauthorization proposal went even further and made enforcement lawsuits optional, eliminated the prevention of significant deterioration program, doubled tailpipe emission standards, and eliminated the durability requirements for motor vehicle emission control equipment. Industry representatives hailed the proposals; as one lobbyist said, "I don't see anything we'd object to yet."[25]

Participants in the Amending Process

Industry groups formed an umbrella organization, the Clean Air Working Group, led by William Fay, to coordinate lobbying efforts. The resources these groups brought to bear on the clean air debate in Congress were enormous. Because clean air legislation threatened to impose new regulatory burdens on virtually every industry, they were able to mobilize concerned citizens in every congressional district.

Environmental groups, organized in the early 1980s as the National Clean Air Coalition under the leadership of Chairman Richard Ayres, began lobbying for a stronger, more comprehensive Clean Air Act. Member groups included representatives of local units and national offices of the Sierra Club and the Environmental Defense Fund; the National Wildlife Federation, and the Audubon Society, church groups and labor unions, particularly the United Steelworkers Union; and groups such as the U.S. Public Interest Research Group and the American Lung Association, whose interests went far beyond environmental regulation. Lawyers and scientists at the Natural Resources Defense Council (in particular, Ayres, David Hawkins, and David Doninger) were indispensable sources of expertise to congressional leaders in drafting the details of environmental law.[26]

The challenge for the members of this coalition was in some ways like that for industry: to decide what stance should be taken, given the compromise that is inevitable in the legislative process. Should they be aggressive in making their demands, vehemently criticizing any compromise, in order to ensure that the final product would be close to their liking, or should they try to help congressional and White House negotiators by trying to come up with reasonable compromise positions?

Policy making for the goal of clean air was further complicated by the division of responsibilities. The economic costs of environmental regulation brought in agencies and officials concerned with economic policy, ranging from the Council on Economic Advisers to the White House Domestic Policy staff. Responsibility for environmental law and regulation in the executive branch is shared by, in addition to the EPA and the Nuclear Regulatory Commission, several branches of the Executive Office of the President, including the Council on Environmental Quality and the Office of Management and Budget, and several cabinet departments, including the Departments of the Interior (public lands, energy, minerals, national parks); Agriculture (forestry, soil conservation); Commerce (oceanic and atmospheric monitoring and research); State (international environmental agreements); Justice (environmental litigation); Energy; Transportation; Housing and Urban Development (urban parks, planning); Health and Human Services (public health); and Labor (occupational health).

A large number of congressional committees share jurisdiction over environmental law. The House Ways and Means Committee and the Senate Finance Committee have responsibility for environmental laws that include tax provisions. The House Appropriations Committee, the Senate

Government Affairs Committee, and the House Government Operations Committee are the primary overseers of the implementation of environmental statutes, but the EPA has identified thirty-four Senate committees and subcommittees and fifty-six House committees and subcommittees that exercise jurisdiction over that agency.[27] The key roles, however, were played by the leaders of the Senate and its Environment and Public Works Committee, and leaders of the House Energy and Commerce Committee.

Table 3-1 is a list of some of the major participants in the amendment process in the 1980s that culminated in the Clean Air Act of 1990.

In 1981, economists, legal scholars, political scientists, and industry officials had three major criticisms of the Clean Air Act. First, they believed that the national ambient air quality standards should be revised so that, in general, the costs of pollution control equipment could be balanced with the benefits of cleaner air. In addition, acceptable pollution levels should protect the general population, not those who were most susceptible to the effects of pollution. Under the existing law, national ambient air quality standards were to protect everyone, with an ample margin of safety, and costs were not to be considered in setting them. Second, the process of obtaining permits for new construction was too slow and expensive and thus stymied economic growth. The provisions of the act aimed at protecting clean air (the prevention of significant deterioration program) were particularly complicated. Third, the auto industry wanted the tailpipe emission standards for carbon monoxide and nitrogen oxides relaxed to enable them to reduce costs, produce more diesel engines, and simplify their efforts to increase fuel efficiency.[28]

Advocates of strengthening the law made major demands on Congress: to include an amendment regulating emissions from coal-burning utility plants that were implicated in acid rain; to accelerate the EPA's regulation of airborne toxic emissions; and to push the EPA to regulate fine particulates—those less than 1/1,000th of an inch in diameter—that pose more serious health threats, in general, than larger particulates.[29]

The Reagan administration had promised to submit to Congress revisions of the law but eventually decided to provide only a set of guiding principles. Bills to delay the imposition of tailpipe emission standards and ease regulation of stationary sources were introduced in the House and soon became mired in committee politics. Henry Waxman, chairman of the Subcommittee on Health and the Environment, led the members who sought to protect the law against industry lobbying; he proposed minor changes to tighten provisions and also broaden them to regulate acid rain. But he was apparently in no hurry to urge passage of amendments, having calculated that as the 1982 elections approached, members of Congress would be unwilling to cast votes that could be construed as being anti-environment. John Dingell, chairman of the Committee on Energy and

Table 3-1   Major Players in Amending the Clean Air Act of 1970

Environmental Groups

National Clean Air Coalition
Sierra Club
Natural Resources Defense Council
Environmental Defense Fund
U.S. Public Interest Research Group
American Lung Association
National Wildlife Federation
Audubon Society
United Steelworkers Union
National Council of Churches

Industry Groups

Clean Air Working Group
Business Roundtable
National Association of Manufacturers
Trade associations (coal, electric utilities, steel, chemicals, and automobile industries)

State and Local Officials

State and territorial air pollution program administrators
Local air pollution control officials
Representatives of individual states

Executive Branch

Office of Management and Budget
Domestic Policy Staff
Chief of staff
Environmental Protection Agency
Department of Energy
Department of the Interior
Department of Transportation

Legislative Branch

House
Speaker
Committee on Energy and Commerce
  Subcommittee on Health and the Environment
  Subcommittee on Energy and Power

Senate
Majority leader and minority leader
Committee on Environment and Public Works
  Subcommittee on Environmental Protection

Commerce, led a bipartisan coalition of members who wanted major changes, including reduction of tailpipe emission standards. A third group consisted of Republicans who sought to defend industrial sources from more stringent regulation and as a consequence supported tighter tailpipe emission standards.[30] The subcommittee reported out a bill in March that relaxed tailpipe emission standards, extended compliance deadlines, and weakened regulations protecting the relatively clean air national parks. In the full Energy and Commerce Committee, however, Dingell's package (reduction in tailpipe emission standards, easing of controls imposed on industrial sources, and retention of the scrubbing requirement for coal-burning utilities) was picked apart by Waxman and his allies, who believed that Dingell did not have control over his committee and that members were hesitant to cast votes that signified a retreat from a clean air position. The Dingell coalition prevailed in its efforts to lower tailpipe emission standards but lost on other issues, and its plan to rewrite the bill had collapsed by the fall. In contrast, the Senate Committee on Environment and Public Works, clearly controlled by supporters of the existing law, had completed a modest revision of the Clean Air Act by August. Committee members were generally content with the Clean Air Act and were interested only in limiting the EPA's discretion. There was, however, little support in the Senate leadership for consideration of their version, and it never reached the floor.[31]

In February 1983, the EPA announced that 218 areas had not met national ambient air quality standards and would be subject to sanctions. This threat provided some motivation for Congress to amend the Clean Air Act. Acid rain received increased attention in 1983 following reports by three major scientific committees that had examined the problem. Neither faction was willing to compromise, however: northeasterners and other members favored controls to reduce acid rain; those representing the Midwest and high-sulfur-coal states opposed any controls. The stalemate continued throughout the year, eventually prompting an amendment to an appropriations bill that imposed a one-year moratorium on EPA sanctions.

Congress was extremely apprehensive about the direction the EPA was taking during the Reagan presidency. Much of its attention was being diverted from legislation to oversight. EPA Administrator Ann Gorsuch and other top administration officials were defiant in their criticisms of the existing law. The EPA had made clear its intent to work closely with industry representatives to help them solve pollution problems so that aggressive enforcement measures could be avoided.[32] This lack of trust between the two branches presented a seemingly insurmountable barrier. The amendments to the Clean Air Act that were eventually passed reflected congressional frustration with the unwillingness of the EPA and many Reagan administration officials to ensure that the law was implemented as forcefully as demanded by Democrats. Part of the administration's strategy to stimulate the economy was to cut back on the enforcement of environmental laws and regulations.

Until 1989, both houses of Congress dealt with the various pollution problems (acid rain, air toxics, and smog) in separate bills. Senate Environment and Public Works Committee bills generally favored imposition of more environmental controls, reflecting the concerns of environmental groups and state and local air quality officials, many of whom pointed to California's experience in going beyond national requirements to develop its own solutions to the state's air pollution problems.

Acid Rain and Congressional Deadlock

By 1984, the problem of acid rain had become the main stumbling block to amending the Clean Air Act. The Reagan administration was firmly opposed to anything more than continued research. Every Democratic contender in the 1984 presidential campaign criticized the president's inaction on the issue, but he was easily reelected and continued to oppose any new regulatory or statutory initiatives throughout his second term. The Senate Environment and Public Works Committee reported out a bill in 1984 that would have imposed stronger controls on midwestern power plants than were included in the bill the Senate passed in 1982 and tightened other provisions of the law, but the Senate leadership refused to bring it to the floor. The House version never got out of subcommittee. Midwestern members deleted the acid rain provision from the bill being marked up, despite efforts of Waxman and members from the Northeast to distribute cleanup costs by imposing a tax on the energy produced by burning coal.[33]

The stalemate continued through 1986 as members of the Senate Committee on Environment and Public Works waited to see if the Dingell-Waxman logjam in the House could be broken. The Subcommittee on Environmental Protection reported out an acid rain bill but it died in the full committee. In 1987, the threat of EPA sanctions for nonattainment areas again prompted congressional attempts to reauthorize the Clean Air Act. The Senate committee, now under the control of the Democrats as a result of the 1986 elections, once again passed amendments to the act that would have given states additional time to clean up urban smog and added new regulatory programs to combat acid rain and air toxics. Democratic Majority Leader Robert Byrd refused to bring the bill to the floor, however, because of his opposition to sulfur dioxide emission controls that would threaten coal mining jobs in his state.

The political dynamics had shifted somewhat in the House. John Dingell, chairman of the Committee on Energy and Commerce, and other industry supporters were not in any hurry to amend the law since the changes were no longer likely to be provisions to weaken the law but rather to strengthen it. Auto tailpipe emission standards had been met by the auto makers, despite their warnings to the contrary, and Waxman and others were pushing for a new round of more stringent provisions. Opponents of acid rain controls continued to block action in the Waxman subcommittee. In a major vote that showed the strength of environmentalists, the House agreed to a Waxman-backed extension to August 31, 1988, for meeting national ambient air quality standards and defeated Dingell's proposal to prohibit the EPA from imposing sanctions until 1989, which had been expected to pass. Environmentalists believed that Congress would be more likely to pass a bill to their liking during the 1988 election year than if they waited until 1989, and wanted to use the threat of sanctions to force passage of amendments that would include new regulatory initiatives.[34]

Despite the August 1988 deadline, Congress failed again to amend the Clean Air Act. Sen. George Mitchell had taken over leadership of the clean air bill in the Environment and Public Works Committee in 1987, but collided with Majority Leader Byrd and was unable to bring the committee's bill to the floor. Progress had been made in talks between Mitchell and the United Mine Workers and a tentative agreement had been struck. But opposition from environmentalists, who argued that the deal would not provide sufficient protection to human health and ecological systems, and westerners, who believed it favored the use of high-sulfur coal at the expense of the low-sulfur coal mined in their states, killed the bill and precipitated an angry outburst by Mitchell, faulting "extremists" on both sides of the issue who were unwilling to compromise.[35]

Consideration of clean air amendments in the House Subcommittee on Health and the Environment extended from February to the summer of 1988. Many of the votes on amendments to the bills proposed by Waxman and by Rep. Gerry Sikorski (D-Minn.) to address nonattainment and acid rain problems were rejected by votes of 10-10 or passed 11-9. Nine moderate-to-conservative members of the Energy and Commerce Committee tried to break the legislative gridlock with a compromise plan for urban smog. The proposal of the Group of Nine was important because these members held the balance of power in the committee, but neither Dingell nor Waxman could be persuaded to agree to it. Dingell sent the group a fifteen-page letter—one page listed items with which he agreed, and fourteen pages outlined those with which he did not. The governors of New York and Ohio proposed a plan to reduce acid rain and distribute the cleanup costs among the states. The Senate was fairly close to agreement on an acid rain proposal, and members of the House claimed to be ready to reach an agreement on ozone as soon as the Senate was ready on acid rain.[36] But no breakthrough occurred. More members were becoming familiar with the intricacies of clean air legislation and increasingly frustrated with the polarization and paralysis that afflicted Congress.[37]

The free flow of money helped stiffen the opposition of some members to a more stringent clean air bill. Members of the House Energy and Commerce Committee, for example, were the recipients of nearly $612,000 from political action committees (PACs) in 1989 (a nonelection year), contributed by industries interested in the bill. As many as 154 PACs were identified as having a "significant stake in the outcome of the clean-air bill." About 5 percent of all money raised by all members of Congress in 1989 came from PACs interested in securing passage of clean air legislation—an average of $14,570 per member. Republican members averaged more than $17,278 in contributions; Democrats averaged $12,729. The PAC money from clean air interests constituted as much as one-third of all PAC money received by some members. The most generous contributors were the electric utilities, who gave more than $150,000. They were followed by the oil, natural gas, automobile, and chemical industries; gas utilities; coal and steel industries; diversified energy companies; construction; and farm equipment manufacturing. Although the amount of PAC money contributed to members supporting clean air was relatively small in terms of total PAC giving, it is illustrative of the way campaign spending chases hot legislative issues. For members such as Rep. Al Swift (D-Wash.), receiving PAC money was not a problem: "There is so damn much money out there that anybody who gives anybody anything for it is an idiot." For industry, PAC contributions have become a cost of doing business, a prerequisite for ensuring that its voice will be heard in committee decision making.[38]

Campaign contributions have raised fears that industry lobbying might weaken key provisions. In October 1989, the House Subcommittee on Health and the Environment passed, by a 12-10 vote, an amendment to weaken a provision in the bill mandating the use of alternative fuels. The auto and oil industries had vigorously lobbied for the amendment. The twelve members who voted in favor of it received an average of $6,021 from oil and auto industry PACs; the ten members who voted against it took an average of $2,755 from these PACs.[39] Some PAC contributions, of course, may be nothing more than a recognition of the already established policy views of members. But many observers and participants alike agree that they pose profound problems for the legislative process.[40]

1989: Clean Air Breakthroughs

The 1990 Amendments to the Clean Air Act were the result of the drafting of numerous bills and countless attempts to negotiate compromise throughout the 1980s. The election of George Bush in November 1988 turned out to be the key event in breaking the congressional logjam over clean air. Bush effectively used environmental issues to distance himself from the Reagan administration, since those issues continued to command widespread public support despite President Reagan's hostility to most governmental regulation. Bush and his campaign advisers had also had some success in co-opting traditional Democratic leadership in support of environmental protection. Bolstered by presidential promises, Congress renewed its efforts to amend the Clean Air Act early in 1989. The second breakthrough that year occurred in the Senate when George Mitchell replaced Robert Byrd as majority leader. The Senate Committee on Environment and Public Works promised to produce a package of bills concerning acid rain, air toxics, and urban area nonattainment by the summer. House Speaker Jim Wright promised to make clean air legislation a top priority, but he was forced to resign in 1989 as a result of a financial scandal and was replaced by Thomas Foley. A number of bills had been introduced in the House that mirrored proposals of earlier years. House Republicans began pressuring the White House to show that Republicans could take the lead on environmental protection issues.[41] An outline of the president's bill was introduced on June 12; the bill itself was released on July 21.

The Bush Administration's Clean Air Bill

The president's bill was the result of a major effort by the White House and the EPA to accomplish several things. The EPA had a growing list of reforms and improvements to the existing law that it felt were necessary. Some provisions, such as the enforcement title, were merely designed to update the Clean Air Act and make it consistent with other environmental laws. Other provisions pertained to the development of alternative-fueled vehicles, a particular interest of some key White House officials. The acid rain provisions emphasized an innovative marketlike approach to environmental regulation.

The administration was in a politically delicate position. If its bill was to have any legitimacy in Congress, it had to be as aggressive in attacking air pollution as other bills proposed by members of Congress. But if it was too aggressive, it would alienate important business constituencies. On the other hand, if the bill was too weak, it would be dismissed as irrelevant to what the president had repeatedly promised to do. Some members of Congress and representatives of environmental groups had argued that the president's bill would have to propose a reduction in sulfur dioxide emissions of at least 10 million tons in order to be taken seriously. Whichever bill he introduced would likely become the minimum position for the bill that Congress would finally enact. As Robert Beck of the Edison Electric Institute put it, "I think whatever George Bush sends up to the

Hill is worse than the budget, it's dead before arrival. It becomes merely the floor." [42] The president's June 12 statement was widely heralded in Congress and by environmentalists as the breakthrough in clean air that everyone had been waiting for. When the bill was actually issued, however, it was immediately attacked by environmentalists as too weak and as signifying a retreat from the promises made earlier, and by industry groups as too expensive and inconsistent with the regulatory flexibility that they were expecting. [43]

In contrast to the usual practice, in which the agency drafts a bill and sends it to presidential aides for review, the bill had been prepared by a team of officials from the White House, the Office of Management and Budget, the Department of Energy, and the EPA. [44] This ensured that economic and energy issues would be central considerations in the formulation of environmental policy. Richard Ayres, chairman of the National Clean Air Coalition, viewed this approach to policy making as a mixed bag:

> The fact that the White House is involved in one sense is a positive sign because it says they regard this issue as one of the big national policies. In another sense, it makes one worry, because a lot of people who are not operating from the base of environmental commitment that the EPA administrator is, are involved in shaping this policy. [45]

The president's bill included three major initiatives concerning non-attainment of national ambient air quality standards, air toxics, and acid rain, and additional provisions concerning permit requirements for sources of pollution and enforcement by the EPA and the states. The most aggressive provision, the one pertaining to acid rain, became the centerpiece of the president's bill and was politically attractive for at least two reasons. First, the public viewed acid rain as one of the most serious environmental problems. Candidate Bush had promised to go beyond the Reagan accomplishment of simply studying the problem further. Acid rain was compatible with the new president's interest in foreign policy. His first foreign trip was to Canada for meetings with Prime Minister Brian Mulroney, in which acid rain was a major topic of discussion. Furthermore, the initiative adversely affected only a relatively limited number of coal-fired power plants in the Midwest—an industry that had been the object of widespread congressional condemnation for failing to support any compromise in the 1980s. One of the many ironies was that the bill that finally passed required much less cost sharing among Midwest utilities than earlier bills that Congress had considered but rejected because of industry opposition.

Second, the acid rain provision's reliance on a marketlike scheme of emissions trading made it the kind of initiative that industry-oriented and conservative members of Congress could accept. It was based on an argument that critics of regulation had been making for decades—that government intervention needed to be more decentralized, flexible, and efficient. The initiative afforded a promising opportunity to demonstrate that environmental law could actually be "reformed" in practice, a goal that many members of Congress, White House officials, and others had come to champion.[46] It also had the endorsement of the Environmental Defense Fund, which was critical in gaining congressional acceptance. And it recommended a higher rate of reductions in the level of sulfur dioxide emissions than had been specified in most of the bills Congress had considered.

The nonattainment and air toxics provisions were important because they helped to structure the debate in Congress. Critics of the president argued that many provisions in his bill were weaker than the existing law. Sen. Max Baucus (D-Mont.), chairman of the Environment and Public Works Committee's Subcommittee on Environmental Protection, complained that "unfortunately, the president stepped up to the problem, blinked, and stepped back" and warned that the bill would "significantly tarnish his ... effort to be the environment president." During the negotiations between the Senate and the administration (discussed below), there was even some discussion about dropping the air toxics provisions because compromise was so difficult to reach. The announcement that John Dingell would sponsor the administration's bill in the House stirred fears that the motor vehicle emission provisions were tied too closely to the auto industry's wish list. Lower tailpipe emission standards meant that controls on stationary sources would have to be tightened to make up the difference. The zero-sum emissions game pitted auto industry-oriented members of Congress (and later those from oil-producing states affected by demands for cleaner fuels) against members representing districts with other major industries. Dingell tried to reach an agreement between these two groups and midwesterners concerned about the costs of acid rain controls, but it became increasingly difficult for him and industry coalition leaders to maintain a united front and to prevent some industries and members of Congress from making separate deals.[47]

The 1986 Emergency Planning and Community Right-to-Know Act required industries to report to local officials and the EPA the amount of certain chemicals they release each year. When Rep. Henry Waxman released an initial estimate of air toxic releases by industry in 1987, industry officials derided his figures as wildly excessive. But when the 1987 *Toxics Release Inventory* was made available in 1988, it became clear that Waxman's estimates were only a fraction of actual emissions. According to the inventory, more than 2.7 billion pounds of air toxics had been released in 1987, but emissions were widely viewed as being underreported because there was no mechanism to ensure that companies reported them.[48] Chemical industry officials, apparently sensing that they had a major public relations problem, dropped their opposition to the new legislation and began working with members of Congress (although not without major differences) to put together legislation that would require major cuts in emissions. The death of Rep. Mickey Leland (D-Texas) in a plane crash while on a humanitarian mission to Africa in 1989 was a major blow to such efforts, for he championed a strong air toxics provision.

Clean Air Act Amendments in Congress

The House.   Clean air legislation in the House fell primarily within the jurisdiction of the Energy and Commerce Committee's Subcommittee on Health and the Environment. John Dingell, chairman of the full committee, was careful to pack the subcommittee with members who supported his efforts to block a stringent clean air bill, especially one aimed at reducing auto emissions. Support for an aggressive clean air bill was therefore weakest in the subcommittee, despite the vigorous efforts of the subcommittee chairman, Henry Waxman. Waxman and his supporters were convinced that once the bill got out of committee, they would find much stronger support for their position because votes lost in the subcommittee and committee would be reversed on the floor. Waxman's subcommittee began marking up the clean air bill on September 19. The bill, which was sponsored by Dingell and Rep. Norman Lent (R-N.Y.), the ranking minority member of the Energy and Commerce Committee, was basically the Bush bill with some thirty-two changes aimed at satisfying the concerns of environmentalists and a number of relatively minor changes or "technical corrections." Strong White House lobbying had resulted in the defeat of several Waxman amendments designed to move up the deadlines for nonattainment of national ambient air quality standards and to increase tailpipe emission limits. The Energy and Commerce Committee's moderates (the Group of Nine) occasionally altered the balance of power between Dingell and Waxman—for example, they successfully challenged Dingell's proposal that the auto manufacturers be able to meet emission standards by averaging emissions from all vehicles, rather than requiring that every vehicle meet them.[49]

An agreement on the length of warranties for motor vehicle pollution control equipment, although it concerned a relatively minor issue, signaled that industry could not continue to assume that it could block clean air legislation. Subcommittee members were stunned in early October when Dingell and Waxman announced a compromise on tailpipe emission standards, one of the most contentious issues. Waxman had wanted higher standards and a shorter timetable for achieving them than had been proposed by Dingell and Lent. For more than a decade Waxman and

Dingell had been arguing over what should be required of the auto industry. Waxman viewed cleaning up auto emissions as the most important step in reducing air pollution in southern California. It was also a major step that needed to be taken to improve public health, and Waxman was the leading proponent of revised health legislation in the House. Dingell thought the auto industry had already borne more than its share of the burden for cleaning up the air. There were real limits to the regulatory costs that could be imposed on U.S. industries without harming their competitiveness in global markets and causing job losses.[50]

The agreement on tailpipe emission standards was a key development; following it, the prospects for passage of the amendments improved considerably. Many people believed that Dingell's subcommittee victories would be short-lived and that Waxman would likely prevail in floor votes; but that outcome was still uncertain, and it would not necessarily determine the conference vote. Committee members disliked having to choose between the powerful committee and subcommittee chairmen and continually pressured them to come up with a compromise. Dingell and Waxman agreed to bind themselves to the compromise throughout the subsequent House-Senate conference committee deliberations and not push for further concessions.[51] Such an agreement deflected criticism that Dingell was trying to block an amendment whose passage was inevitable. It also showed that Waxman could compromise and solve problems. And it produced some political capital for both that could be used in future debates over clean air issues as well as other issues.

The second battle in the House subcommittee was fought over clean fuels. When tailpipe emission standards were increased, attention naturally turned to fuels that pollute less and can be used in older cars not subject to the new tailpipe emission limits. In one skirmish in September, Waxman, the environmentalists, and EPA head Reilly were pitted against Dingell, Detroit, and Chief of Staff John Sununu. The Bush administration had included in its bill a requirement that one million clean-fuel vehicles be produced each year by 1997. Waxman embraced the proposal, but strong lobbying by the auto industry caught the White House in a bind. Waxman reported that he had spoken with Reilly shortly before the subcommittee meeting and that he had voiced support for the production mandate. Ranking minority member Lent reported that he had just spoken with Sununu, who supported an amendment to strike the mandate. Members then debated over who was better able to represent the president's views—Bill Reilly, calling from a phone booth in Chicago, or John Sununu, calling from his desk next to the Oval Office. The Lent-Sununu position prevailed in a 12-10 vote. The White House was quick to argue that the administration remained united and that there had only been a misunderstanding.[52]

The House subcommittee had lost its momentum by mid-October, and a number of contentious issues remained unresolved. The Energy and Commerce Committee's Subcommittee on Energy and Power had jurisdiction over the acid rain provisions in the clean air bill. Philip R. Sharp (D-Ind.), subcommittee chairman, led midwestern members in an attempt to stall the legislation so they could generate support for the notion that cleanup costs should be borne not just by utilities and ratepayers in their district.[53] The midwesterners, originally aligned with the Dingell-Lent team, began complaining that nothing was being done to solve their problems and let it be known that they would lend their support in key committee votes on other issues to whatever faction would best help them minimize the costs of acid rain controls. But coalition building in the committee was further complicated by the opposition of members from "clean" states, primarily westerners, who feared a limit on sulfur dioxide emissions that would inhibit local economic growth.[54] The conflict reached a peak in November, when Dingell warned that the "public bloodletting" in his committee threatened to "turn close friends into lasting enemies, and divide [the committee] on many issues for years to come." But midwesterners led by Sharp warned that "this time we're talking about high stakes for us." His threats were explicit: "Perhaps there are going to be other costs to be paid . . . on this or other legislation, if [rolling the Midwest] is going to be the game." [55] Members and lobbyists were asking each other if Dingell's complex deal making on so many different issues could produce results. The House leadership did not push for action on clean air, given other legislative priorities and the rush to adjourn by Thanksgiving.

The Senate. The clean air bill moved much more quickly in the Senate. Throughout the history of the Clean Air Act, both industry and environmental lobbyists have perceived the Senate Committee on Environment and Public Works as a bastion of support for environmental regulation. To industry, the committee was (and continues to be) "a wholly owned subsidiary of the environmental community"; industry lobbyists have gone outside the committee to find sympathetic ears in the Senate. To environmentalists, the committee was "the conscience of the Senate on environmental matters." The committee's majority and minority staffs, particularly Katharine Kimball and Jimmie Powell, who directed the Senate bill through the committee debates, negotiations, floor debate, and House-Senate conference, were virtually indistinguishable in terms of their commitment to aggressive environmental regulation. Some observers believe the committee's clout was, paradoxically, somewhat diminished by its fierce bipartisan dedication to environmental protection. There was relatively little compromise when the committee did markups, but of course the makeup of the committee does not reflect the range of views in the entire Senate. When the committee's bills were attacked on the floor, its influence was further diluted. As one industry lobbyist pointed out, "they don't have to cut any compromises in committee level . . . [but] that makes their job twice as hard when they get to the floor." [56] The committee's clean air bill, many believed, had simply failed to be subjected to any real test, and it had to be extensively revised in negotiations with the White House.

The Subcommittee on Environmental Protection began marking up three separate bills—air toxics, acid rain, and urban smog in mid-October. The air toxics bill, with more stringent provisions than those in the president's bill, was passed with the subcommittee's usual bipartisan cooperation on October 19. The nonattainment provisions of the urban smog bill took less than an hour to approve on October 26. The first big split in the subcommittee occurred in November, when a Republican proposal to include an alternative fuels program in the smog bill patterned after the Bush administration's initiative was rebuffed by the Democrats, who were eager to report a bill before Thanksgiving. In general, the Democrats on the subcommittee favored tougher tailpipe emission standards; the Republicans emphasized alternative fuels and the development of new cars that used them. The Democrats prevailed in a series of close votes and the bill was reported out to the full committee. An acid rain bill was reported on November 14 after a half day of discussion. The full committee, under pressure from Majority Leader Mitchell, combined the three bills into one and passed it in less than a day.[57] Despite the rapid movement of the bill in the Senate, many observers doubted that a coalition could ever be put together to break the House deadlock.[58]

1990: Toward the Finish Line

The Senate took the lead in pushing the clean air bill forward in 1990, and Senate Majority Leader Mitchell made it his top legislative priority. The bill, managed by Max Baucus, arrived on the Senate floor on January 23. Minority whip and Environment and Public Works Committee member Alan Simpson (R-Wyo.) had warned that the floor debate would be a "riotous occasion" full of "anguish and horror." The main criticism of the bill was that the costs of compliance made it simply too expensive. Forty senators, led by Steve Symms (R-Idaho), had written to the Congressional Budget Office, the Congressional Research Service, and the Office of Technology Assessment asking for cost estimates. Industry calculations put the cost as high as $104 billion a year, but environmentalists argued that the health costs of air pollution were just as high.[59] The major issues to be resolved included how to lessen the impact of acid rain controls on midwestern utility consumers and high-sulfur coal miners and whether the production and sale of alternative fuels and clean-fueled vehicles should be mandated by law.[60]

By the second week of floor consideration, White House officials, industry lobbyists, and Senate critics were arguing that the committee's bill was much more expensive than the president's version but that it offered no real additional environmental benefit. Members, staff, and lobbyists for both sides began counting votes in anticipation of a motion to end a filibuster that many believed to be inevitable. Majority Leader Mitchell and Senator Baucus believed that they had enough votes to pass the bill but not enough to cut off a filibuster. Even if the bill passed, however, a presidential veto loomed. The EPA estimated that the cost of the committee bill was more than double that of the administration bill, and Bush had promised to veto any bill whose estimated compliance costs exceeded those of his version (estimated at $20 billion) by more than 10 percent. The administration identified twenty-four "priorities" for amending the Senate bill.[61]

The White House-Senate Summit

Fearing a filibuster, Mitchell withdrew the bill from the floor and called a series of extraordinary closed-door meetings with officials of the Bush administration for a second markup of the bill. Environmentalists were quick to oppose the process, because their strength lies in identifying the pro-environment votes and holding members publicly accountable for their votes on certain issues. Many members were glad to escape that accountability and used the closed-door process to obtain concessions for important interests in their states that would have been difficult to obtain in the open. This process favors certain interests and weakens the influence of others. Its defenders legitimately argue that, at least in theory, private talks free participants from the need for political posturing and may facilitate the kind of negotiations that are essential to resolve highly contentious issues. But skeptics fear that the process favors industry interests at the expense of broader public concerns.

The negotiations that began on February 2 in Mitchell's office were intense and contentious; an impasse on mobile source limits, for example, was broken only after a full day of hard bargaining. They continued for one month (some two dozen meetings spanning more than 250 hours) and took an enormous amount of the majority leader's time. He presided over the talks, apparently because of his sincere interest in and commitment to the bill but also because Senator Baucus was believed to lack sufficient familiarity with the complicated bill to be able to manage it. Some members of the Senate Environment and Public Works Committee and a few key White House and EPA officials were the major participants (dubbed by some the Group of Fifteen), but hundreds of staff members and dozens of administration officials participated at some point; nearly half of the Senate membership came in at one time or another to ask for concessions important to their states or to satisfy their objections.[62]

The agenda was set primarily by administration demands for changes in the committee bill so that the total cost of the final package could be estimated.[63] Central to the White House strategy was the threat to veto a bill that was too expensive. Some believed that the "environmental" president would never carry out such a threat, particularly when there was such strong support for the Clean Air Act among the public and in Congress. Nevertheless, it seemed to be a useful mechanism by which administration negotiators could avoid provisions they did not want included in the package. The White House was in a strong position because it had delivered on its promise to propose a clean air bill and was in no hurry to accept a bill that included provisions it did not want. If the bill died, the Senate Democrats and not the president would bear the brunt of criticism. Another key White House strategy was not to bind senators to an agreement through the conference with the House of Representatives, but only through the final Senate vote. The White House apparently believed that it was in a strong position to get what it wanted in the House, where ally John Dingell was in control of the legislation.

Mitchell believed that the president's bill was not strong enough or broad enough to deal with the problems of air pollution. His strategy was to push for passage of an aggressive committee bill that could then be used to pressure the president to support a stronger legislative package than the one he had proposed. He viewed the committee bill as including about 80 percent of what the president had introduced, with stronger provisions regulating air toxics, stratospheric ozone, and motor vehicle emissions. But Mitchell was caught off guard by opposition to his strategy on the part of environmental groups, for whom the Environment and Public Works Committee's bill was the minimum acceptable measure. "Rather than praising the Committee for getting the president to move beyond his bill," Mitchell complained, "they criticized us for accepting anything less than our bill." The media joined in the attack on the secret negotiations, making it harder, according to Mitchell, to get the bill passed.[64]

Industry groups were relieved that the two bills had been taken into closed-door negotiations; they argued that the issues were too volatile for public debate and that environmentalists would vilify anyone who proposed changes in the committee's bill. Environmentalists, anxious for the bill to remain on the floor because they feared that negotiations would only weaken it, canvassed the Senate, hoping to garner enough votes to invoke cloture on the filibuster, but they could not obtain sixty commitments.[65] Not everyone assumed that a filibuster was inevitable; many believed that Mitchell and Baucus should have forced floor votes. Environmentalists were hesitant to criticize the two senators for failing to do so and tried to place the blame on Bush for weakening the committee bill; nevertheless, their criticism of the majority leader's strategy angered Mitchell and Baucus.

By February 23, the negotiations had produced agreements on regulations concerning toxic air pollutants, use of alternative fuels, and stationary sources of air pollution. Mitchell had set February 26 as the deadline for completion of the talks. On March 1 he and the other negotiators emerged with a substitute bill that was somewhere between the bill passed by the committee and the Bush administration's proposal. It delayed the phase-in time for meeting motor vehicle emission standards, provided a less stringent means of assessing the risks posed by air toxics, added a requirement that alternative fuels be used in the most polluted cities, gave additional time and incentives for midwestern utilities to reduce emissions, and deleted proposed increases in fuel efficiency standards aimed at reducing carbon dioxide emissions that were thought to contribute to global warming. Industry groups were generally pleased with the proposed changes. Leaders of environmental groups debated whether to support the substitute bill or to try and defeat it, and organized a grass-roots effort to push for strengthening amendments.[66]

The Bill Returns to the Senate Floor

An initial canvas of senators by the National Clean Air Coalition identified 225 possible amendments to the substitute bill, but only a few posed major challenges. Industry-backed senators proposed a series of amendments that would further weaken the air toxics provisions and the permit program.[67] (The permit program, discussed more fully in Chapter 4, was an important addition to the Clean Air Act that required all major stationary sources to obtain permits specifying how much pollution they could release.) The National Clean Air Coalition concentrated on passage of two key amendments: one that would raise the tailpipe emission and clean fuel standards, and one that would bolster the nonattainment provisions. The Senate leadership's strategy was to defend the compromise by attacking these and other amendments as "deal-busters" that would kill the bill if passed, since the changes would increase the cost of the legislation beyond the limit set by the president. The committee bill, for example, had required a second round of higher tailpipe emission standards that were to take effect in the year 2003. The substitute bill proposed that the second round of standards not take effect unless at least twelve cities failed to meet national ambient air quality standards for ozone. Many senators believed that the second round was inevitable; White House officials predicted that it would not be needed. Because these standards were contingent on future decisions, they were not considered mandatory and thus were not included in the cost estimates.

Members of the Environment and Public Works Committee now found themselves in the awkward position of opposing amendments that they had put in their own bill a few months earlier. Some unusual political coalitions were produced by the votes on these deal-buster amendments, particularly the vote on an amendment to restore the second round of tailpipe emissions standards and require clean fuels in sixty to seventy cities rather than the nine mandated in the substitute bill. Sponsored by Senators Tim Wirth (D-Colo.) and Pete Wilson (R-Calif.), the amendment was viewed by the National Clean Air Coalition as the key environmental vote of 1990—a classic, clear-cut choice between industry and environmental interests. The Senate leadership thought passage of the Wirth-Wilson amendment would kill the substitute bill and defeat any chance for revising the clean air legislation. Some senators who normally took a position in favor of environmental protection voted against the Wirth-Wilson amendment in order to preserve the chances of getting a bill; proponents of the amendment dismissed the president's veto threat as a political impossibility. Members who found the substitute bill still too burdensome and expensive voted for the amendment, hoping that it was indeed a deal-buster. Farm state senators supported the amendment because it promoted the use of ethanol, a clean fuel made from grain. Champions of small business voted for it as a way to reduce pressure for controls on industry. Particularly grating on some members was the warning from environmental lobbyists that this was a scorecard vote—one that would be used by the League of Conservation Voters to evaluate members. Labeling votes in that way had become an increasingly common tactic used to pressure members.[68]

In the end, strong lobbying by the administration and EPA officials who buttonholed members on their way to vote enabled the Senate leaders to keep their deal together. The Wirth-Wilson amendment was shelved by a 52-46 vote to table the motion. For many members, the key argument was that if the deal broke apart, the hope for revising clean air legislation would vanish into dirty air. Other amendments that ran counter to provisions in the substitute bill were passed once they were defined as non-deal-breakers. But the defeat of the Wirth-Wilson vote still required some serious arm twisting by Mitchell and Dole. "You could hear the arms snapping all the way down the mall," said Wirth. "I know of seven guys who switched in the last hour." [69]

A couple of Senate votes in late March entailed more complicated maneuvers than simply trying to protect the substitute bill from deal-breaking amendments. An amendment proposed by Sen. Tom Daschle (D-S.D.) requiring that reformulated gasoline be used by all vehicles in the nine most polluted cities (rather than used only by new vehicles in those cities) was passed despite warnings that it was a deal-breaker.[70] The White House had lobbied for another amendment, to ease the requirements for the permit program and enforcement by the states, but Mitchell, Baucus, and Chafee opposed it as an unacceptable weakening of the law. On the morning of March 27, a motion to table the amendment lost by a vote of 47-50. When the amendment came to a vote, several members had reversed their votes as a result of hours of patient work by Mitchell and others, and the amendment itself was defeated by the same 47-50 count.[71]

The final obstacle to Senate passage of the substitute bill was Sen. Robert Byrd's amendment to give job training and other assistance to miners who lost their jobs as a result of new clean air legislation. Byrd had helped block passage of clean air amendments for years in order to protect the jobs of West Virginia miners, whose high-sulfur coal was a key element in the production of acid rain. He viewed this effort as critical to the survival of their communities. Byrd held the floor during much of the week of March 19, describing in detail the lives and deaths of coal miners. He had originally proposed that displaced miners be given from 50 percent to 100 percent of their average salary and benefits over a six-year period, at a cost to the government of nearly $1.4 billion. By the end of March Byrd had twice scaled down the cost of his proposal. He noted that the White House, which had been outspoken in its criticism of his amendment, refused to negotiate with him.[72]

The debate dragged on, and Mitchell issued an ultimatum: by April 3 the Senate would vote on the clean air bill. They would meet evenings and weekends until all amendments had been proposed and voted on. As former Senate majority leader and now president pro tempore and chairman of the Appropriations Committee, Byrd had many political chits to call in. Mitchell viewed Byrd's amendment as the final challenge to the bill he had so painstakingly nurtured for so long. Passage of the clean air bill was a test of his leadership and a measure of how well he was filling the job Byrd had just vacated. Members squirmed as they faced choosing between the majority leader and the Appropriations Committee chairman. Minority whip Simpson lamented in a speech on the Senate floor that members who voted against Byrd would still have to petition him for money for projects in their states. This was one issue where industry and environmental alliances did not have much influence.[73] The National Clean Air Coalition, after a series of lengthy discussions, decided to endorse the amendment as the kind of accommodation that was generally necessary to ensure the passage of environmental legislation, and as a recognition of the importance of organized labor in the coalition.

Neither Byrd nor Mitchell would yield. On April 3 the Senate voted on Byrd's amendment to authorize an appropriation of $500 million over three years to be paid to miners as job loss benefits and retraining assistance. Byrd believed he had fifty votes lined up, including that of Spark M. Matsunaga (D-Hawaii), who was dying of cancer and had been brought from the hospital to the Senate chamber in a wheelchair to cast his vote. Byrd lost the vote of Bennett Johnston (D-La.), who had gone home to attend a funeral and was delayed in returning because of bad weather. "Three of my votes took wings," Byrd later mourned, "with the help of the boys downtown." The White House veto threats had been repeated by Minority Leader Robert Dole of Kansas, although he softened somewhat in warning that the amendment would "probably lead" to the president's veto. As Sen. Joseph Biden entered the chamber to vote, he was ushered to the cloakroom where Chief of Staff John Sununu's phone call was waiting. Sununu, Biden said later, "guaranteed me the president would veto the bill." [74] Senator Symms initially voted for the amendment, believing that it would kill the bill. He was then convinced by Sununu that the amendment would not lead to a veto but would simply make what was, in Symms's view, a bad bill worse, and he switched his vote.[75] That made the vote 49-49; Senator Alfonse D'Amato (R-N.Y.), a member of the Appropriations Committee, voted against its chairman and the amendment lost by one vote.[76] The Senate voted to approve its clean air bill on April 3.

Meanwhile, Back in the House

Many White House officials were confident that a powerful committee chairman such as John Dingell would protect their interests as well as those he represented.[77] House negotiations centered on efforts to strike political deals to gain passage of legislative packages. Members who wanted to weaken provisions affecting the coal-fired power plants blamed for acid rain, for example, were willing to exchange votes of support with other members who wanted to protect the oil industry from demands for reformulated fuels that would be expensive to produce. Other proposals, such as the stratospheric ozone depletion initiative, were dealt with individually.

The House clean air bill resurfaced for a markup in February 1990, after four months of negotiations among House members. Discussion of acid rain controls lasted only a half day in the Energy and Commerce Committee's Subcommittee on Energy and Power. No votes were taken, but it was clear that there was little support for the kind of cost sharing wanted by subcommittee Chairman Phil R. Sharp and other midwesterners. Some subcommittee members, such as Jim Cooper (D-Tenn.), argued that the bill already included cost sharing, in the form of grants for research on clean coal technology and extra allowances to midwestern utility companies. Sharp and his allies had failed to support Waxman earlier in full committee votes, thus preventing the formation of a coalition by those two groups.[78] Midwesterners worked for another month to get support for cost sharing, to no avail. The subcommittee finally decided not to mark up the bill, and it went to the full committee for markup on March 14.

One week later, after three days of negotiations among the members and their staffs concerning nonattainment of air quality standards, the Energy and Commerce Committee made a surprise announcement that an agreement had been reached on urban air quality. Title I of the House bill was now almost as aggressive as the similar title in the Senate Environment and Public Works Committee bill, and it included provisions that had been voted down on the Senate floor as deal-breaking amendments. Industry and administration officials had expected Chairman Dingell to prevail in the House negotiations, and everyone was surprised to see that the House bill that was beginning to take shape was in some respects more stringent than the Senate version. Dingell, Waxman, and Lent agreed to support the agreement through the conference. This title, along with the provision on tailpipe emission standards that had been agreed to in the fall, significantly increased the prospects for House passage of the bill.[79]

Committee members again retreated behind closed doors to review the alternative fuels provisions the subcommittee had agreed to in October. White House officials did not participate in these negotiations as they had in the Senate. On March 29 they emerged without having reached a compromise and began voting on amendments. One amendment, requiring the sale of reformulated gas in more than thirty of the most heavily polluted cities, was defeated by a vote of 21-22. A substitute provision concerning alternative fuels and related programs, offered by Representatives Ralph Hall (D-Texas) and Jack Fields (R-Texas), who had close ties to the oil industry, finally passed, but some members warned that they would try again for more aggressive amendments on the floor.[80]

Intensive talks were then held among Energy and Commerce Committee members and staff. A compromise was reached regarding toxic air pollutants that eased the controls for any residual risk in the second round, but increased the sources covered in the first round of technological controls. Representatives of both industrial and environmental groups were pleased with the deal, favoring it over the Senate version. The compromise was approved by the full committee by a 43-0 vote. Two days of round-the-clock talks were then held on acid rain, involving as many as thirty-five of the forty-three members of the committee. The session that started at 10:00 A.M. on April 4 continued until 4:30 A.M. the next day. After a break of a few hours, the talks resumed and an agreement was reached early in the afternoon. But the staffs discovered some problems with the agreement and the details were not worked out until 8:00 P.M. that evening. A markup meeting was hastily called to approve the acid rain title. Sharp and his allies had finally relented; no express cost sharing would be included in the bill, but midwestern and clean states would be given additional allowances to help soften the impact of controls. The negotiations had been driven by fatigue as much as anything else as the committee struggled to meet a deadline Dingell had agreed to with the Speaker for completing markup of the bill.[81]

The progress made in the House was largely the result of guesses Waxman and Dingell made about how much success they would have on the floor. Both seemed confident that they would prevail in key votes, but both were willing to hedge their bets by striking a deal in committee. Dingell believed that legislation must not impose unnecessary costs or make impossible demands, and that the auto industry had done more than its share to reduce pollution. He was in a strong position when he went to the House-Senate conference because both the committee and the House were united behind him. Some members believed that his ability to obtain some concessions in a bill that was destined to pass enhanced his power in the committee.[82] Waxman tried to avoid the uncertain developments of contentious floor vote by locking Dingell into positions before the conference. In so doing, he also won the gratitude of members who were not forced to choose between himself and Dingell.[83]

The House votes were anticlimactic. The members took only two days to pass the bill, and they spend much of that time making speeches in which they congratulated each other for their willingness to compromise and expressed relief that there were no tough votes. One of the few recorded votes (274-146) was on an amendment to create a five-year, $250 million assistance program for workers displaced as a result of the Clean Air Act. The White House had fought hard and successfully to delete a similar provision from the Senate bill, but House members largely ignored White House threats to veto the bill if the program was included. Other amendments were added with little controversy to require use of reformulated gas, maintain visibility in national parks, and protect the stratospheric ozone layer. Dingell and Waxman spent several hours in a corner of the House chamber arguing over the unresolved issue of whether to include the clean-fuel vehicles mandate that had been part of the original Bush bill. Speaker Tom Foley sat and listened passively to the two antagonists and their staffs as they argued, refusing to leave until they had come up with a deal both could support. The Speaker did not threaten or cajole, but did roll his eyes once at the bickering. As one staff member described the scene, "It looked like he wasn't going to leave until there was a deal. That's a powerful influence. It's like when someone's sitting on your throat." When the deadlock was finally broken, the bill was quickly passed by a 415-15 vote.[84]

The House-Senate Clean Air Conference

The conference chairmanship alternates between the House and Senate in each major category of legislation (such as environmental regulation) discussed. The chairman of the Senate Committee on Environment and Public Works, eighty-two-year old Quentin Burdick (D-N.D.), had been largely uninvolved in the debates leading to passage of the bill in the Senate and was not believed to be up to the challenge of directing the proceedings of the Senate conference committee. Instead, the task was assumed by Max Baucus, chairman of the Senate Subcommittee on Environmental Protection of the Environment and Public Works Committee. Baucus was widely viewed as relatively inexperienced and no match for the chairman of the House conference committee, John Dingell, however. (Senate Majority Leader George Mitchell, and not Baucus, had led the Senate negotiations with the White House in February.)

The House passed its clean air bill on May 23, but conferees were not named until June 28. The delay was a result of disagreements between John Dingell and members of his committee over who would be permitted to participate. House tradition calls for the chairman of the committee with jurisdiction over the legislation to select the conferees and for the Speaker to ratify the selection. The chairman is to be constrained in the selection, however, and to choose members whose views reflect the basic orientation of the bill to be passed. Dingell claimed that the list he had submitted was geographically balanced and represented the diversity of interests of members of the Energy and Commerce Committee. But Dingell had again proved to be a tough negotiator, as he did not choose members of his committee who had earlier challenged his position. Some members whose names had been omitted appealed to Speaker of the House Tom Foley to force Dingell to include them. Only as a result of the Speaker's unusual intervention were Gerry Sikorski of Minnesota and Mike Synar of Oklahoma, both Democrats who had crossed Chairman Dingell earlier in the clean air debate, included in the conference.[85] Despite Foley's help, Henry Waxman, leader of the members who wanted the most stringent provisions to protect the environment, could count on only five solid votes for his position among the 26 conferees from the Energy and Commerce Committee. The House group also included about 140 members from eight committees: the Public Works, Ways and Means, Education and Labor, and Science, Space, and Technology committees each sent 26 members; the Interior and Merchant Marine committees each sent 5 members; and 2 other members were named to work on specific amendments and given limited participation rights in the conference. In contrast, the 9 Senate conferees came from two committees: Environment and Public Works, and Finance.

Political Motivations.   Dingell's motives were questioned frequently throughout the conference. He had been the primary proponent in the House of minimal regulation of industry, but his efforts in the early 1980s to obtain enactment of legislation that would weaken provisions of the Clean Air Act had been stymied by Henry Waxman and others. Some thought he was now making a last attempt to scuttle the clean air bill. Environmentalists feared that he planned to delay the conference and pressure those with opposing views to accept his positions as the price of the bill's passage. Delay would play into his hands, according to this view, since he would have been content to have no bill emerge, whereas champions of the bill would be willing to compromise whenever necessary in order to gain passage. But Dingell's motives were more complex. Because he had been widely blamed for the failure of Congress to update the Clean Air Act and would bear the brunt of criticism if it failed again, there was a clear incentive for him to show that he could lead and not just obstruct.[86] The fact that the amendments were passed, and that they included a host of provisions in response to industry concerns, is evidence of Dingell's considerable legislative power. He was able to accommodate many industry demands yet was also credited with gaining passage of the bill.

There were notable differences between the House and Senate delegations. The Senate Environment and Public Works Committee, from which conferees were taken, was dominated by members favoring environmental protection. The bill that was passed by the Senate committee in the fall of 1989 was the most aggressive version passed by any subcommittee or any committee during the sixteen-month odyssey of the Clean Air Act Amendments. Although senators had made numerous concessions to the White House in negotiations held during the winter of 1990, those agreements were not binding beyond the Senate vote. In some cases, the conference committee senators sought stronger language than had been in the Senate bill. Henry Waxman later wrote that the administration's insistence that the Senate agreement not be binding through the conference with the House (it apparently assumed that industry interests would dominate in the House bill) was "one of the most striking miscalculations of the clean air fight. . . . As a result, key Senators from the Environment and Public Works Committee were free to pursue the strongest environmental bill possible at Conference."[87]

The Senate conferees' demands were tempered, however, by two political considerations. First, Baucus was up for reelection in 1990 and faced a strong challenger. His positions were shaped by a disquieting sense that some provisions might be unpopular in Montana. Second, western senators had threatened to filibuster and block a final vote on the compromise if it included the House provision intended to protect the relatively clean air in national parks. Sen. Jake Garn had blocked final passage of the clean air bill that had been approved by both houses in 1976 and claimed credit for eliminating a strong visibility provision in 1990.

In contrast, the House conferees were bound through the conference to agreement on several issues, including the plan to reduce smog and air toxics; this meant that they could change their position in conference only as a group. Some members believed that the agreement on tailpipe emission standards and acid rain was also binding, but others disagreed.[88] When they had some leeway, the Dingell-led majority opposed efforts by Waxman's minority contingent and the Senate conferees to adopt the more aggressive positions of the House and Senate versions.

A preliminary question that had to be resolved was the role of the White House in the conference. Norman F. Lent, the ranking House Republican at the conference, requested that White House domestic policy adviser Roger Porter be permitted to take part in the negotiations on the regulation of chlorofluorocarbons. In 1990, the United States had participated in talks to amend the 1987 Montreal Protocol on CFCs, and Lent and others wanted to be able to compare what the White House had agreed to with the congressional provisions. Waxman and others feared that Dingell and Lent would use a formal White House presence to strengthen their hand, as they had done at the 1986 conference on Superfund legislation by giving EPA head Lee M. Thomas a role in the talks.[89] The conferees eventually decided not to permit White House participation beyond simply being available on the sidelines to consult with conferees.

Nevertheless, the White House tried to maintain some influence by regularly reminding the conferees of the president's threat to veto the bill if its projected costs exceeded those of the president's original bill by more than 10 percent. The executive branch was somewhat divided in its view of the clean air bill; apparently most advisers favored its passage, but a few were responsive to industry lobbyists and others who argued that it was simply too expensive. Projections of high costs and the threats of a veto were an important political strategy. Cost estimates that put the total over the president's ceiling put pressure on conferees to reject the more stringent options being considered, for they feared that the president might veto the bill. But there was also a countervailing pressure to underestimate the probable costs of compliance with the bill so that the "environmental" president would sign it.

The clean air conference was unusual in two respects. The first was that both House and Senate conferees were familiar with the legislation. House members usually enjoy an advantage in conference because they have fewer committee assignments and are likely to be more familiar with the legislation than members of the Senate. But in this case, senators had engaged in intensive negotiations with the White House and were thus familiar with the legislation. Second, the structure and key provisions of the House and Senate bills were quite similar; although there were many differences, most pertained to details such as dates for compliance or the number of allowances permitted different sources. Legislation often changes markedly as it winds its way through the House and Senate labyrinths, because members of the two chambers fiercely guard their institutional prerogative to shape legislative provisions to their own liking. These two bills had developed in roughly the same time periods, and lobbyists had furthered the cross-fertilization of basic approaches and ideas between the two chambers.

Proposals and Counterproposals. The conference had to resolve a number of contentious issues raised by each major title of the bill. The nonattainment provisions differed concerning the responsibility of the EPA to step in when states failed to act to reduce urban smog. With regard to motor vehicle emissions, three important questions were still unanswered: (1) How strict should the requirements be for alternative fuels and the vehicles using them? (2) Should a specific formula for reformulated gas be included in the bill or should oil companies simply be given a goal to meet? (3) Should a second round of stricter emission standards be imposed on new motor vehicles early in the next century? The key issues pertaining to sources of toxic air emissions were how the residual risk existing after technological controls are in place should be regulated, and how the emission allowances that were part of the acid rain cleanup provisions should be distributed among the states.

When the conference opened on July 13, the senators made offers on two sections of the bill (stratospheric ozone depletion and permits and enforcement) that were similar in the House and Senate versions, in the hope that a quick agreement might generate some momentum and result in early completion of the conference.[90] The senators' request for a response from the House within a week was rebuffed by Dingell, and the House did not make a counteroffer until July 25. The Senate made another offer two days later, and staff members then met to hammer out a compromise, which was announced on August 3.[91] The slow pace of negotiations was attributed in part to the House conferees' unfamiliarity with the CFC provisions, since they had been added to the bill on the House floor. Dingell had effectively killed the provisions in his committee by arguing that the United States should not go beyond the provisions of the Montreal Protocol on Substances That Deplete the Ozone Layer.

The conference adjourned and Congress recessed in mid-August for its Labor Day holiday. Staff meetings resumed during the week of August 27 and conference members came to an agreement on provisions to reduce urban smog and permits on September 14. The urban smog package was largely the one passed by the House, including the requirement that the EPA issue cleanup plans if states did not and an extension of areas within states that could be encompassed by cleanup plans. During its January-February negotiations with the Senate, the administration had rejected the suggestion that members be bound by agreements through conference, so Senate conferees were free to accept the more ambitious House provisions. Since that agreement had been between the Senate negotiators and the administration, other senators did not perceive the conferees' acceptance as a breach of an agreement with fellow senators. For many senators, the greater concern was the impact on their states of the emission allowances for acid rain that had been painstakingly allocated in Senate talks in the spring; they hoped that, in the words of conferee Sen. John H. Chafee (R-R.I.), a "mood of reciprocity" would result from the urban smog compromise.[92]

The back-and-forth process of making offers and counteroffers continued throughout September. The House delegation led with an offer on tailpipe emission limits; the Senate delegation responded with its own suggestions, and the House delegation then took eleven days to renegotiate the language in its own bill concerning alternative fuels, since many conferees believed they were bound only to the tailpipe emissions agreement for motor vehicles. Lobbyists were giving no better than 50-50 odds that a bill would emerge before the October recess. A breakthrough occurred when negotiators agreed to work from the House title on motor vehicles and alternative fuels and the Senate air toxics provisions.[93]

The primary roadblock was that the House conferees representing oil states demanded that the House position be changed to require that only reformulated gas be sold in the nine smoggiest cities, that oil companies be given three additional years to use cleaner fuels, and that the EPA be able to delay or weaken other requirements. Oil company lobbyists argued successfully that some of the provisions in both House and Senate bills were not technologically feasible. Dingell had demanded that only the EPA, and not the states, be authorized to enforce the California tailpipe emission standards, a provision that was in neither bill. After an all-night session on October 6 and 7, the House conferees accepted the oil delegation's demands. Dingell dropped his proposal in exchange for other concessions. The Senate conferees then accepted the provisions worked out among the House members.[94]

The chaos surrounding the budget talks in the fall of 1990 generated increased pressure for congressional Democrats to show they could legislate effectively, and the clean air bill was one of the most visible pieces of draft legislation that still had a chance of passage. Congress extended its session to complete the budget talks, thus giving the clean air conferees additional time to position themselves to get what they wanted before

Congress adjourned. The strategy of the Dingell-led House conferees was clear: to delay issuance of counterproposals to offers made by others as long as they could.

When the Speaker imposed a deadline of midnight October 14 for completion of their work, the conferees began moving more quickly to review the hundreds of pages of bills that remained. The House delegation again became deadlocked, this time over a special extension given to the steel industry to clean up coke oven emissions. There were only minor differences between the House and Senate provisions that called for technological controls on air toxics. But the Senate bill included a less stringent residual risk provision and a special thirty-year exemption for the steel industry. In an unusual reversal, the Senate conferees favored the House provisions, whereas Dingell and the House conferees representing midwestern states wanted the weaker Senate version. The deadlock was finally broken in an early morning (3:00) meeting; the steel industry was given a thirty-year extension in exchange for some additional controls to be imposed in the next several years.[95]

All-night negotiating sessions focusing on acid rain controls continued through the middle of October; House conferees resisted acceptance of the Senate version favored by the senators and the administration. (Waxman later argued jokingly that the key to passage of the Clean Air Act Amendments of 1990 was that three members of his staff—administrative assistant Philip Schiliro and subcommittee counsel Philip Barnett and Gregory Wetstone—were in better physical shape than other staff members with whom they negotiated and simply outlasted them. Some of the best deals they made, observed Waxman, were in the early morning hours when other staff members were exhausted.)

In a session that concluded about 5:00 A.M. on October 22, the conferees gave midwesterners some additional allowances to ease the cleanup required in their states and largely accepted the Senate acid rain package. Two contentious issues remained. The first was the provision in the House bill establishing a five-year, $250 million program to assist displaced workers, to which the Bush administration had objected. The conferees accepted the provision but added language that limited participation in the program; White House officials then signaled from outside the conference room that they were not opposed. The second issue, a measure to protect air quality in national parks, was dropped because of opposition by key senators, who were backed by threats from western senators that they would filibuster if the compromise included it.[96] The House overwhelmingly passed the bill on October 26 by a vote of 401-25 and the Senate passed it the next day. The clean air bill was signed by President Bush on November 15, 1990.[97]

The passage of the bill was a remarkable event after a decade of deadlock, particularly in view of the bill's scope and the stringency of its provisions, in comparison with earlier versions. The provisions concerning vehicle emission standards in the 1990 act, for example, are more stringent and cover more vehicles than the provisions of the clean air bill introduced in the 100th Congress (1987-1988).[98] The act also includes a new clean fuels package. The auto industry had argued that "achievement of the mobile source requirements in [the earlier bill] is simply beyond the reach of any known or envisioned technology." Oil companies complained that the bill was "cumbersome, expensive, and unworkable" and would "trigger economic downturns in many areas." [99] Industry and Reagan administration opposition delayed passage of the 1990 clean air legislation, but, ironically, resulted in a much more ambitious bill than had been proposed before 1989.

Given industries' economic clout, ranging from honoraria paid to members to campaign contributions, one might expect that lobbyists could have freely worked their will in the legislative process. But business lobbying is rarely, if ever, united, since competitive pressures cut in many different directions. Small businesses might fight regulations that larger businesses have the resources to accommodate, and big companies seek to ensure that the regulatory costs they have borne are shared by all their competitors. The interests of producers of pollution control equipment are obviously different from those of the polluting industries. Every require-ment that control equipment be installed in some industry also means sales for the companies that produce such equipment. Heightened public concern over environmental protection in recent years has also fragmented industry unanimity.

Chemical companies have borne the brunt of public criticism and fear concerning air toxics, frequently manifested by consumer backlash. They have recently been uncharacteristically aggressive in arguing that they now want to clean up and they have become rather willing participants in the clean air debate. Company reputations have been damaged by adverse publicity concerning toxic waste dumps and the accidental release of massive amounts of chemical pollutants into surrounding communities.[100] Utilities, in contrast, are widely perceived as having resisted acid rain controls too long. The utilities' intransigence despite relatively generous accommodations to them ultimately resulted in a bill that was much less sympathetic to their concerns than any earlier version.

Notes

1. George Hager, "Smog Bill Toughens Standards for Car, Truck Emissions," *Congressional Quarterly Weekly Report*, May 13, 1989, 1113.
2. Bruce A. Ackerman and William T. Hassler, in *Clean Coal/Dirty Air* (New

Haven, Conn.: Yale University Press, 1981), discuss how some of these themes were reflected in the 1977 amendments to the Clean Air Act of 1970.

3. Environmental Protection Agency, *Environmental Progress and Challenges: EPA's Update* (Washington, D.C.: EPA, 1988), 13.
4. Pub. L. No. 84-159, 69 Stat. 322 (1955).
5. Pub. L. No. 88-206, 77 Stat. 392 (1963).
6. Pub. L. No. 89-272, 79 Stat. 992 (1965).
7. For a review of these efforts, see Charles O. Jones, *Clean Air: The Policies and Politics of Pollution Control* (Pittsburgh: University of Pittsburgh Press, 1975); and Paul Portney, "Air Pollution Policy," in Paul Portney, ed., *Public Policies for Environmental Protection* (Washington, D.C.: Resources for the Future, 1990): 27-96.
8. Pub. L. No. 90-148, 81 Stat. 485.
9. *New York Times*, January 23, 1970, 22.
10. Testimony of James W. Jeans at a hearing of the Senate Public Works Subcommittee on Air and Water Pollution, March 23, 1970, quoted in *Congressional Quarterly Almanac, 1970* (Washington, D.C.: Congressional Quarterly, 1971), 480.
11. Reorganization Plan no. 3, 1970 5 U.S.C.A. App. (Supp. 1992).
12. Congressional Quarterly, *Congressional Quarterly Almanac, 1970*, 482-483.
13. Ibid., 478.
14. Ibid., 485-486.
15. Ibid., 472-488.
16. Ibid., 472.
17. 42 U.S.C. sec. 7401(a) (1988, Supp. 1990).
18. Congressional Quarterly, *Congressional Quarterly Almanac, 1970*, 472-474.
19. Pub. L. No. 92-157, 85 Stat. 464 (1971); Pub. L. No. 93-15, 87 Stat. 11 (1973); Pub. L. No. 93-319, 86 Stat. 249, 256, 261, 265 (1974); and 90 Stat. 2069 (1976).
20. Congressional Quarterly, *Congressional Quarterly Almanac, 1976* (Washington, D.C.: Congressional Quarterly, 1977), 128-132.
21. Ibid., 132.
22. See Ackerman and Hassler, *Clean Coal/Dirty Air*.
23. National Commission on Air Quality, *To Breathe Clean Air* (Washington, D.C.: Government Printing Office, 1981). Regarding establishment of the National Commission on Air Quality, see 42 U.S.C. sec. 7409(a) (1988).
24. National Commission on Air Quality, *To Breathe Clean Air*, 55-66.
25. Quoted in Henry A. Waxman, "An Overview of the Clean Air Act Amendments of 1990," *Environmental Law* 21 (1991): 1724-1725.
26. See *Wall Street Journal*, April 4, 1990, 6, for a profile of the Natural Resources Defense Council.
27. Environmental Protection Agency, Office of Legislation, "List of Committees and Subcommittees of Interest to EPA" (Washington, D.C.: EPA, 1987).
28. Congressional Quarterly, *Congressional Quarterly Almanac, 1981* (Washington, D.C.: Congressional Quarterly, 1982), 505-507.
29. Ibid.
30. Ibid. The balance of this chapter is based largely on interviews with a number of House and Senate staff members who were involved in the evolution of the clean air bills in Congress. They specified that their comments were not for attribution.

31. Congressional Quarterly, *Congressional Quarterly Almanac, 1982* (Washington, D.C.: Congressional Quarterly, 1983), 425-434.
32. In 1983, some key members of the Reagan administration began to favor action. William Ruckelshaus, who was appointed EPA administrator in May to replace the embattled Ann Gorsuch, who had been forced out, tried to develop support for an acid rain program, but opposition to controls, including that by OMB Director David Stockman, who ridiculed an expensive regulatory program aimed at saving fish, killed the initiative.
33. Congressional Quarterly, *Congressional Quarterly Almanac, 1984* (Washington, D.C.: Congressional Quarterly, 1985), 340-342. "Marking up" a bill refers to the revision process in committee that includes careful examination and editing of every detail.
34. Congressional Quarterly, *Congressional Quarterly Almanac, 1987* (Washington, D.C.: Congressional Quarterly, 1988), 299-302.
35. Congressional Quarterly, *Congressional Quarterly Almanac, 1988* (Washington, D.C.: Congressional Quarterly, 1989), 145, 148.
36. Richard E. Cohen, "Breaking through the Political Smog," *National Journal,* February 18, 1989, 421.
37. Congressional Quarterly, *Congressional Quarterly Almanac, 1988,* 144-148.
38. Chuck Alston, "As Clean-Air Bill Took Off, So Did PAC Donations," *Congressional Quarterly Weekly Report,* March 17, 1990, 811-813.
39. Ibid., 813-817.
40. See, for example, Brooks Jackson, *Honest Graft* (Washington, D.C.: Farragut Publishing, 1990); David B. Magleby and Candice J. Nelson, *The Money Chase* (Washington, D.C.: Brookings Institution, 1990).
41. George Hager, "Acid Rain Controls Advance on Both Sides of Aisle," *Congressional Quarterly Weekly Report,* April 1, 1989, 688-691.
42. Margaret E. Kirz, "Politics in the Air," *National Journal,* June 5, 1989, 1102.
43. George Hager, "Bush Sets Clean-Air Debate in Motion with New Plan," *Congressional Quarterly Weekly Report,* June 17, 1989, 1460-1464.
44. White House officials who played a key role included Roger B. Porter, assistant to the president for economic and domestic policy; Boyden C. Gray, the president's counsel; and Chief of Staff John H. Sununu. Also influential were Robert E. Grady, associate director for natural resources, energy, and science at OMB; Robert W. Hahn, senior staff economist at the Council of Economic Advisers; Secretary of Energy James D. Watkins; EPA Administrator William K. Reilly; and Assistant EPA Administrator for Air and Radiation William G. Rosenberg.
45. Kirz, "Politics in the Air," 1100.
46. "Project 88, Harnessing Market Forces to Protect Our Environment: Initiatives for the New President," a report written by a panel of academics, environmentalists, corporate executives, and government officials and sponsored by Senators Tim Wirth (D-Colo.) and John Heinz (R-Pa.), helped to focus attention on market-oriented approaches to regulation.
47. George Hager, "Critics Disappointed by Details of Bush Clean-Air Measure," *Congressional Quarterly Weekly Report,* July 22, 1989, 1852-1853.
48. George Hager, "Clean-Air Package, Part 1: Toxic Air Pollutants," *Congressional Quarterly Weekly Report,* April 22, 1989, 888-889.
49. George Hager, "Bush Scores Early Victory in Clean Air Markup," *Congressional Quarterly Weekly Report,* September 23, 1989, 2451-2452.
50. George Hager, "Energy Panel Seals Pact on Vehicle Pollution," *Congres-*

sional Quarterly Weekly Report, October 7, 1989, 2622-2623.

51. Ibid., 2621-2624.

52. George Hager, "Bush's Plan for Cleaner Fuels Scaled Back by House Panel," *Congressional Quarterly Weekly Report,* October 14, 1989, 2700.

53. George Hager, "Tougher Air-Toxics Standards Get Quick Nod from Panel," *Congressional Quarterly Weekly Report,* October 21, 1989, 2783-2784.

54. George Hager, "Senate Panel One-Ups Bush on Clean Air Controls," *Congressional Quarterly Weekly Report,* October 28, 1989, 2864-2865.

55. George Hager, "Bush's Tough Acid Rain Bill Puts Midwest on the Spot," *Congressional Quarterly Weekly Report,* November 4, 1989, 2934-2937.

56. Margaret E. Kris, "The Impassioned Panel," *National Journal,* June 15, 1991, 1504-1505.

57. George Hager, "Clean-Air Bill Loses Steam in Rush to Adjournment," *Congressional Quarterly Weekly Report,* November 11, 1989, 3045-3046.

58. Christopher Madison, "Clean Air Plans Go Up in Smoke," *National Journal,* November 18, 1989, 2832.

59. George Hager, "Senate Takes Up Clean Air But Doesn't Get Very Far," *Congressional Quarterly Weekly Report,* January 27, 1990, 230.

60. George Hager, "The 'White House Effect' Opens a Long-Locked Political Door," *Congressional Quarterly Weekly Report,* January 20, 1990, 141.

61. George Hager, "Senate's Clean-Air Struggle Goes Behind Closed Doors," *Congressional Quarterly Weekly Report,* February 3, 1990, 324.

62. George Mitchell, *World on Fire* (New York: Scribners, 1991), 1-11.

63. George Hager, "Closed-Door Talks on Clean Air Anger Environmental Groups," *Congressional Quarterly Weekly Report,* February 10, 1990, 386-387.

64. Mitchell, *World on Fire,* 1-11.

65. Hager, "Closed-Door Talks on Clean Air," 386-387.

66. George Hager, "Senate-White House Deal Breaks Clean-Air Logjam," *Congressional Quarterly Weekly Report,* March 3, 1990, 652-654.

67. Ibid., 654.

68. George Hager and Phil Kunz, "Senate-White House Deal Survives Another Test," *Congressional Quarterly Weekly Report,* March 24, 1990, 900-906.

69. Phil Kunz, "The 'Super-Tuesday' of Clean Air: Nothing but a Quirky Footnote," *Congressional Quarterly Weekly Report,* March 24, 1990, 902-903.

70. Phil Kunz and George Hager, "Showdown on Clean-Air Bill: Senate Says 'No' to Byrd," *Congressional Quarterly Weekly Report,* March 31, 1990, 986-987.

71. Ibid.

72. Byrd said that he had therefore been forced to negotiate with himself. Although these negotiations had been "rather amicable," he wryly observed, "I think I have voluntarily retreated about as far as I can go backward." One morning, Byrd observed that many of his colleagues had gone home before he had completed his speech late the night before, so he repeated it, noting simply that "I feel that they are entitled to some enlightenment." George Hager, "Byrd vs. Byrd," *Congressional Quarterly Weekly Report,* March 24, 1990, 901.

73. George Hager, "Clean-Air Deal Survives First Senate Assaults," *Congressional Quarterly Weekly Report,* March 10, 1990, 738.

74. Kunz and Hager, "Showdown on Clean-Air Bill," 984-985.

75. Phil Kunz, "Was Senator Byrd's Plan Veto Bait? Sununu Signaled Yes and

No," *Congressional Quarterly Weekly Report*, April 14, 1990, 1136-1137.
76. Kunz and Hager, "Showdown on Clean-Air Bill," 985.
77. Some members of Congress were expected to represent a wide range of interests in the debate on each major issue. The interests represented by Rep. Terry Bruce (D-Ill.), for example, ranged from environmentalists who were active in a movement centered at local universities to managers of coal-powered electric plants. Members oriented toward industry sometimes had to choose between the demands of large industries and the concerns of small businesses. But in general, the members represented specific industries or economic interests and the task was to put together majority coalitions concerning key issues. Environment-oriented members usually took their cues from the positions championed by the National Clean Air Coalition. See Julie Kosterlitz, "Twin Powers," *National Journal*, June 15, 1991, 1431.
78. George Hager, "House Makes No Headway," *Congressional Quarterly Weekly Report*, February 10, 1990, 387.
79. Hager and Kuntz, "Senate-White House Deal," 900-902.
80. Kuntz and Hager, "Showdown on Clean-Air Bill," 985-987.
81. George Hager, "Clean Air: War About Over in Both House and Senate," *Congressional Quarterly Weekly Report*, April 7, 1990, 1057-1063.
82. Janet Hook, "By Shifting Tactics on Clean Air, Dingell Guarded His Power," *Congressional Quarterly Weekly Report*, May 12, 1990, 1453-1446.
83. George Hager, "Easy House Vote on Clean Air Bodes Well for Bill's Future," *Congressional Quarterly Weekly Report*, May 26, 1990, 1643-1645.
84. Ibid.
85. "Clean Air Conferees Finally Named," *Congressional Quarterly Weekly Report*, June 30, 1990, 2044.
86. George Hager, "Cannons of the Conference Room Draw Clean Air Battle Lines," *Congressional Quarterly Weekly Report*, July 21, 1990, 2291-2293.
87. Waxman, "An Overview," 1739.
88. Hager, "Easy House Vote on Clean Air," 1644.
89. George Hager, "Conferees in Holding Pattern over Clean Air Proposals," *Congressional Quarterly Weekly Report*, July 28, 1990, 2399-2400.
90. George Hager, "Clean Air Conference Opens with Two Senate Offers," *Congressional Quarterly Weekly Report*, July 14, 1990, 2214.
91. George Hager, "Compromise on CFCs 1st Step in Slow-Moving Conference," *Congressional Quarterly Weekly Report*, August 4, 1990, 2507.
92. Alyson Pytte, "Conferees Reach Agreement on Urban Smog Provision," *Congressional Quarterly Weekly Report*, September 15, 1990, 2903.
93. Alyson Pytte, "Clean Air Conferees to Talk But Differences Loom," *Congressional Quarterly Weekly Report*, October 6, 1990, 3210.
94. Alyson Pytte, "Clean Air Conferees Agree on Motor Vehicles, Fuels," *Congressional Quarterly Weekly Report*, October 13, 1990, 3407-3409.
95. Alyson Pytte, "Clean Air Conferees Agree On Industrial Emissions," *Congressional Quarterly Weekly Report*, October 20, 1990, 3496-3498.
96. Alyson Pytte, "A Decade's Acrimony Lifted in the Glow of Clean Air," *Congressional Quarterly Weekly Report*, October 27, 1990, 3587-3592.
97. Pub. L. No. 101-549 (S. 1630), 104 Stat. 2399 (November 15, 1990). See *Congressional Record*, October 26, 1990, S-17118-17125, S-17232-17256, H-13101-13203; *Congressional Record*, October 27, 1990, S-16878-16999, S-18264-18268, E-3663-3714.
98. H. R. 3054, introduced by Representatives Henry A. Waxman and Jerry

Lewis (R-Calif.).
99. Waxman, "An Overview," 1812.
100. Interview with Bill Roberts, senior attorney for the Environmental Defense Fund, April 9, 1990. See, generally, the text of advertisements by the Chemical Manufacturers Association in the *Washington Post* throughout the clean air debate in 1990.

4 Issues in Formulating Clean Air Policy

The Clean Air Act of 1990 is an intricate mix of traditional approaches to environmental regulation and some important innovations. Because it is such a complicated and detailed piece of legislation, full examination of all of its provisions is beyond the scope of this book. The main titles or sections of the law concern some of the most difficult policy issues in environmental regulation. This chapter explores the most important issues and problems addressed by the 1990 act and their implications both for environmental policy and for public policy making in general.

Structure of the Clean Air Act of 1970

As required by the Clean Air Act of 1970, the EPA has issued health-based standards for six traditional or ambient air pollutants (sometimes referred to as "criteria" pollutants): total suspended particulates, sulfur dioxide, carbon monoxide, lead, ozone, and nitrogen dioxide. These national ambient air quality standards specified the acceptable level of concentration of these pollutants in the ambient (outside) air (see Chapter 2). *Primary standards* are intended to "protect the human health," with an "adequate margin of safety"; *secondary standards* are intended to protect public welfare and are aimed at crops, property, and plant and animal life. For most pollutants, the secondary standard is the same as the primary standard. The standards for some pollutants pertain to maximum levels that are permitted for from 1 to 24 hours; standards for other pollutants limit average annual concentrations. Concentrations of pollutants in the ambient air are measured in micrograms per cubic meter ($\mu g/m^3$) of air or in parts of pollutant per million parts of air (ppm). Table 4-1 lists the national ambient air quality primary (health-related) standards for the six traditional or ambient air pollutants.

States are required to formulate cleanup plans, called state implementation plans, for meeting, maintaining, and enforcing the national ambient air quality standards. These plans generally impose emission limitations on existing stationary (industrial, commercial, and household) sources of pollution. They may also include transportation control measures to reduce traffic and to require the inspection and maintenance of pollution control

Table 4-1   National Ambient Air Quality Primary (Health-Related) Standards

Pollutant	Averaging time	Maximum concentration (approximate equivalent)
Particulate matter (PM_{10})	Annual arithmetic mean	50 $\mu g/m^3$
	24-hour	150 $\mu g/m^3$
Sulfur dioxide (SO_2)[a]	Annual arithmetic mean	80 $\mu g/m^3$ (0.03 ppm)
	24-hour[c]	365 $\mu g/m^3$ (0.14 ppm)
Carbon monoxide (CO)[b]	8-hour[c]	10 mg/m^3 (9 ppm)
	1-hour[c]	40 mg/m^3 (35 ppm)
Nitrogen dioxide (NO_2)	Annual arithmetic mean	100 $\mu g/m^3$ (0.053 ppm)
Ozone (O_3)	Maximum daily 1-hour averaged[d]	235 $\mu g/m^3$ (0.12 ppm)
Lead (Pb)	Maximum quarterly average	1.5 $\mu g/m^3$

Source: Environmental Protection Agency, *National Air Quality and Emissions Trends Report,* 1989, 2-2.
[a] Secondary standard for SO_2: averaging time of 3 hours, concentration of 1300 $\mu g/m^3$ (0.50 ppm).
[b] There is no secondary standard for CO.
[c] Not to be exceeded more than one day a year.
[d] Standard is attained when the maximum hourly average concentrations above 0.12 ppm occur no more than one day a year.

equipment on motor vehicles. Each state is divided into air quality regions; state officials are required to identify which air regions are not in compliance with federal standards. Once the plans have been approved by state officials, they become binding *state* regulations and have the force of *state* law. Once they are approved by the EPA, they become binding *federal* regulations and have the force of *federal* law.

New stationary sources of pollution, or expansions of existing ones, are expected to be cleaner than older sources. The EPA issues New Source Performance Standards for categories of industrial facilities that are generally more stringent than the state standards limiting existing sources, since the retrofitting of older facilities is assumed to be more expensive than the installation of control equipment as new facilities are built. New sources of pollution cannot be constructed until permits are granted by the state in which they will be located. States are to issue permits only for new facilities that demonstrate they will meet these new source standards, and that they will not cause the air quality area in which they are located to exceed any national ambient air quality standard. If the facility is to be built in an area that already fails to meet one or more of those standards, any new major pollution must be offset by reductions in emissions from existing sources. To achieve that result, companies proposing new construction can close down old facilities they own, purchase existing sources and reduce or eliminate their emissions, or buy from other sources part of their authorization to emit pollutants.

Motor vehicles, a major cause of pollution, are also regulated by a federal-state partnership. The Clean Air Act of 1970 specified maximum tailpipe emissions from new automobiles and authorized the EPA to enforce those standards. States are responsible for developing inspection and maintenance programs to ensure that vehicles meet the standards imposed on them at the time of manufacture. State implementation plans can include specific regulations to reduce air pollution, such as those controlling traffic and parking or encouraging car pooling.

States are also required to develop a program for the prevention of significant deterioration in areas where air quality is relatively good and meets the national ambient air quality standards (such as national parks and wilderness areas). More stringent standards are to be imposed on existing and proposed sources in these areas than in nonattainment areas.

The Clean Air Act Amendments of 1990: A Summary

The 1990 amendments to the Clean Air Act of 1970 constitute a major addition, but the basic structure of the act was not changed. Two new provisions were added, concerning acid rain and stratospheric ozone protection. A workers' compensation program for those who lose their jobs or are laid off as a result of compliance with the act was also included—the first in any environmental statute. The main provisions of the amendments are summarized in this section and in Table 4-2.

Title I: Nonattainment

If Title I had been passed alone, it would rank as one of the most detailed and complex laws ever enacted by Congress. It is a monument to the efforts of congressional and EPA staff members and state and local regulatory officials to provide to the states all the regulatory powers that could be devised to help them meet the national ambient air quality standards.

One of the most important innovations, included in Title I, is an elaborate system of classifying pollutants: six categories of ozone non-attainment areas, from marginal to extreme, and two each for carbon monoxide and particulate matter. Deadlines of from three to twenty years are set for meeting the standards. The more serious the pollution problem, the more regulatory steps states must take, and the more aggressive they

Table 4-2   Summary of 1990 Amendments to the Clean Air Act

Title I: Nonattainment

    Adds new classifications of air quality areas
    Imposes deadlines that vary with severity of pollution problems
    Requires revised state implementation plans
    Covers more pollution sources
    Tightens controls on many pollution sources
    Lowers thresholds for major pollution sources
    Requires specific, measurable progress

Title II: Mobile Sources

    Imposes new, stricter emission standards for new motor vehicles
    Requires production of clean-fueled vehicles for use in fleets and pilot programs
    Requires sale of clean fuels in severely polluted areas

Title III: Hazardous Air Pollutants

    Requires regulation of 189 air toxics by technology-based controls
    May require additional controls based on residual risk
    Requires risk management plans for accidental release of air toxics

Title IV: Acid Deposition Control

    Reduces electricity-generating power plant emissions of sulfur dioxide by 10 million tons/year and nitrogen oxides by 2 million tons/year
    Sets a cap on the amount of sulfur dioxide to be emitted by year 2000
    Creates a market-based system of emission allowances to help finance cleanup costs

Title V: Permits

    Establishes a comprehensive new state-administered permit program
    Limits permits to 5 years
    Requires states to charge permit fees ($25/ton)
    Requires review of permits by EPA and neighboring states

Title VI: Stratospheric Ozone Protection

    Phases out production and consumption of CFCs and other chemicals that deplete the ozone layer
    Requires recycling and imposes other controls on various CFC-containing products

Title VII: Enforcement

    Establishes $25,000/day penalties and $5,000 field citations
    Establishes criminal penalties for violations knowingly committed
    Expands citizen suit provisions

Source: Clean Air Act Amendments, November 15, 1990.

must be. The most difficult air quality standard to meet has been that for ground-level ozone, a main ingredient of urban smog. Title I brings more sources under the act's coverage. Reductions are required by sources emitting 100 tons of precursors of ozone per year in marginal and moderate areas; 50 tons per year in serious areas; 25 tons per year in severe areas; and 10 tons per year in extreme areas. Furthermore, the definition of major source is changed so that smaller sources can be regulated in areas where there is serious air pollution. Another key provision requires establishment of annual emission reduction goals. Under the 1970 law, states were to make "reasonable further progress," but no minimum, quantitative targets were specified. The amendments state that areas of moderate to extreme ozone pollution must reduce emissions by 15 percent within the first six years and 3 percent per year thereafter. The 15 percent goal is difficult but not impossible to meet, according to state and local air quality officials, and many states should be able to meet it.[1] But one sponsor of the bill points out that "the emphasis in the bill . . . is not on the deadlines. The emphasis is on achieving steady progress before the deadlines." [2]

Title II: Mobile Sources

Title II, which regulates motor vehicle emissions, specifies more than ninety emission standards. Statutory provisions concerning use of reformulated fuels include detailed performance standards and fuel content requirements. Tailpipe emissions of hydrocarbons and nitrogen oxides are to be reduced by 35 percent and 60 percent, respectively, in some new cars by the 1994 model year and in all new cars by 1996. Beginning in 1998, pollution control equipment in all new cars will be required to have a 10-year, 100,000-mile warranty. Auto manufacturers are required to produce a fleet of experimental cars for sale in southern California (150,000 cars by 1996, 300,000 cars by 1998). Using new technologies, they are to meet even more stringent emission standards than those listed above. Oil companies are required to offer alternative formulations of gasoline that produce fewer pollutants when ignited. They are to be used in areas with the worst carbon monoxide pollution problems by 1992, and in all areas with ozone problems by 1995. In areas with serious ozone problems, fleets of ten or more vehicles that can be centrally fueled are required to use clean fuels such as methanol, ethanol, and natural gas. A new program, stage II controls, requires that equipment be placed on service station gasoline pumps to capture vapors released during refueling.

Title III: Hazardous Air Pollutants

The requirement in Title III that emission limits be established for all major sources of hazardous or toxic air pollutants represents a major departure from the 1970 law. Title III also lists 189 chemicals to be regulated as hazardous air pollutants; Congress did not leave that determination to the EPA. The agency is required to list the categories of industrial processes in chemical plants, oil refineries, steel plants, and other facilities that emit these pollutants and to issue standards for each of them by the deadlines specified and using as a basis minimum regulatory standards provided in the title. Within eight years of establishing the emissions standards for industrial processes, the EPA is required to establish a second round of health-based standards for each chemical that is believed to be a carcinogen and represents a risk of at least one cancer case for every million exposed individuals. The EPA cannot impose health-based or residual risk standards on coke ovens at steel mills until 2020 if they meet interim, technology-based standards between 1993 and 1998. The major sources of hazardous air pollutants, defined as those emitting at least 10 tons per year of any one toxic pollutant or at least 25 tons per year of any combination, are required to achieve the same level of emissions reduction reached by existing sources. These reductions are to be achieved between 1995 and 2003 and are expected to reduce the emission of toxic air pollutants by as much as 90 percent by 2003. Finally, the title establishes an independent agency, the Chemical Safety Board, to investigate chemical accidents to determine their causes. The EPA will require industrial plants to prepare formal safety reviews to be made available to the public and will set new safety standards for plants where the bulk of toxic chemicals are used.

Title IV: Acid Deposition Control

An important innovation included in Title IV is an emissions trading program for sulfur dioxide (the major precursor of acid rain). The EPA is to allocate to each major coal-fired power plant an allowance for each ton of emission permitted; sources cannot release emissions beyond the number of allowances they are given. Allowances may be traded, bought, or sold among allowance holders. Additional allowances are to be given to certain midwestern utilities that they can sell to help finance their cleanup efforts. The EPA is required to create an additional pool of allowances to permit construction of new sources or expansion of existing ones. The sulfur dioxide emission allowances for each of the major power plants in twenty-one states are listed in the law. Emission allowances for other power plants are to be computed by means of detailed formulas that are provided.

Sulfur dioxide emissions are to be cut in half by the imposition of these emission limitations. A reduction from 1980 levels of 10 million tons annually is to be achieved by the year 2000. Half of the reduction is to take place by January 1, 1995, when the 110 largest sulfur dioxide-emitting electric utility plants in twenty-one states will be required to meet more stringent emission standards.

Emissions of nitrogen oxides, the other major cause of acid rain, are to be reduced by 2 million tons a year from 1980 levels. The first emission limits will become effective within eighteen months of enactment of the 1990 amendments. Additional reductions are required by 1997.

Title V: Permits

The amendments establish a new permit program to facilitate enforcement of the Clean Air Act. All major stationary sources must have EPA-issued operating permits that specify what emissions they can release and at what levels, and what control measures they must employ.

Title VI: Stratospheric Ozone Protection

The destruction of the stratospheric ozone layer was not considered a problem when the Clean Air Act of 1967 was enacted. The 1990 amendments are a means of implementing the Montreal Protocol on Substances That Deplete the Ozone Layer in the United States. Some sections of Title VI commit the nation to a more rapid phaseout of some of these chemicals than is required by international agreement. The title lists specific ozone-depleting chemicals and provides a schedule for the phaseout of the production and use of those chemicals. The production of chlorofluorocarbons and carbon tetrachloride is to be phased out throughout the 1990s and outlawed by January 1, 2000; methyl chloroform cannot be produced after January 1, 2002. The use of hydrochlorofluorocarbons in aerosol cans and insulating material is prohibited after January 1, 1994, and their production is prohibited after 2030. The title also requires the EPA to issue new rules for the recycling and disposal of ozone-depleting chemicals recovered from air conditioners, refrigerators, and other appliances and equipment.

Title VII: Enforcement

Enforcement provisions require more monitoring by sources and by state agencies, update the penalties imposed by the law to make them consistent with those in other environmental statutes, and increase the role of the public in enforcing the law through citizen suits to be filed against polluters and government agencies.

Title XI: Clean Air Employment Transition Assistance

The secretary of labor is authorized to establish a program to provide compensation for workers whose jobs are lost or who are laid off as a consequence of compliance with the Clean Air Act, including grants for retraining and allowances for job searches and relocation. The cost of the program is expected to reach $250 million by 1995.

The 1990 amendments also include a number of provisions that address relatively less important issues. Title VIII orders the EPA to regulate air pollution resulting from activities such as oil exploration on the outer continental shelf, study air pollution that impairs visibility in national parks and other areas that have relatively clean air, develop a program to monitor and improve air quality along the United States border with Mexico, and compare the environmental regulations that U.S. trading partners impose on firms within their borders with EPA regulations. It provides grants for state air pollution planning and control programs and for research on hydrogen fuel cells and requires that all sources subject to acid rain controls report to the EPA their carbon dioxide emissions to facilitate the agency's effort to gather information on gases that are believed to contribute to global climatic change. Title IX authorizes establishment of a program to monitor and analyze air pollution production and its health effects. Title X requires that no less than 10 percent of funds expended by the EPA on research be made available to businesses that are at least 51 percent owned by "one or more socially and economically disadvantaged business concerns."

Clean Air Law and Regulation: Defining the Issues

The decisions incorporated in the Clean Air Act Amendments of 1990, and the way its provisions are implemented, will have a major impact on American business and Americans' health. The precedents it establishes will have important implications for environmental law and for regulation in general. Several key issues are discussed below.

Broad Goals and Detailed Provisions

The Clean Air Act as amended is a statement of broad, aggressive goals. The summary of the amendments in the preceding section does not begin to convey the technicalities and minutiae in the seven main titles. The amendments list hundreds of specific chemicals to be regulated, establish precise deadlines for virtually every regulatory step to be taken by the EPA and the states, and specify exactly how much pollution can be emitted by new and old motor vehicles.

Henry Waxman, a proponent of such a detailed approach, is optimistic that it will result in stricter enforcement:

> To an extent unprecedented in prior environmental statutes, the pollution control programs of the 1990 Amendments include very detailed mandatory directives to EPA, rather than more general mandates or broad grants of authority that would allow for wide latitude in EPA's implementation of the CAA's programs. In addition, statutory deadlines are routinely provided to assure that required

actions are taken in a timely fashion. More than two hundred rule-making actions are mandated in the first several years of the 1990 Amendments' implementation.[3]

Title I of the 1990 amendment is Congress's response to the failure of the 1977 Clean Air Act to produce attainment of the national ambient air quality standards for the six traditional pollutants. Under the 1970 law, states were to have their attainment programs, or state implementation plans, in place by 1972. It became increasingly clear in the early 1980s, however, that the law was not having the intended effect. Many states failed to meet deadlines for coming into compliance and for formulating and implementing their cleanup plans. The EPA and the Reagan administration were widely viewed as trying to weaken the law and minimize industry compliance costs. Many members of Congress became increasingly frustrated because the EPA was slow to issue documents to guide state regulatory efforts and either failed to impose sanctions in noncomplying states that were required by law (although members of Congress representing industrial states did not want the sanctions to be imposed either), or was unwilling to enforce the sanctions as aggressively as the law seemed to require.

The challenge confronting state regulatory officials was immense. There were tens of thousands of sources to be regulated, monitoring data were usually scarce, and many states had little idea of which sources needed to be regulated and how to regulate them. Aggressive regulatory initiatives were often met by industry predictions that factories would be closed down and there would be massive layoffs. In a series of congressional hearings, state air quality officials supported a stronger Clean Air Act and a stronger threat of federal intervention in recalcitrant states as a way to improve their regulatory position vis-à-vis other state officials who feared that environmental regulation would harm the economy.

By the mid-1980s, it was obvious that the standards for emission of ozone, carbon monoxide, and particulates would not be met unless the act was strengthened. Although the most serious problems were concentrated in large urban areas, physicians and health researchers warned in congressional hearings and elsewhere that the health of children, the elderly, and those with respiratory diseases in all areas of the country was endangered by poor air quality.[4] Members of Congress and the subcommittee staff agreed that the law needed to be more complicated because the task of regulating the different pollutants was so daunting; they also believed that Congress needed to limit the discretion of the EPA and the states. The questions they debated included what burdens, if any, should be imposed on small businesses, what kinds of sanctions for noncompliance were appropriate, how the EPA and the states were to go about enforcing compliance with the national ambient air quality standards, how far to extend the deadlines for compliance with those standards, what constitutes a major source of emissions in determining which sources are to be regulated, how to establish a new program of permits to regulate emissions from major sources, and how to prevent significant deterioration of air quality in and near national parks and wilderness areas. Most of these details were worked out in the House bill, and the House-Senate conference committee largely adopted that version.[5]

Members of Congress were always preoccupied with the possibility that "without detailed directives, industry intervention might frustrate efforts to put pollution control steps in place. . . . History shows that even where EPA seeks to take strong action, the White House will often intervene at industry's behest to block regulatory action."[6] The agency's actions are circumscribed by the amendments' detailed provisions; its inaction can be challenged by citizen suits (Title VII). These are usually straightforward cases that can be won simply by showing that an action required by a certain date has not been taken, and their outcomes can shape the EPA's regulatory agenda. If the agency fails to act, statutory default requirements, or "hammers," go into effect. For example, after January 1, 1995, no gasoline can be sold in certain areas unless it is in compliance with EPA regulations; if no regulations have been issued, no gasoline can be sold. The petroleum industry will be as interested as environmentalists are in ensuring that the EPA issues these regulations. States are authorized to issue their own control technology regulations for major sources of air toxics if the EPA fails to do so, and the threat to industry of a number of different state standards will likely prompt it to support EPA efforts.[7]

Despite the widespread criticism of the traditional command-and-control form of regulation, where Congress orders the EPA to issue regulations and the states implement them, as discussed in Chapter 1, the Clean Air Act of 1990 is based largely on that approach. The continued reliance of Congress on deadlines for state and EPA action, and the specificity of the amendments' provisions, reflect its continuing distrust of the executive branch and its belief that many environmental laws are not being fully or aggressively implemented by state and federal agencies. Many of the deadlines included in the 1990 amendments will be used in citizen suits brought by environmental groups and others to force implementation of the law. Congress tried to limit the EPA's discretion in every way it could because many members, particularly Democrats, had come to believe that if the agency had any leeway, it simply would not act. Or, if it tried to exercise some initiative and discretion in taking an action that was not absolutely required by law, its OMB overseers would quickly clamp down.

The EPA continues to be caught in the middle of the constitutional tug-of-war between Congress and the president over how environmental laws are to be implemented. This poses tremendous challenges for the agency in managing its workload and setting priorities for the allocation of its resources. Agency officials have relatively little flexibility; they are committed by law to policies that reflect Congress's 1990 understanding of air pollution regulation and that will probably impede agency adjustments as new research and new scientific developments alter our understanding of the causes and consequences of air pollution and present possible alternatives. The 1990 amendments, as they are implemented, will provide another test of whether Congress can enact laws that effectively compel agencies to pursue an aggressive regulatory agenda.

Technology Forcing

Throughout the two decades of debate over the Clean Air Act, a basic expectation has been that laws and regulations will provide clear incentives for industry to develop cleaner technologies and use them more widely. Air pollution from mobile sources has been regulated under the Clean Air Act in two ways: directly, through emissions standards, and indirectly, through transportation control measures designed to reduce traffic. One of the successes of the Clean Air Act of 1970 is that it helped force the development and use of new control technologies such as the catalytic converter for motor vehicles. Despite its frequent praise for technology forcing, however, Congress has generally been hesitant to push industries beyond what they claim is technologically possible. Consequently, technology forcing has often meant forcing the more widespread *use* of already existing new technologies, rather than forcing the *creation* of new technologies required to meet stringent standards. Two prominent examples of technology forcing in the 1990 law include regulating tailpipe emissions and encouraging use of clean fuels.

Tailpipe Emission Standards.   The Clean Air Act of 1970 established tailpipe emission standards for three pollutants: nonmethane hydrocarbons, carbon monoxide, and nitrogen oxides. To implement the standards, the EPA established in the 1970s the Federal Motor Vehicle Control Program, under which it issues national emission standards for fuel evaporation, carbon monoxide, nitrogen oxides, volatile organic compounds, and particulates. New vehicles must meet these standards; EPA officials test emissions of sample vehicles from production lines to ensure their compliance. The states assume responsibility for enforcing tailpipe emission standards of vehicles once they are in use. Many states have included in the sections of their state implementation plans pertaining to ozone and carbon monoxide a motor vehicle inspection and maintenance program. The inspection includes an examination of the catalytic converter and other control equipment to ensure its proper functioning as well as a test of tailpipe emissions to determine whether they meet the standards.

From 1940 to 1970, motor vehicle emissions of volatile organic compounds more than doubled; from 1970 to 1988 they declined by 46 percent, despite an 81 percent increase in national vehicle miles traveled in that period. Figure 4-1(a) shows the decline of motor vehicle VOC emissions from 1970 to 1988. Motor vehicle emissions of carbon monoxide nearly tripled between 1940 and 1970; they decreased by 48 percent between 1970 and 1988 (see Figure 4-1(b)). The decrease in emissions of both pollutants was a result of the imposition of tailpipe emission standards; older cars were replaced by those using cleaner fuels. Nitrogen oxide emissions, however, peaked around 1980 and have declined since then, as shown in Figure 4-1(c).[8]

The battle between the auto industry and clean air advocates over the extent to which cleanup can be achieved through technological controls on tailpipe emissions has dominated the debate over clean air policy for two decades, overshadowing other efforts such as the reduction of motor vehicle traffic. Aware that technological changes are less difficult to bring about than changes in the driving habits of Americans, Congress has hesitated to impose aggressive transportation control measures. The steady increase in national vehicle miles traveled since 1980 (Figure 4-2, p. 134) has largely offset the progress made in reducing tailpipe emissions. It is clear that the imposition of strict tailpipe emission standards and the production of vehicles that emit fewer pollutants are not enough. If national ambient air quality standards are to be met, states with severe pollution problems will have to develop and enforce transportation control measures to reduce the number of vehicle miles traveled.

The progress made in the 1970s renewed demands in the 1980s that even more stringent controls be placed on tailpipe emissions. As mentioned in Chapter 3, Rep. John Dingell believed that auto company officials had borne the brunt of the effort to clean up the air and were justified in resisting further controls. Environmental groups and state and local officials were just as adamant; pointing to the reduction in motor vehicle emissions as a cost-effective way to reduce pollution levels, they championed a new round of technology-forcing emission standards. Some compromises reached between Representatives Waxman and Dingell early in the debates of the 1990 amendments resolved this issue and made House passage of the clean air bill possible. Rather than delegating such policy details to the EPA, Congress has determined what emission standards new vehicles must meet. Table 4-3 (p. 135) lists the tailpipe emission standards that have been established beginning with the 1967 Clean Air Act. It suggests the amount of detail in the 1990 law.

The Clean Fuels Program. The 1990 amendments established a program to clean up motor vehicle fuels that is also based on the idea of technology forcing. Oxygen-containing additives are required in fuels used

Figure 4-1   Emissions by Motor Vehicles, 1970-1988

(a) Volatile organic compounds

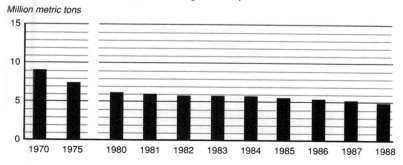

(b) Carbon monoxide

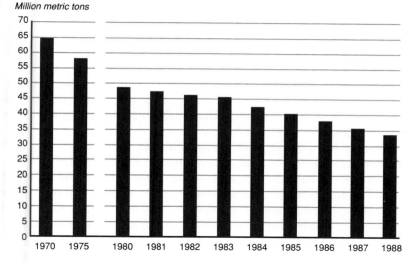

(c) Nitrogen oxides

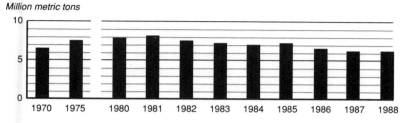

Source: Environmental Protection Agency, *National Air Pollutant Emission Estimates, 1940-1988* (Washington, D.C.: EPA, 1990), 58, 61, and 62.

Figure 4-2 Total National Vehicle Miles Traveled and Carbon Monoxide Emissions, 1980-1989

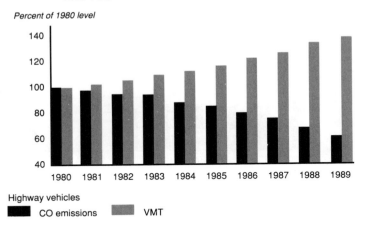

Percent of 1980 level

Highway vehicles

■ CO emissions   ▨ VMT

Source: Environmental Protection Agency, *National Air Quality and Emissions Trends Report, 1989* (Washington, D.C.: EPA, 1991), 3-18.

in communities with high levels of carbon monoxide. Reformulated (cleaner) gasoline must be sold in cities with the most serious ozone problems. Fleet vehicles must produce substantially less pollution than other vehicles.

Probably the toughest battle fought in the debate over the 1990 amendments centered on fuels. No group lobbied harder against those provisions of the bill than the oil companies. One of the many ironies of clean air politics is that no one in Congress or in the EPA had pushed for development of reformulated gasoline. A variety of reformulated and alternative fuels have been developed in response to the problems posed by traditional fuels. Some have been developed expressly for motor vehicles; others are part of a much broader effort to develop renewable, less polluting energy sources. A major breakthrough that encouraged passage of the clean fuel provisions was the 1989 announcement by ARCO that it had developed a reformulated gasoline for use in older cars that were not equipped with catalytic converters. The announcement caught policy makers by surprise. According to one EPA official, the OMB never would have approved inclusion of a requirement for reformulated gasoline in the clean air bill, but once ARCO made the announcement, there was no way to block it. When the company introduced reformulated gas in 1990, its market share shot up by 10 percent.[9] But ARCO suffered the wrath of the American Petroleum Institute and the rest of the oil industry for breaking rank.

Congress quickly responded by requiring use of both reformulated

Table 4-3   1990 Amendments' Tailpipe Emission Standards, by Model Year (grams per mile)

Model year	Hydrocarbons	Carbon monoxide	Nitrogen oxides	Particulate matter
1968-1969	6.30	51.0		
1970-1971	4.00	34.0		
1972	3.00	28.0		
1973-1974	3.00	28.0	3.0	
1975-1976	1.50	15.0	3.0	
1977-1979	1.50	15.0	2.0	
1980-1993	0.41	7.0	2.0	
1994-2003				
5 yr/50,000 mi	0.25	3.4	0.4[a]	0.08
10 yr/100,000 mi	0.31	4.2	0.6[a]	0.10
2004-				
10 yr/100,000 mi	0.125	1.7	0.2	0.08

Source: "Major Clean Air Amendments Enacted," *Congressional Quarterly Almanac, 1977* (Washington, D.C.: Congressional Quarterly, 1978), 627; Clean Air Act, Amendments, Pub. L. No. 101-549 (November 15, 1990), sec. 203; Thad Godish, *Air Quality* (Chelsea, Mich.: Lewis, 1991), 262.

Notes: The 1970 Clean Air Act required the following standards to be met beginning with the 1978 model year: hydrocarbons, 1.5 grams per mile; carbon monoxide, 3.4 grams per mile; nitrogen oxides, 0.4 grams per mile. The 1977 act changed the standards for subsequent years. The 1990 amendments' standards take effect beginning with the 1994 model year but are phased in: the standards change after the first 5 years or 50,000 miles, whichever comes first. To be certified, 40 percent of the 1994 model-year vehicles, 80 percent of the 1995 model-year vehicles, and 100 percent of the 1996 model-year vehicles must comply with these standards. The standards for the year 2004 take effect unless the EPA determines that the previous standards should be maintained or issues different ones.

[a] Standards for diesel-fueled vehicles are 1.0 grams per mile for 5 years or 50,000 miles and 1.25 grams per mile for 10 years or 100,000 miles.

gasoline and alternative fuels. States with serious air pollution problems were to begin replacing traditional gasoline formulas with alcohols such as ethanol and methanol, alcohol-gasoline blends, liquefied petroleum gas, liquefied natural gas, and hydrogen that produce fewer hydrocarbons and air toxics. Table 4-4 lists the major alternative fuels, their sources, and uses.

Reformulated gasoline promises to reduce levels of ozone and air toxics in automobile emissions and can be used in many vehicles without having to modify them, a major advantage. But its benefits are relatively modest compared with those of alternative fuels. The production of reformulated gasoline and alternative fuels will likely require new refining equipment and processes. Difficult trade-offs must be made: fuels with higher oxygen content result in reduced carbon monoxide emissions and higher octane levels, but may result in increased emissions of volatile organic compounds,

Table 4-4 Sources and Uses of Alternative Fuels

Alternative fuel	Source	Uses				
		Internal combustion engines	Diesel engines	Turbine engines	Electric motors	Fuel cells
Reformulated gasoline	Petroleum, natural gas	x				
Methanol and methyl tertiary butyl ether	Biomass, natural gas, coal	x	x	x		x
Ethanol and ethyl tertiary butyl ether	Biomass	x	x	x		
Compressed natural gas	Natural gas	x	x	x		
Electricity	Solar energy, hydroelectric power, nuclear energy, natural gas, biomass, coal, geothermal energy				x	
Hydrogen	Solar energy, nuclear energy, coal	x		x		x
Synthetic gasoline	Biomass, coal, oil shale	x				
Synthetic diesel fuel	Biomass, coal, oil shale		x	x		

Source: Adapted from Department of Energy, *Interim Report: National Energy Strategy* (Washington, D.C.: Department of Energy, 1990), 16.

nitrogen oxides, and toxic chemicals. They also reduce fuel economy and are more expensive to produce.

Methanol and ethanol have been touted by many as the fuels of the future; they may burn more completely and release fewer hydrocarbons because they contain less oxygen and carbon than regular gasoline, and they may evaporate more slowly because their vapor pressure is lower. Methanol can be produced from coal or natural gas, but conversion of vehicles is expensive. Engine performance is at least as good as that of gasoline and diesel engines, but methanol contains only about half the energy of the same quantity of gasoline. Both fuels eliminate some of the additives that are precursors of air toxics, although methanol use results in formaldehyde, a possible human carcinogen. Ethanol or ethanol blends are attractive because they are produced from agricultural products, but they cost more to produce and have their own dangerous by-products. Liquid natural gas and liquefied petroleum gas produce significantly fewer pollutants but require large fuel tanks and expensive conversion. Hydrogen is clearly the fuel of choice. It has no carbon atoms, so carbon monoxide and hydrocarbon emissions are eliminated. It is very combustible and can be used in lean air-fuel mixtures, reducing emissions of nitrogen oxides. Its source is virtually inexhaustible. But the cost of producing and storing hydrogen is quite high, so it is not yet feasible for use as a fuel.[10] Table 4-5 compares some of the advantages and disadvantages of reformulated and alternative fuels.

One congressional sponsor of the clean air bills continues to be optimistic about the gains that will result from the inclusion of technology forcing in environmental legislation:

> The nature and severity of the air pollution problems addressed in the CAA are so daunting that immediately available technologies are not, in themselves, sufficient to assure protection of America's public health and environmental resources. In fact, in the case of ozone depletion, new technologies must be developed for protection of the planet itself.

In addition to its environmental benefits it gives a "competitive edge to American companies in a global economy where nations are increasingly concerned about environmental protection" and are looking for cleaner, more efficient technologies.[11]

The Importance of Political Coalitions

Although environmental issues like clean air have considerable political clout, the legislative process is still influenced to a great extent by traditional interests. Clean air politics in the 1980s was discussed in Chapter 3. The formation of political coalitions around specific issues deserves additional exploration, however, because it gives us some perspective on major provisions of the 1990 law.

Table 4-5   Advantages and Disadvantages of Reformulated and Alternative Fuels

Methanol
  Advantages:

  May reduce ozone-forming hydrocarbon emissions by up to 40 percent when used as a mixture of 85 percent methanol and 15 percent gasoline
  In 100 percent concentration, may reduce ozone-forming hydrocarbon emissions by up to 90 percent
  Eliminates benzene and other toxic emissions

  Disadvantages:

  May increase formaldehyde emissions
  Requires significant expenditures for new production and distribution systems
  Reduces vehicle driving range and is corrosive to engine parts
  Makes vehicles difficult to start in cold temperatures

Ethanol
  Advantages:

  May reduce ozone-forming hydrocarbon emissions and toxic emissions to extent and in concentration similar to methanol
  Reduces carbon dioxide emissions

  Disadvantages:

  Emits more acetaldehyde
  Would cost consumers substantially more without federal tax exemption
  Requires vehicle modifications estimated at $300 per vehicle

Liquefied petroleum gas
  Advantages:

  Produces an estimated 50 percent fewer hydrocarbons, which have less ozone-forming potential
  May reduce carbon monoxide emissions by an estimated 25 percent to 80 percent

  Disadvantages:

  Reduces vehicle driving range and causes refueling inconveniences
  Requires pressurized fuel tanks, which restrict vehicle cargo space
  Increases new car cost by up to $1,000

(Continued on next page)

Table 4-5   *(Continued)*

Compressed natural gas
  Advantages:

  Reduces hydrocarbon emissions by an estimated 40 percent to 90 percent
  Reduces carbon monoxide emissions by an estimated 50 percent to 90 percent
  Reduces emissions of benzene and other toxic pollutants

  Disadvantages:

  Emits more nitrogen oxides
  Requires installation of new distribution system
  Reduces vehicle driving range and causes refueling inconveniences
  Requires large, heavy, pressurized fuel tanks
  May increase vehicle costs by up to $2,000

Oxygenated fuels
  Advantages:

  Reduce carbon monoxide emissions by an estimated 12 percent to 22 percent
  Increase gasoline octane levels, thus decreasing the need for harmful additives
    such as benzene

  Disadvantages:

  Increase evaporative emissions of volatile organic compounds
  Oxidize to form toxic chemicals such as formaldehyde
  May increase emissions of nitrogen oxides
  May contribute to auto fuel system problems and reduce fuel economy
  Increase the cost of gasoline

Reformulated gasoline
  Advantages:

  Deliverable to consumers through existing distribution system
  May reduce levels of ozone and air toxics in automobile emissions
  Requires few, if any, vehicle modifications

  Disadvantages:

  May require purchase of significant amounts of refinery equipment and
    construction of refinery units
  Emission benefits not comparable with those of fuels such as pure methanol and
    compressed natural gas
  Extensive reformulation may result in substantial consumer price increases

Source: General Accounting Office, *Air Quality Implications of Alternative Fuels,* GAO/RCED-90-143, July 1990, 8-9.

Environmentalists were strong supporters of reformulated gas, but the key political support came from midwestern agricultural interests, since one way of cleaning up fuels is to add alcohol (particularly ethanol), made from grain. As a result of the efforts of two midwestern senators, Thomas Daschle (D-S.D.) and minority leader Robert Dole of Kansas, who pushed hard for addition of the reformulated gas provisions, oxygenated or reformulated gasoline is required in every carbon monoxide nonattainment area. In contrast, methanol had no real congressional champions; consequently, there are few provisions specifically requiring its use. The lesson is clear: if a powerful economic and political interest can be harnessed to environmental goals, inclusion of the relevant provisions is virtually guaranteed. Initiatives aimed at improving air quality that were coupled with subsidies generated strong political support but upset many long-standing political alliances; conservative, agriculture-oriented members of Congress were pressured to support new regulatory requirements promoted by ardent environmentalists.

Much more complicated was the politics of acid rain. That the acid rain provision was included in the Clean Air Act Amendments of 1990 is remarkable, given ten years of deadlock over the issue. Acid rain is an important international issue and continues to be a major source of contention between the United States and Canada. Informal discussions between officials of the two countries began in 1978. The Canadians argued that they had already taken significant steps to reduce their contribution to the problem of acid rain, including a plan to reduce sulfur dioxide emissions by 50 percent of their 1980 levels (67 percent in Ontario) by 1994, and called on the Americans to do the same. But U.S. officials were hesitant to make a commitment to such reductions, claiming that this country had already done much more than Canada to reduce sulfur emissions and that more research was necessary before making major investments in pollution control technologies. After three years of negotiations Canada proposed reducing sulfur dioxide emissions by 50 percent of current levels in both countries, but the United States rejected that initiative.[12] A 1986 agreement called for $5 billion to be spent in the United States over five years, to be split equally by industries and the federal government, to retrofit plants with new control technologies.[13]

At least as important to Congress as foreign relations, however, was the domestic politics of acid rain, which transcends partisan politics and provides an illustrative case study of how members of Congress deal with regional conflicts. Legislation proposed in the early 1980s, as the Clean Air Act of 1977 was about to expire, called for a 40 percent reduction (10 million tons) of sulfur dioxide emissions below 1980 levels over a ten-year period. The Reagan administration and congressional opponents argued that there was insufficient information to link sulfur dioxide emissions from power plants and factories in the Midwest with acid rain damage in Canada and New England and that, in any event, the problem would be remedied as old power plants were replaced by less polluting ones.[14]

There were three central issues in the congressional debate over acid rain in the 1980s. First, how much reduction in sulfur dioxide emissions should take place? In order to protect ecologically sensitive areas, reductions in acid deposition of 50 percent were suggested, which translated into an annual reduction in sulfur dioxide emissions of about 11 million tons. But since some areas are more sensitive than others, the distribution of reductions may be more important than an average reduction.

A second divisive issue was the means of reducing sulfur dioxide emissions. If public utilities and industries were permitted to choose the most cost-effective means of reducing emissions, many would likely have substituted low-sulfur coal for high-sulfur coal. But the 1977 amendments to the Clean Air Act prohibited states from achieving national ambient air quality standards for sulfur by using low-sulfur coal and required companies to install flue gas desulfurization or "scrubbing" equipment.[15] A shift to low-sulfur coal would probably not have decreased the total number of mining jobs, and might even have increased it, but the distribution of jobs would have shifted from eastern to western coal states. Some communities in the East would have been particularly hard hit and could have lost from 20,000 to 30,000 mining jobs.[16] If scrubbers were installed to reduce emissions by 10 million tons a year, an estimated 45 million tons of scrubber sludge would also be generated each year, posing another major environmental challenge. Scrubbers also increase carbon dioxide emissions and thus contribute to global warming because they require more coal to be burned to produce the same amount of electricity, although some believe that alternative technologies will soon be available that will reduce sulfur dioxide emissions without the negative environmental by-products.[17]

The third issue was who would pay for the reduction in sulfur dioxide emissions. The EPA estimated that a 50 percent reduction in the emissions causing acid rain would cost from $16 billion to $33 billion over twenty years.[18] Other estimates were higher, putting the cost at from $3 billion to $6 billion each year well into the twenty-first century, if utilities were to switch to another fuel, install scrubbers, and build new facilities.[19] Electric rates in Ohio were projected to increase from 8 percent to 12 percent if emission reductions were required. A shift away from high-sulfur coal would threaten as many as one job in four in some areas of Kentucky and would have adversely affected other sectors of the local economy dependent on the coal industry. States such as Ohio, West Virginia, and Indiana would face similar economic problems.[20]

Three options discussed in Congress in the 1980s were (1) to subsidize with federal tax revenues the capital expenditures required to achieve the reductions, (2) to increase taxes in the northeastern and midwestern states so that those most affected by the problem would bear the burden, and (3) to levy a tax on all electricity generated by public utilities, to be contributed to a trust fund to subsidize new investment. Midwesterners argued that federal subsidies had been used to develop sources of electricity in other areas of the country, such as hydroelectric plants in the Northwest; therefore, funds should be made available to help build coal-powered generating plants in the Midwest.

Legislation reported out by the Senate Environment and Public Works Committee in the mid-1980s required that polluters bear the burden of controls to reduce sulfur dioxide emissions. The federal subsidies that would pay for control equipment were to be funded by a surtax on electricity based on the amount of such emissions produced by each power plant. This agreement promised to protect the jobs of high-sulfur coal miners. In June 1988, a bipartisan group of twenty-eight senators proposed a compromise on acid rain that was similar to the one that had been proposed by the governors of New York and Ohio in May. Governors Mario Cuomo and Richard F. Celeste had proposed that the costs of the control equipment necessary to achieve major reductions in sulfur dioxide emissions be divided equally between the midwestern states and the federal government, the federal share coming from the proceeds of a tax on oil imports.[21]

By October 1988, however, despite the previous summer's heat, the most severe urban smog in a decade, and letters signed by majorities in both chambers calling for reauthorization of the Clean Air Act, Senate sponsors of the legislation abandoned their efforts. Environmentalists rejected the concessions made to industry, and some key senators on the Environment and Public Works Committee withdrew their support of the compromise. Senator Byrd continued to refuse to bring the bill up for a floor vote in order to protect the West Virginia high-sulfur coal industry.

In the House, the Group of Nine on the Energy and Commerce Committee had begun working on a compromise bill in the mid-1980s, hoping to break the logjam between members favoring industry and those favoring environmental concerns. Rep. Jim Cooper, a Democrat from a Tennessee coal-mining district, met with the Alliance for Acid Rain Control, a group of governors led by then governor John Sununu of New Hampshire and Governor Anthony Earl of Wisconsin, and with representatives siding with industry and environmental groups. The House compromise bill included a fifteen-year cleanup period and was a modest attempt to encourage the development of clean coal technologies instead of requiring scrubbers. One of the first bills to set a cap on total emissions, it included a minimal trading program that allowed public utilities to trade emissions allowances within their regions but did not require offsets for companies that wanted to build new plants. States that had already cleaned up or that did not really have significant pollution problems were not affected by the bill; the limits applied only to the states with high emission pollutant rates. Emissions were projected to decrease to 10 million tons by the year 2000, but could then grow over time.

Sponsors of the reauthorization legislation in both chambers blamed members favoring industry and environmental groups for taking extreme positions and causing rejection of the compromise bill. Representative Sharp, for example, argued in 1988 that

> advocates at polar ends of the issue prevented action this year. Some concerned environmentalists wanted more action sooner, but there is insufficient support in Congress for their position. Many in industry fear the high costs of compliance, and want fewer legal requirements. That position is insufficient to protect the public health. Together, they essentially made it impossible to move legislation.[22]

Senator Mitchell blamed the extremism of those whose

> principal weapon is the exaggerated claim that if anything is required of them to prevent pollution—anything at all—the cost will be so high that whole industries will have to shut down, whole States will suffer, whole regions will decline [and others] who say they support the Clean Air Act [but] joined with the many who oppose it. They remained rigid and unyielding, wholly unwilling to compromise, even when faced with the certainty that their rigidity would result in no action this year.[23]

The unwillingness of both groups to compromise might be attributed to their perception of the benefits of delay. The alliance between members representing the high-sulfur coal industry and environmentalists that facilitated passage of the 1977 amendments (which made mandatory the installation of scrubbers in new power plants and the use of local rather than western low-sulfur coal) was severely criticized[24] and may have discouraged subsequent compromise. Much of the progress in reducing pollution during the years immediately following enactment of those amendments was achieved by sources that were easiest (and cheapest) to control. As the control of emissions became increasingly expensive for each unit of pollution reduced, the opposition of industrial groups also increased. The decline of American competitiveness in international markets was less of a concern to these groups in 1970 and 1977 than in 1990. Members of Congress have been quick to give such interest groups a veto over possible compromise positions and are frequently unable or unwilling to make commitments until their assent is forthcoming. Legislators who see themselves as brokers between outside parties cannot exercise creative leadership in crafting solutions to difficult problems.

When the Bush administration released its proposed amendments to the Clean Air Act in the summer of 1989, the debate over whether new acid rain controls were necessary was essentially concluded. Environ-ment-oriented members of Congress quickly accepted the Bush initiative as the minimum position; much of the public viewed acid rain as the worst of the environmental problems. The Bush proposal took on only one constituency, the electric utilities, and let industrial polluters off the hook. Since electric utility executives are not likely to desert the Republican party, it was a relatively safe political action to take. The proposal knocked representatives of the utilities for a loop, because they had been lobbying against a bill of any kind, and their allies in Congress had demanded cost sharing before any new requirements were imposed. The president's plan was to be tough on the acid rain title and more flexible on the smog and air toxics titles. The opposition to acid rain controls was led by Democrats in both chambers; the Bush initiative upset these and other political coalitions.

Economic Incentives in the Regulation of Acid Rain

One of the most important innovations in the Clean Air Act of 1990, which was contained in the Bush proposal, was a market-based incentive system to reduce emissions from coal-fired power plants that contribute to acid rain.[25] This approach to regulation gained the support of all but the most stubborn defenders of midwestern electric utilities and high-sulfur coal miners in Congress. Title IV has three provisions. First, it requires 107 electricity-generating power plants in 18 states, primarily in the Midwest, to reduce their annual emissions of sulfur dioxide by 10 million tons and nitrogen oxides by 2 million tons from 1980 levels. Each utility is to reduce its emissions to 2.5 pounds of SO_2 per million Btu in phase I; the standard is stricter in phase II (to begin January 1, 2000) to ensure a total reduction of 10 million tons. Second, utilities are given allowances, each one permitting them to emit one ton of sulfur dioxide. Utilities must obtain permits indicating their SO_2 emissions allowance. The total level of emissions permitted is not to exceed the 10 million ton limit. Third, the allowances can be banked for future use, traded, bought, or sold. If utilities exceed their allowances, they are subject to an excess emission fee and must offset the excess emission the following year. Utilities that are able to control their emissions below the levels permitted them can trade their excess emission allowances so that reductions can be made at the lowest possible cost.[26]

Title IV provides for special allocation of allowances. Some states with high-polluting plants are given extra allowances that can be sold to help generate revenues to offset cleanup costs. Power plants in Illinois, Indiana, and Ohio are given an additional 200,000 allowances during each year of phase I. Plants that are part of a utility system that reduced its use of coal by at least 20 percent between 1980-1985 and that rely on coal for less than

50 percent of the total electricity generated may also receive extra allowances. Clean states are given additional allowances to facilitate economic growth.[27]

Some 2,000 utilities will be required to reduce their emissions further to ensure that no more than 8.9 million tons of SO_2 will be emitted by the year 2000, when phase II of the control program begins. In that phase, a number of additional special allowances are given companies to help them raise money for cleanup efforts. The EPA is to sell 25,000 allowances a year at a price of $1,500 (adjusted using the Consumer Price Index). The balance of the allowances are to be sold in a public auction, the proceeds from which (as well as any unsold allowances) are to be returned to the utilities providing the allowances.[28]

The enforcement mechanism is relatively simple and similar to that of other regulatory programs. The EPA allocates annual emission limits for individual plants based on the formula included in Title IV. At the end of each year, each source must demonstrate that its allowances match its emissions. If emissions exceed allowances, sources must pay a fine for each ton and subtract the excess tons of emissions from their permissible allowance for the coming year. Companies that buy, sell, or trade to obtain the required allowances need not do so throughout the year. It is only at the end of the year that the SO_2 budget must be balanced, and there will likely be a short period after December 31 of each year for such transactions.

There was more agreement in Congress about the basic approach to controlling acid rain in Title IV than about any other main provision of the Clean Air Act Amendments, primarily because the Bush administration's proposals were as stringent as those in many of the bills supported by environmentalists. The disagreements, criticisms, and concerns that had surfaced during the debate were primarily economic. Representatives from the Midwest were concerned about the impact of regulation on the costs of electricity. Representatives of western states were concerned that utilities that had already cleaned up would not be able to obtain allowances by cleaning up that could facilitate economic growth in their states and that most of the allowances would be concentrated in the Midwest. Representatives from states with high-sulfur coal reserves sought provisions that would protect those industries and their workers. Offset required to compensate for excess emissions was criticized as being so tough that it would inhibit economic growth. A question also arose whether the legislation should include subsidies to help defray the costs of cleanup in the Midwest. Although some members argued that the trading system provided sufficient subsidies, concessions were made to increase the number of allowances in those states.

In many ways, the congressional debates over the acid rain provisions were a classic case of distributive politics, involving the kinds of horse trades and deals that are made in many other policy areas. Much time was spent working out the complicated allocations of sulfur dioxide allowances that provided the financial incentives for cleanup. From another perspective, however, Title IV is a testament to the power of public ideas and policy analysis. The Bush proposal to combine a 10 million ton emissions limit with a market-based incentive system provides an opportunity to test market-based approaches to regulation. Although earlier acid rain bills included some provisions for trading of allowance, the idea was really advanced in the "Project 88" report of Senators Tim Wirth and John Heinz (R-Pa.), which called for market incentives in a wide range of environmental protection areas. It was essential that the administration be able to get the support of environmentalists if its bill were to be taken seriously in Congress, and adopting the strict emissions limit bought the endorsement of the Environmental Defense Fund. A member of the National Clean Air Coalition (which included most of the environmental organizations in the United States), the EDF was the only environmental group willing to negotiate with the Bush administration. The Republicans were especially interested in market-oriented pollution controls.

The key to the acid rain emissions allowance trading system is the idea of a cap; the actual distribution of emissions is unimportant. It is not clear whether or how such a system could be used for achieving the national ambient air quality standards for traditional pollutants, or for regulating air toxics, since the nationwide distribution of these pollutants is critical. If air quality standards are not achieved in specific areas, then the health of residents of those areas is endangered, even if levels are reduced nationwide. Even within a facility, trading may not work if it means that more dangerous emissions can be substituted for less dangerous ones.[29]

There may be some additional lessons to be learned from the acid rain provisions in the 1990 Clean Air Act that would have some relevance for other problems related to air pollution. Most proposals for a global warming agreement argue for a reduction in greenhouse gas emissions of from 20 percent to 60 percent of current levels by early in the next century.[30] They usually also recommend establishment of an international reporting and monitoring system to ensure that emission reductions actually occur, and an international tribunal to adjudicate conflicts. Trade sanctions for noncompliance are considered the most feasible coercive measure, and grants to the poorer nations are perceived as an essential part of ensuring that goals are met. Specific provisions for achieving the goal, monitoring emissions, and enforcing limitations are usually included in subsequent protocols.

The economic incentives and trading system specified in the acid rain provisions have been used in other areas as well. Marketable permits will be used to phase out the manufacturing of chemicals that deplete the ozone layer, for example. States are required to levy emission fees on sources in serious ozone nonattainment areas that fail to meet the deadline for attainment, and are authorized to charge emission fees, auction emission rights, and make other innovations in their regulatory programs. Under these provisions, California announced a plan in 1992 that requires oil refiners and other large industrial polluters to reduce their emissions of different pollutants by from 6 percent to 8 percent a year. Companies that reduce pollution by more than the required amount can sell pollution credits to other companies that have exceeded their limits.[31]

The Clean Air Act of 1990 and Global Environmental Agreements

Once international treaties are signed, the participating nations implement them by means of their own legislation and administrative regulations. A number of bills were proposed in Congress in the late 1980s and early 1990s that addressed the global problems of stratospheric ozone depletion and global warming. Ozone provisions were included in the House and Senate bills that were finally agreed upon, but global warming provisions were not (except to require some monitoring of greenhouse gas emissions), largely because the scientific consensus concerning the threat posed by CFCs to the ozone layer does not yet exist with regard to global warming. The debate focused mostly on economics, however, particularly on the implications for the competitive position of U.S. industries if this nation unilaterally imposed new controls rather than waiting for global agreements to be signed.

The provisions aimed at preventing further depletion of the stratospheric ozone layer were among the most environmentally aggressive in the clean air bill; unlike other provisions, they required not merely the control but the elimination of certain substances. The opposition had claimed that the ability of the United States to encourage future international agreements would be undermined by unilateral action. Industry groups such as the National Association of Manufacturers and the Alliance for Responsible CFC Policy also argued against domestic imposition of tougher reduction schedules without corresponding international action. "Any unilateral action taken by the United States," the alliance contended, "would have an all but insignificant effect upon the global environment and severely hinder U.S. industry while placing the American economy at an unfair disadvantage in the global market, to say nothing of the loss of American jobs.[32] But industry had already demonstrated its ability to come up with alternatives, and the widespread support in both houses of Congress for more vigorous action to protect the ozone layer virtually ensured passage of the provisions.

The provisions for reducing CFC emissions contained in the 1990 Clean

Air Act Amendments and the Montreal Protocol are a sobering example of the dilemma of dealing with uncertainty. Subsequent research has identified an even further depletion of the ozone layer than was apparent in 1990. If an agreement to limit the manufacturing and use of CFCs had been concluded in the 1970s, in response to initial scientific warnings, much less damage to the ozone layer would doubtless have occurred. Many scientists fear that the Montreal Protocol is too little, too late, because the emissions released during the past decade and those that will be released in the decade to come will damage the ozone layer far into the future because CFC molecules can stay in the stratosphere for decades. Ozone depletion is a relatively simple problem compared with global warming, however. The modest progress made as a result of passage of the Clean Air Act and conclusion of the international accords is not necessarily a cause for optimism about our ability to solve other global environmental problems.

Federal Regulation and the Preemption of State Efforts

Many states have developed regulatory programs that are stricter and more aggressive than those mandated by federal law, and have thus greatly complicated the compliance efforts of many industries. Industry groups have lobbied strongly for the inclusion of provisions in federal law that would preclude states from doing so. Industry fears of state and local regulation of manufacturing and use of CFCs, for example, generated support for federal regulation of the ozone-depleting chemicals. The 1977 Clean Air Act prohibited states from issuing such regulations, but that did not keep some states and localities from taking actions in the past few years to limit or prohibit CFC use within their boundaries. By 1990, some two dozen ozone protection bills had been introduced in state legislatures. A bill was passed by the Hawaii state legislature that banned the sale of recharge cartridges for car air conditioners that use CFCs as a coolant.[33] In May 1989, the Vermont state legislature passed a bill that, beginning with the 1993 model year, would prohibit the sale or registration of any car with an air conditioner using CFCs as a coolant. This "landmark legislation," remarked Governor Madeleine M. Kunin, made Vermont "a role model for the U.S. Congress." [34] Vermont law also requires the recycling of CFCs in auto air-conditioning systems and their elimination from those systems by 1993.[35]

The attorney general of Massachusetts announced in August 1988 that a foam producer had agreed to pay $700,000 in civil penalties for emitting approximately 1,300 tons of CFCs in violation of state regulations.[36] In Irvine, California, a city ordinance was enacted in July 1989 that prohibited businesses from buying, selling, or using products containing CFCs beginning July 1, 1990. It also banned the use of halons, used in fire extinguishers, and two solvents, carbon tetrachloride and methyl chloroform. When Irvine became a CFC-free area, auto repair shops advertised their CFC-recovery equipment for servicing air conditioners. Critics predicted that the higher costs would drive business to other cities, but just the opposite happened. Residents from other communities came to Irvine shops to have their air conditioners serviced, demonstrating strong public support for environmental protection and providing powerful economic incentives for other businesses to offer "green" services.[37] Styrofoam packaging containing CFCs has been banned in Suffolk County, New York; Newark, New Jersey; Tempe, Arizona; and Los Angeles, San Francisco, Berkeley, and Palo Alto, California. Iowa forbids the sale of plastic foam products that contain or are manufactured by a process producing ozone-depleting substances. Missouri prohibits the use of any product whose container or packing material is manufactured by such a process. Florida law requires that polystyrene foam sold in the state must be manufactured with material that will degrade within twelve months. Maine prohibits the use in schools and government agencies of all polystyrene that is manufactured from ozone-depleting substances. Portland, Oregon, bars the service of prepared food in any polystyrene foam products.[38]

The Clean Air Act hearings did not address federal preemption of state and local law. The preemption provision in Title VI repealed the 1977 preemption clause and replaced it with the following provision: "during the 2-year period beginning on the enactment of the Clean Air Act Amendments of 1990, no State or local government may enforce any requirement concerning the design of any new or recalled appliance for the purpose of protecting the stratospheric ozone layer."[39] State and local governments thus are apparently free to continue to regulate the manufacturing and sale of such appliances thereafter. But new research findings concerning the risk of further ozone depletion may intensify pressure for more aggressive action.

Federal preemption of state regulatory actions is a subject of Title II, which establishes motor vehicle emission standards. One of the most contentious issues in the debate was whether states should be permitted to adopt the emissions standards that California already had in place for new cars sold in that state, which were more stringent than the federal requirements existing before 1990. New York had adopted the California requirements before the 1990 amendments were passed, and other northeastern states planned to do so. Auto manufacturers warned that permitting states to issue their own standards would create a patchwork of requirements that would be impossible to enforce. State officials feared that federal legislation might create barriers to effective state regulation of auto emissions and make it easier for car manufacturers to challenge state enforcement decisions. The amendments effectively limit states to either adopting the new round of California standards or accepting the federal standards.

Balancing the demand for federal standards with the urgent need to reduce emissions in California was one of the primary challenges confronting Congress and the executive branch in formulating the 1990 amendments. Five of the seven areas with the most serious ozone pollution problems in the nation are in California. The California Air Resources Board's old tailpipe emission standards for new cars and light-duty trucks sold in that state were adopted by Congress in 1990 as the standard to be met by all new vehicles.

The requirements in the 1990 amendments are modest in comparison with California's program for regulating auto emissions. Title II adopts the technology-forcing approach of the 1970 Clean Air Act. But the technology for lowering tailpipe emissions has already been developed; consequently, the 1990 law forces more widespread use of new technologies rather than the development of new ones. The first round of controls specified in the 1990 Clean Air Act, to be phased in beginning with the 1994 model year, are the same as California's 1993 standards for new cars. A second round of controls might be imposed beginning in the year 2004. But California will launch an aggressive program requiring that by the year 2000, all new cars sold in California must meet at least the standards for low levels of emission. By 2003, 10 percent of the new cars will be required to have zero emission, 25 percent will have to have ultralow levels of emission, and the balance must have low levels of emission. California will also require the sale of more than 1.5 million vehicles that run on alternative fuels by the year 2000.[40]

Assessing Acceptable Levels of Risk from Air Pollution

Two approaches—national ambient air quality standards and technological controls—have been emphasized at different times throughout the history of the Clean Air Act. The first approach entails determining what levels of pollution do not pose a health risk and then developing sophisticated air quality models to determine what reductions in pollution are needed to achieve those standards. The second approach—simply requiring all sources to install pollution control equipment—has usually been easier to implement. The debate then centers on the question of what technological controls should be required. Should they be reasonably effective, widely used controls? Or should they be the best controls available and used by the cleanest sources? Similar questions have been debated with regard to other environmental laws as well. The Clean Water Act of 1972, for example, required every municipal and industrial source to install the best available technology; more recently, attention has shifted to the use of models to determine what is needed to ensure clean water. Critics of the national ambient air quality standards argue that they are too complicated and difficult to enforce, but at least the approach does focus on air quality and the health risks involved. Technological controls may not always lead to achievement of air quality standards or protection of human health. The 1990 amendments maintain the national ambient air quality standards of the 1970 Clean Air Act but also impose a wide variety of technological controls on pollution sources.

When it rewrote the Clean Air Act in 1990, Congress rejected its earlier approach to the regulation of hazardous air pollutants in favor of a two-tiered approach. The first round of controls imposed by the EPA are technology-based, much like those Congress has used in regulating other forms of pollution. A second round, of health-based national ambient air quality standards, will be issued by the agency if technological controls do not reduce to minimum levels the risks posed by exposure to these chemicals.

The 1970 law was widely viewed as being very stringent and under-implemented. But addition of any provisions that weakened the requirement of meeting the absolute standard of protecting public health "with an ample margin of safety" was criticized by environmentalists as a retreat from that law. In the 1990 amendments, however, such provisions were coupled with the imposition of technological controls that were more likely to be enforced than the old standards, and thus more likely to result in significant reductions in air toxic emissions. So the retreat was, in reality, a step forward. But environmentalists were reluctant to lose the requirement for a commitment to the protection of public health, even though they agreed it had not always been adhered to. They saw clear indications that industry could do more than had been required of it.

Because some companies were already committed to zero emissions, there was, in that respect, no need to weaken the law. Reductions in emissions from chemical plants (the source of nearly one-half of all air toxics), for example, had begun to take place in 1984 after the chemical spill in Bhopal, India. The enforcement of disclosure laws and the imposition of fines and new regulations jolted corporate executives into realizing that there were major economic gains to be made by reducing emissions and, conversely, pollution represented economic loss. Processes were made more efficient, waste was reduced, and uses were found for by-products. A Dow Chemical plant in Louisiana spent $15 million on waste reduction and saved $18 million within a year. A DuPont plant in Texas realized a savings of $1 million a year simply by using less of one raw material. The chairman and chief executive officer of Monsanto predicted that his company's "initiative and commitments to environmental protection will, over the long term, make us more efficient, more cost effective and more competitive." [41]

Environmental regulations ultimately push companies to do what is in their own economic interest. It is no small irony that the regulations resisted by industry for years have led to reduced costs and may increase competitiveness. If regulators had been more aggressive in the past, American industry might today be more efficient and competitive. Congress might have done more in the 1990 amendments to encourage prevention of pollution than simply impose technological controls. But the costs of technological controls can create incentives to change processes.

Title III represents a significant increase in regulatory authority over the sources of air toxics. The Bush administration's bill had required regulation of only 50 percent of the source categories (smaller sources such as chemical process vents, storage tanks, and fugitive emissions) and gave the EPA discretion to regulate the remainder if it wished to. But members of Congress were hesitant to give the EPA any discretion in regulating air toxics, given the experience of the past two decades, so they included in the law a list of 189 pollutants to be regulated.

The technological standards are detailed and complicated. Emission standards for sources of hazardous air pollutants require the "maximum degree of reduction . . . achievable for new or existing sources in the category or subcategory," taking into account the "cost of achieving such emission reduction" and "energy requirements." Regulations may require process changes or material substitutions, changes in design of equipment or work practices, or other measures.[42] The EPA is to consider a number of factors in establishing a compliance schedule and setting priorities for issuance of the standards: the "known or anticipated adverse effect on human health and the environment," the "quantity and location of emissions," and the "efficiency of grouping the categories by the pollutants emitted or by the processes or technologies used."[43]

Congress required the EPA to submit within six years of the amendments' enactment a report on the residual risks to public health from exposure to hazardous air pollutants—that is, the risks that remain after technological controls are installed. The study is to assess methods of calculating residual risks, their significance as well as that of the adverse health effects that are likely with respect to persons living in the vicinity of the sources, and the availability and cost of additional technological controls. The EPA is also to commission a study by the National Academy of Sciences on risk assessment methodologies and to establish a Risk Assessment and Management Commission that will provide recommendations to the EPA and other federal agencies for assessing and managing risks from exposure to carcinogens and other chronic human health threats.[44]

If Congress takes no action to instruct the EPA on how to assess and reduce residual risks, the agency is to promulgate, within eight years of issuing the technology-based standards for each category and subcategory of sources, health-based standards for all hazardous air pollutants to "provide an ample margin of safety to protect public health" or "to prevent, taking into consideration costs, energy, safety, and other relevant factors, an adverse environmental effect." The agency must also impose standards for sources emitting a "known, probable or possible human carcinogen" where technological controls have not reduced the "lifetime excess cancer risks to the individual most exposed to emissions from a source in the category or subcategory to less than one in one million." [45]

The voluntary reductions program included in Title III is an innovative attempt to speed up reduction of air toxics. Like other titles of the amendments, the air toxics title outlines an extended schedule for compliance. The early reduction program permits companies that agree to reduce emissions by 90 percent to obtain a six-year extension before a maximum achievable control technology (MACT) standard is applied to them. To qualify for such a waiver, companies will have to make an enforceable commitment by January 1994 and will have to achieve the reduction before the standard is proposed. Companies thus have a real incentive to inflate their emission levels in order to reduce the amount of cleanup necessary. Nevertheless, this program promises to result in immediate, significant reductions in air toxic emissions over the next few years. Even if the MACT standard were to require an emissions reduction of more than 90 percent, the early reduction program might achieve as much as four times more emissions reduction than would occur if companies waited until the MACT standards were issued before reducing their emissions. [46] Some data are available from the *Toxics Release Inventory*, and the voluntary reductions program will probably yield more detailed data, but the making of comparisons is presently difficult. The more numerous the categories, the less likely that the standards issued will be based on the best plants. The EPA may look at the emissions reduction record of plants in other countries, but there are apparently political pressures not to do so. Industry groups complain that regulations will make them less competitive with industries in other countries, but they do not want to be compared with them because foreign industries might be found to be cleaner.

Given the past problems with the attempt to develop a risk-based standard for regulating air toxic emissions, the technology-based approach may be the most effective way to gain control of air toxics. But the law presents the EPA with a tremendous challenge in preparing the technology-based standards, and Congress will likely have to review these provisions within a few years. As the EPA has begun to implement the 1990 Clean Air Act and to establish the Risk Assessment and Management Commission, the debate over risk assessment has intensified. Skeptics charge that risk assessment is a "sham science" that can be used to justify any conclusion, usually "to justify pollution," and that it causes us to ignore potentially serious or even catastrophic problems because we lack sufficient data. Proponents argue that risk assessment is essential if we are to know "when a regulatory expenditure is not a good investment, and decide whether we want to spend money elsewhere to save a lot of lives." [47]

The Bottom Line: Permits and Enforcement

Whether and to what extent the Clean Air Act achieves its goals will be determined in large part by the effectiveness with which the EPA and the states implement and enforce it. Pollution sources may not comply with regulations if they are not given effective incentives to do so. As indicated earlier in this chapter, the state implementation plans to achieve national ambient air quality standards failed to work in many states. Some critics blamed the states' slowness in developing and approving the plans and pointed to the confusion over what exactly was required of specific sources of pollution. Others argued that the implementation process promoted inefficiency (since sources were not permitted to choose the most efficient way to reduce emissions), was too rigid and complicated, and failed to encourage improvements as new knowledge and new technologies became available. [48]

These criticisms led to a package of innovative reforms, introduced in the Bush administration's clean air bill and ultimately adopted by Congress, whose core proposal was the requirement that every major stationary source of pollution regulated under any provision of the law (traditional pollutants, air toxics, power plants emitting pollutants that were precursors of acid rain) have an operating permit issued by the state in which it is located. Each permit was to specify all the regulations that applied to that source, including emission limits, monitoring requirements, and maintenance procedures.

Permits were viewed by EPA officials and members of Congress as a way to facilitate the enforcement of air quality provisions by the EPA, states, and communities. Because all the requirements applicable to a stationary source are conveniently brought together in one document, permits can eliminate confusion and ambiguity over which requirements apply to what sources and can facilitate efforts to assess compliance.

A permit program could be a first step in the more aggressive use of marketlike incentives to reduce emissions (even though the permit fees to be collected under Title V do not really constitute an incentive to emit less). As states gain experience with administering a comprehensive permit program, they can experiment with other uses of permits. Polluting companies, for example, could be required to purchase an emissions permit for each unit of each pollutant they are allowed to release. The size or number of permits could be reduced each year or less often, in order that incremental reductions could be made until the national ambient air quality standard was met. Similarly, because of adverse meteorological conditions or other factors, the program was found to be inadequate, the allowable emissions or the number of permits could be reduced until the national ambient air quality standard was met.

Emissions that exceeded the limit set for each facility could be taxed at a much higher rate to discourage such violations. Companies would be given the flexibility to develop the most cost-effective changes. Revenues from permit fees could be used to finance enforcement efforts and research programs.

Permits are also important because they strengthen the powers of states as the primary enforcers of environmental laws and regulations. The federal government has only about one-fifth of the enforcement resources possessed by the states. More aggressive federal enforcement is likely to occur when federal and state officials agree that federal enforcement is the most appropriate strategy or when states have not successfully enforced major provisions of the law. A permit-based system may have significant positive implications for enforcement because it clarifies the requirements imposed on every major source of emissions.[49] The fear of permit delays (because of bureaucratic red tape) will provide a strong incentive for industry representatives to support effective implementation of the law.

The permit and enforcement provisions of the House and Senate clean air bills were seen as highly technical and detailed and initially aroused little interest. Unlike the other major titles of the 1990 amendments, they were not discussed in the negotiations between the Senate and the administration in the majority leader's office in February and March of 1990. Permits were the subject of separate but unsuccessful negotiations between members of the Senate Environment and Public Works Committee, the administration, and other senators.

Industry lobbyists came to realize fairly late in the process the possibility that permits would result in more aggressive enforcement as well as the inevitability of costs and delays arising from compliance with a new regulatory procedure. They also resisted the new enforcement provisions, but since these changes really only made the Clean Air Act's sanctions as strict as those of other environmental laws, their opposition to them was muted.

By the time the bill reached the Senate floor, the permit requirement had aroused considerable industry opposition. The permit and enforcement title was the only one opposed by the National Association of Manufacturers, which estimated that 362,000 firms would require permits.[50] Industry groups warned that if permits were to place a limit on every source of emissions, permit writers would be crushed in a mountain of detail. Permits would be unwieldy and unworkable; moreover, companies that constantly change their processes and mix of materials would constantly have to renegotiate their permit provisions unless permits were worded to provide for operational flexibility. Some feared that regulatory requirements such as reporting and monitoring would enable competitors to discover proprietary information such as the composition of products and processes. Others charged that the inevitable delay in state and EPA approval of permits would make new construction or modification of existing sources all but impossible. This was a critical issue because if the EPA rejected a permit for being incomplete or inconsistent with the law, the source could not legally operate. The amendment was the subject of three close Senate votes. The motion to table or kill the amendment was defeated by one vote. After some maneuvering, the motion to pass the amendment was also defeated by one vote. A slightly modified version was again defeated by one vote before the bill was finally passed.[51] In the House, changes were made in the Energy and Commerce Committee and in negotiations between key members before the bill was introduced on the floor.

State and local regulatory officials were opposed to EPA review and veto of permits. Environmental groups favored EPA review but feared that industries would claim that compliance with the provisions of its permit would shield a source against charges of violating any Clean Air Act regulations or standards not included in that permit. The idea of a possible "permit shield" aroused a fair amount of controversy as the bill moved through Congress. According to the conference report,

> Permit compliance also may be deemed compliance with other applicable provisions of the Clean Air Act if the permit has been issued in accordance with Title V and includes those provisions, or if the permitting authority includes in the permit a specific determination that such provisions are not applicable.[52]

The uncertainty about the meaning of compliance may be cleared up only through litigation, but it is an important issue that will affect the efficacy of the permit system in reducing emissions.

The 1990 amendments updated the Clean Air Act's enforcement provisions to make them consistent with those of other environmental statutes. Under the 1970 act, all enforcement proceedings took place only in federal district courts. Calculation of penalties was to be based on the economic benefit to the source of not complying with emission limitations, which was sometimes difficult to determine. Criminal violations were considered misdemeanors and thus of little interest to the Justice Department prosecutors, who focused on felony violations.

The most important change effected by the 1990 amendments was to make most criminal violations felonies.[53] The EPA may now initiate a civil action in a federal district court against the owner or operator of a stationary source who "knowingly violates any requirement or prohibition" included in an applicable state implementation plan, permit, or any provision of the act to obtain a permanent or temporary injunction or to assess and recover a civil penalty of up to $25,000 per day for each violation. Criminal penalties include fines and imprisonment of up to five years. Any person who misrepresents, omits, alters, conceals, fails to file or maintain information required, or tampers with or fails to install monitoring equipment is subject to up to two years' imprisonment. Any person who knowingly fails to pay a required fee can be sentenced to up to one year in prison. The maximum prison term and fine double if the person charged has been convicted of the same violation in the past. The agency may also issue an administrative order and impose a civil penalty of up to $25,000 for each day of violation if it acts within one year of the violation.[54]

Additional penalties are aimed at the release of hazardous air pollutants regulated under the act. Any person who "negligently places another person in imminent danger of death or serious bodily injury" by releasing hazardous air pollutants is subject to a fine and imprisonment of not more than one year; the maximum penalties are doubled after the first conviction. Any person who "places another person in imminent danger of death or serious bodily injury" by knowingly releasing a hazardous air pollutant is subject to fines and imprisonment of up to fifteen years. Fines assessed against an organization cannot exceed $1 million. Maximum fines and imprisonment are doubled for subsequent convictions. Serious bodily injury is defined as involving a "substantial risk of death, unconsciousness, extreme physical pain, protracted and obvious disfigurement or protracted loss or impairment of the function of a bodily member, organ, or mental facility."[55] The act defines the "operator" or person legally liable for criminal penalties as anyone classified as "senior management personnel or a corporate officer" rather than the employees who actually operate the equipment.[56]

The EPA may award up to $10,000 to any person (excluding any employee of the federal, state, or local government performing in an official capacity) who "furnishes information or services which lead to a criminal conviction or a judicial or administrative civil penalty" for any violation of the act.[57] Under the Clean Air Acts of 1970 and 1977, the EPA could require any person who may have "information necessary for the purposes" of the enforcement provisions of the act to establish and maintain records, submit reports, install and use monitoring equipment and auditing procedures, sample emissions, and submit compliance certifications and other information that the agency might need. The agency could also subpoena witnesses and relevant documentation.

Suits under the 1990 Clean Air Act may be brought in U.S. district courts by any person against state or federal officials for failing to take an action required under the law, and against any source that is believed to be in violation of a provision of the act, a regulation, or a permit provision. A court may enforce any emission standard or order, and direct the EPA to perform any duty and to impose appropriate civil penalties. These fines are to be deposited in a special fund in the U.S. Treasury to be used by the EPA to finance "compliance and enforcement activities." A court may award the "costs of litigation (including reasonable attorney and expert witness fees) to any party, whenever the court determines such award is appropriate." [58]

The citizen suit provisions are particularly important because, as mentioned earlier in this chapter, EPA and state compliance with virtually all of the requirements and deadlines specified in the law can be compelled by court order. In addition, citizens can bring lawsuits to enforce specific permit requirements applicable to individual sources. In the past, it has been difficult to file suits against sources because their emission limits were difficult to ascertain and emission data were often not available. The permit system in the 1990 law solves both problems; one document includes all the control measures the source is required to implement, and sources must monitor and report their emissions and file reports on their compliance. All provisions of the permits are to be considered "emissions standards or limitations" and are thus subject to citizen suits. Citizens can also seek civil penalties, instead of merely an injunction as under the 1970 law, and although most fines are deposited in the U.S. Treasury, courts can allocate up to $100,000 of the fines to "mitigation projects which are consistent with the Act and enhance the public health or the environment." [59]

The Clean Air Act Amendments of 1990 also include specific provisions concerning areas that have failed to attain the national ambient air quality standards for ozone, carbon monoxide, and particulates; require establishment of research programs to be conducted or funded by the EPA; require the EPA to monitor and attempt to improve air quality of areas near the U.S.-Mexican border; order the EPA to assess the need for new regulatory initiatives to protect visibility in national parks and other areas with relatively unpolluted air; and authorize the EPA to begin collecting data on carbon dioxide emissions that contribute to the threat of global warming. [60] The 1990 law extends to a number of small sources of pollution that have never been regulated, since regulating only the largest sources is clearly insufficient to achieve compliance with national ambient air quality standards. Gas stations, dry cleaners, and consumer solvents are a significant source of ozone and air toxic emissions and will be regulated in the most polluted regions.

One of the most potentially significant provisions is Title XI establishing the workers' compensation program, for it may bring together labor and environmental interests that have sometimes been at odds over the consequences of environmental regulation, such as job loss. Although the program may be an expensive way to achieve compromise with regard to environmental laws, it may prove to be politically powerful.

The expectations regarding the potential of this remarkably ambitious and far-reaching law may be unrealistically high in view of the limited actions the EPA and the states are likely to take in implementing it. Chapter 5 examines their prospects for accomplishing the intended purposes of the 1990 Clean Air Act.

Notes

1. Comments by William Becker at the Conference on Clean Air Act Implementation, sponsored by *Inside EPA* and by Morgan, Lewis & Bockius, Washington, D.C., March 26, 1991.
2. Statement of Sen. Max Baucus, *Congressional Record*, October 26, 1990, S17233.
3. Henry A. Waxman, "An Overview of the Clean Air Act Amendments of 1990," *Environmental Law* 21 (1991): 1742.
4. See, for example, James S. Cannon, *The Health Costs of Air Pollution: A Survey of Studies Published 1978-1983* (Washington, D.C.: American Lung Association, 1985); U.S. Congress, House, Committee on Energy and Commerce, *Clean Air Act Amendments of 1990*, H. Rpt. 101-490, Part 1, 101st Cong., 2d sess., 1990.
5. U.S. Congress, House, *Clean Air Act Amendments of 1990*, conference report on S. 1630, H. Rpt. 101-952, 101st Cong., 2d sess., 1990, 335. See also U.S. Congress, House, Committee on Energy and Commerce, Subcommittee on Energy and Power, *Clean Air Act Reauthorization (Part 1)*, Serial No. 101-111, 101st Cong., 1st sess., 1990; U.S. Congress, House, Committee on Energy and Commerce, Subcommittee on Energy and Power, *Clean Air Act Reauthorization (Part 2)*, Serial No. 101-114, 101st Cong., 1st sess., 1990; U.S. Congress, House, Committee on Energy and Commerce, Subcommittee on Energy and Power, *Clean Air Act Reauthorization (Part 3)*, Serial No. 101-120, 101st Cong., 1st sess., 1989; U.S. Congress, House, Committee on Energy and Commerce, Subcommittee on Health and the Environment, *Air Quality Standards in Southern California*, Serial No. 100-5, 100th Cong., 1st sess., 1987; U.S. Congress, House, Committee on Energy and Commerce, Subcommittee on Health and the Environment, *Clean Air Act Amendments (Part 1)*, Serial No. 100-129, 100th Cong., 1st sess., 1987; U.S. Congress, House, Committee on Energy and Commerce, Subcommittee on Health and the Environment, *Clean Air Act Amendments (Part 2)*, Serial No. 100-130, 100th Cong., 1st sess., 1987; U.S. Congress, House, Committee on Energy and Commerce, Subcommittee on Health and the Environment, *Clean Air Act Amendments (Part 3)*, Serial No. 101-116, 101st Cong., 1st sess., 1989; U.S. Congress, House, Committee on Energy and Commerce, Subcommittee on Health and the Environment, *Clean Air Act Amendments (Part 1)*, Serial No.

101-100, 101st Cong., 1st sess., 1989; U.S. Congress, House, Committee on Energy and Commerce, Subcommittee on Health and the Environment, *Clean Air Act Amendments (Part 2)*, Serial No. 101-101, 101st Cong., 1st sess., 1989; U.S. Congress, House, Committee on Energy and Commerce, Subcommittee on Health and the Environment, *Clean Air Standards*, Serial No. 100-6, 100th Cong., 1st sess., 1987; U.S. Congress, House, Committee on Energy and Commerce, Subcommittee on Health and the Environment, *Environmental Issues*, Serial No. 99-28, 99th Cong., 1st sess., 1985; U.S. Congress, House, Committee on Energy and Commerce, Subcommittee on Oversight and Investigations, *Air Quality Standards*, Serial No. 98-189, 98th Cong., 2d sess., 1984; U.S. Congress, House, Committee on Energy and Commerce, Subcommittee on Oversight and Investigations, *EPA: Ozone and the Clean Air Act*, Serial No. 100-25, 100th Cong., 1st sess., 1987; U. S. Congress, Senate, Committee on Environment and Public Works, *Clean Air Act Amendments of 1989*, S. Rpt. 101-228, 101st Cong., 1st sess., 1989; U.S. Congress, Senate, Committee on Environment and Public Works, *The New Clean Air Act*, S. Hrg. 99-910, 99th Cong., 2d sess., 1986; U.S. Congress, Senate, Committee on Environment and Public Works, Subcommittee on Environmental Protection, *Clean Air Act Amendments of 1987, Parts 1-3*, S. Hrg. 100-187, 100th Cong., 1st sess., 1987; U.S. Congress, Senate, Committee on Environment and Public Works, Subcommittee on Environmental Protection, *Clean Air Act Amendments of 1989, Parts 1-6*, S. Hrg. 101-331, 101st Cong., 1st sess., 1989; U.S. Congress, Senate, Committee on Environment and Public Works, Subcommittee on Environmental Protection, *Health Effects of Air Pollution*, S. Hrg. 101-79, 101st Cong., 1st sess., 1989; U.S. Congress, Senate, Committee on Environment and Public Works, Subcommittee on Environmental Protection, *Ozone and Carbon Monoxide Standards: Nonattainment Issues*, S. Hrg. 100-54, 100th Cong., 1st sess., 1987.

6. Waxman, "An Overview," 1744.
7. For a fuller discussion, see ibid., 1742-1754.
8. Environmental Protection Agency, *National Air Pollutant Emission Estimates, 1940-1988* (Washington, D.C.: EPA, 1990), 56-62.
9. Comment by William Rosenberg at the Conference on Clean Air Act Implementation, March 26, 1991.
10. Thad Godish, *Air Quality* (Chelsea, Mich.: Lewis, 1991), 296-298.
11. Waxman, "An Overview," 1751-1752.
12. Canadian Environmental Law Research Foundation (Toronto) and the Environmental Law Institute (Washington, D.C.), *The Regulation of Toxic and Oxidant Air Pollution in North America* (Toronto: Commerce Clearing House of Canada, 1986), 177-179.
13. Interview with Drew Lewis in *EPA Journal*, June-July 1986, 4-7.
14. American Enterprise Institute, *The Clean Air Act: Proposals for Revision* (Washington, D.C.: AEI, 1981), 76-78.
15. For a history of this provision, see Bruce Ackerman and William T. Hassler, *Clean Coal/Dirty Air* (New Haven, Conn.: Yale University Press, 1981).
16. Nancy M. Davis, "Acid Rain: No Truce Is in Sight in the Eight-Year War between the States," *Governing*, December 1988, 50.
17. Philip Shabecoff, "An Emergence of Political Will on Acid Rain," *New York Times*, February 19, 1989, D5.
18. Ibid.
19. Davis, "Acid Rain," 50.

20. Ibid., 54.
21. Philip Shabecoff, "Senators Announce Accord on Acid Rain Bill," *New York Times*, July 14, 1988, A30.
22. Quoted in Shannon J. Kilgore, "Muddling Through: Congressional Activity in 1988," *Environmental Law Reporter*, January 1989, 10018.
23. Quoted in ibid., 10018-10019, 10026.
24. See particularly Ackerman and Hassler, *Clean Coal/Dirty Air*.
25. The following hearings held in Congress in the 1980s addressed acid rain: U.S. Congress, House, Committee on Energy and Commerce, Subcommittee on Energy and Power, *Acid Rain Oversight*, Serial No. 100-222, 100th Cong., 2d sess., 1988; U.S. Congress, House, Committee on Energy and Commerce, Subcommittee on Energy and Power, *Clean Coal Technologies*, Serial No. 100-70, 100th Cong., 1st sess., 1987; U.S. Congress, House, Committee on Energy and Commerce, Subcommittee on Energy Conservation and Power, *Acid Deposition Control Act*, Serial No. 99-153, 99th Cong., 2d sess., 1986; U.S. Congress, House, Committee on Energy and Commerce, Subcommittee on Fossil and Synthetic Fuels, *Clean Coal Technologies, Part 2*, Serial No. 99-111, 99th Cong., 2d sess., 1986; U.S. Congress, House, Committee on Energy and Commerce, Subcommittee on Fossil and Synthetic Fuels, *Future of Coal*, Serial No. 98-146, 98th Cong., 1st sess. (1983), and 98th Cong., 2d sess., 1984; U.S. Congress, House, Committee on Energy and Commerce, Subcommittee on Health and the Environment, *Acid Deposition Control Act of 1986 (Part 1)*, Serial No. 99-85, 99th Cong., 2d sess., 1986; U.S. Congress, House, Committee on Energy and Commerce, Subcommittee on Health and the Environment, *Acid Deposition Control Act of 1986 (Part 2)*, Serial No. 99-86, 99th Cong., 2d sess., 1986; U.S. Congress, House, Committee on Energy and Commerce, Subcommittee on Health and the Environment, *Acid Deposition Control Act of 1986 (Part 3)*, Serial No. 99-87, 99th Cong., 2d sess., 1986; U.S. Congress, House, Committee on Energy and Commerce, Subcommittee on Health and the Environment, *Acid Deposition Control Act of 1987*, Serial No. 100-96, 100th Cong., 1st sess., 1987; U.S. Congress, House, Committee on Energy and Commerce, Subcommittee on Health and the Environment, *Acid Rain Control Proposals*, Serial No. 101-25, 101st Cong., 1st sess., 1989; U.S. Congress, House, Committee on Energy and Commerce, Subcommittee on Health and the Environment, *Acid Rain in the West*, Serial No. 99-49, 99th Cong., 1st sess., 1985.
26. The EPA is also required to establish limits for emission of nitrogen oxides from utility boilers and to issue revised New Source Performance Standards for fossil-fuel-fired steam-generating facilities. Standards are to require the "best system of continuous emission reduction, taking into account available technology, costs and energy and environmental impacts." The EPA is to report to Congress by 1994 on the economic and environmental consequences of permitting the trading of SO_2 and NO_x allowances. Clean Air Act Amendments, Publ. L. No. 101-549, 104 Stat. 2399 (November 15, 1990), secs. 406, 403(c).
27. Ibid., sec. 404.
28. Ibid., sec. 405.
29. Waxman, "An Overview," 1750. Interestingly, there are sufficient opportunities for trading; commodities exchanges such as the Chicago Board of Trade plan to run markets for sulfur dioxide, nitrogen oxides, and volatile organic compounds in 1993. Jeffrey Taylor, "New Rules Harness Power of Free

Markets to Curb Air Pollution," *Wall Street Journal*, April 14, 1992, A1.

30. One of the most ambitious recommendations, from the Intergovernmental Panel on Climate Change's working group on the science of climate change, was for an immediate reduction in current levels of "long-lasting" greenhouse gases of 60 percent and a reduction of 15 percent to 20 percent in emissions of methane. The 1990 Interparliamentary Conference on the Global Environment, attended by parliamentarians from thirty-five countries, called on all nations to commit themselves to a 50 percent reduction in greenhouse gases from 1990 levels by the year 2010. The 1988 Toronto Conference on the Changing Atmosphere proposed a 20 percent reduction in world CO_2 emissions from current levels by the year 2005; other groups have recommended similar goals. Natural Resources Defense Council, *Slowing Global Warming* (Washington, D.C.: NRDC, 1989).

31. Richard W. Stevenson, "Trying a Market Approach to Smog," *New York Times*, March 25, 1992, C1.

32. Mike Mills, "Ratification of Ozone Pact Recommended," *Congressional Quarterly Weekly Report*, February 20, 1988, 370.

33. "Vermont to Ban Autos' Use of Ozone-Depleting Chemical," *New York Times*, May 10, 1989, B6.

34. Ibid.

35. Robert Reinhold, "Frustrated by Global Ozone Fight, California City Offers Own Plan," *New York Times*, July 19, 1989, A1.

36. "Ozone Depletion Penalty Set," *New York Times*, August 25, 1988, A21.

37. Comments by Jim Jenal of the Citizens for a Better Environment of Venice, California, at the Natural Resources Council of Maine/Natural Resources Defense Council clean air strategy session, Washington, D.C., May 30, 1991.

38. Nancy D. Adams, "Title VI of the 1990 Clean Air Act Amendments and State and Local Initiatives to Reverse the Stratospheric Ozone Crisis: An Analysis of Preemption," *Environmental Affairs* 19 (1991): 183-184, 187-190, 194, 203-205.

39. 42 U.S.C. sec. 7671m (1990 Supp.).

40. Presentation by Tom Cackette of the California Air Resources Board at the Conference on Clean Air Act Implementation, March 27, 1991.

41. Scott McMurray, "Chemical Firms Find That It Pays to Reduce Pollution at Source," *Wall Street Journal*, June 11, 1991, A1.

42. The maximum degree of emissions reduction is defined in different ways. For new sources, the reduction must not be less than the control achieved by the "best controlled similar source." For existing sources, if there are thirty or more sources in the same category or subcategory, the standard is the average level of control achieved by the best 12 percent. If there are fewer than thirty sources, the standard is the average level of control attained by the best five sources. Sources that met the lowest achievable emissions rate thirty months before the standard was issued are not included in the calculation of these averages.

Source categories can be deleted if the EPA determines that, for carcinogens, no source in the category emits pollutants that result in a lifetime risk of cancer greater than 1 in 1 million to the most exposed individual in the population. For other air toxics, no source can threaten public health with an "ample margin of safety" or cause any adverse environmental effect. Clean Air Act Amendments, sec. 301(d).

43. Ibid., sec. 301.

44. Ibid., amending sec. 112(f) of Clean Air Act of 1970, Pub. L. No. 91-604, 84

Stat. 1676-1713 (December 31, 1970).

45. Ibid. Health-based standards go into effect and must be complied with as soon as they are issued, except for existing sources, which must comply within 90 days of the effective date. Existing sources may also apply for a waiver of up to two years if necessary to install controls and if they agree to take whatever steps are necessary to protect the public from "imminent endangerment." These standards do not revoke or alter the national emission standards for hazardous air pollutants already issued by the EPA.
46. Comment by David Doninger, senior attorney for the Natural Resources Defense Council, at the clean air strategy session, May 30, 1991.
47. Graeme Browning, "Taking Some Risks," *National Journal*, June 1, 1991, 1279-1282.
48. William F. Pedersen, Jr., "Why the Clean Air Act Works Badly," *University of Pennsylvania Law Review* 129 (1981): 1059-1109.
49. Comments by Michael Alushin, EPA associate enforcement counsel for air, at the Conference on Clean Air Act Implementation, March 26, 1991.
50. Comments by Alan Eckert of the National Association of Manufacturers at the Conference on Clean Air Act Implementation, March 26, 1991.
51. U.S. Congress, Senate, *Congressional Record*, daily ed., 101st Cong., 2d sess., March 26, 1990, S 3162-3163; March 27, 1990, S 3132-3141; April 3, 1990, S 3796.
52. U.S. Congress, House, *Clean Air Act Amendments of 1990*, 345.
53. Comments by Michael Alushin at the Conference on Clean Air Act Implementation, March 26, 1991.
54. Clean Air Act Amendments, 701, amending secs. 113(c) and (d) of Clean Air Act of 1970.
55. Ibid., sec. 701, amending sec. 113(c)(4) and (5).
56. Ibid., sec. 701, amending sec. 113(h). Responsible officers are not to include an "engineer or technician responsible for the operation, maintenance, repair, or monitoring of equipment and facilities," or any employee "who is carrying out his normal activities" or "acting under orders from the employer," and who is not classified as "senior management personnel or a corporate officer," except in the case of "knowing and willful violations."
57. Ibid., sec. 701, amending sec. 113(e).
58. Ibid., sec. 707(f), amending sec. 304(a). Whenever an action is brought under this provision, a copy of the complaint must be given to the EPA and the U.S. attorney general. No consent agreement can be entered into unless the EPA and the attorney general have received a copy of the proposal; they may also submit comments on the proposed agreement to the court The EPA may intervene at any time in any citizen suit. The court may also compel agency action that has been "unreasonably delayed."
59. Clean Air Act of 1970, sec. 304(g)(2). For more on this subject, see Waxman, "An Overview," 1806-1810.
60. See, generally, Titles VIII and IX of the Clean Air Act Amendments for these provisions.

5   Assessing the Clean Air Act

The passage of the Clean Air Act Amendments of 1990 is an important achievement for several reasons. The amendments address many problems that were not resolved by the 1970 law. They also make the law more comprehensive (smaller or area sources have been brought under regulation, and explicit requirements have been imposed on acid rain, air toxics, and CFCs) and more consistent with other environmental laws. (Penalties for violations of the law have been made equivalent to those of the Clean Water Act, for example, and a permit system has been established that parallels, to some extent, that of the Clean Water Act.) The amendments provide an extensive set of new deadlines that more accurately reflect the seriousness of the pollution problems facing many areas and that generally allow more time for compliance than did the deadlines of the 1970 act (most of which were never met). Provisions are included that specify the schedule to be followed and the steps to be taken by the EPA and the states in implementing the law. Administrative discretion is further limited by the use of legislative hammers. These provisions are usually so inflexible and so stringent that, at least in theory, they provide a strong incentive for the EPA, the states, and the regulated industries to do what is expected of them. In some areas, the amendments require standards to be met that will force the development of new technologies; in others, the amendments require that existing technologies (such as the maximum achievable control technologies required for sources of hazardous air pollutants) be adapted and employed more widely.

Act 1 of the Clean Air Act has ended; Act 2 will be devoted to establishing the regulatory framework. Between 1990 and 1993, the EPA's main task is to issue regulations to establish regulatory programs at the state and local levels, although some regulations will directly and immediately affect industries and consumers. Will Congress and the Bush administration achieve all of their objectives? It is for the most part too early to tell, since the EPA and the states must put in place and then enforce a series of complex regulations covering a wide range of activities. The agency's performance during the first year and a half indicates that it will not come close to meeting its deadlines for issuing regulations and as a result, state and local efforts to implement and enforce the law will also be delayed. Given the history of implementation of the Clean Air Act, it is unlikely that the amendments will be an unqualified success. Their ambitious mandate exceeds the expertise, resources, and political will that now would seem to be required. One way to assess the amendments more fully is to return to the four steps of the policy-making process, and seek answers to four questions: (1) How well did Congress and the executive branch understand the nature of air pollution in drafting the 1990 amendments to the Clean Air Act? (2) How well did they manage the political pressures and to what extent did they consider the economic and scientific analyses that emerged during the legislative process? (3) How well did they provide for the effective implementation of the law by the EPA and the states? (4) To what extent will they be willing to assess the effectiveness of the law and to make adjustments as new technologies are developed and new problems emerge? Underlying these questions is a broader one: What will be the impact of their experience in drafting and enacting the 1990 law on the capacity of governments to achieve important public policy goals such as environmental protection?

Initiation and Definition

There is still some debate over whether air pollution problems are so serious that new regulatory controls are needed, or whether they will be resolved with changes in industrial activity (as a result of technological innovations, for example). But a rapidly growing body of literature (some of which was cited in earlier chapters) points to the conclusion that community air pollution is a major public health concern, responsible for tens of thousands of premature deaths and many more cases of hospitalization, illness, and lost work, as well as other social costs. People do not always choose to subject themselves to community air pollution, and the beneficiaries of the pollution-producing activities are usually not the individuals who bear the heaviest health burdens. These distributional consequences create pressure on governments to act despite limited scientific knowledge.

The economic consequences of compliance with air pollution laws and regulations continue to attract widespread attention. It is clear that, in the short run, there are some economic advantages to be gained from utilizing processes that release pollution. In the long run, however, environmental degradation threatens the viability of industrial activity; therefore, investments to ensure environmental quality make economic sense. But an orientation to long-run concerns is not characteristic of many corporate executives and politicians.

Concerns about the decreased competitiveness of U.S. firms have frequently been heard in the debate over clean air. But a more powerful argument might be that incentives and sanctions to encourage or force U.S. firms to become more efficient and less polluting or wasteful will, in the long run, yield significant economic benefits. Other countries are already moving in this direction. Japanese and German companies are very active in the market for pollution control equipment, but U.S. firms still have an opportunity to make real progress in capturing global markets. As resources become more scarce, prices will increase, and more efficient, less wasteful processes will translate to lower prices. Economic and environmental goals can be pursued together if both sides adopt a creative and flexible approach.

Historically, there has been no choice but to accept the counterbalancing of increased economic activity by the inevitability of pollution. But there are tremendous opportunities for achieving environmental goals in ways that promise benefits as well. Regulation results in a redistribution of economic benefits and burdens, however. The challenge facing political leaders is to manage that distribution so that it promotes public health and economic activity. Some practices and approaches will have to be temporarily suspended. Policies can be enacted that facilitate this process, and thus reduce the opposition to change. The workers' compensation program (Title XI) is a good example. There will be short-term dislocations but in the long run, the reduced waste and improved environmental conditions that will result are essential to economic viability.

The initial successful attempts to reduce emissions of air toxics and ozone-depleting substances have emphasized the economic advantages of reducing pollution. These gains are likely to continue as more companies develop new technologies and comply with the regulations, and if some state regulatory initiatives continue to exceed what the federal government requires. It will become harder to take seriously dramatic predictions by industry representatives that environmental regulation means the destruction of American business.

The Bush administration's obsession with the costs of regulation, which led to its ninety-day moratorium on new federal regulations in January 1992, is an example of short-run economic and political pressures taking precedence over long-run concerns. The moratorium, renewed in April and August, along with the president's announcement describing specific regulations that would not be imposed on industry, were widely dismissed as an election-year ploy intended to attract business support and campaign contributions.[1] They were defended as necessary to protect jobs and bolster the competitiveness of American industry. But their primary impact is to allow existing industries to delay making the investments necessary to modernize their facilities, reduce their waste, and adjust to fundamental global change. Such efforts to insulate industry can delay the emergence of new, cleaner industries and new technologies that prevent or reduce pollution.

The real costs of full compliance with the Clean Air Act may be even greater than the costs industry complains about. The real costs will constitute a burden for old, dirty industries, especially those that have delayed modernization, and will produce layoffs, job loss, and other problems because some sources of pollution must be eliminated to protect public health. Companies that are having trouble competing in global markets will readily point to environmental laws and regulations as the explanation, when the real problems have been poor management and maximizing short-run returns at the expense of long-run productivity.[2] In the short run, effective environmental regulations will be disruptive; that is one reason they are often not enforced. But once industries get beyond the short-run disruptions, they will find that most economic and environmental objectives are compatible. Companies that are more efficient and use less energy will be more competitive in the long run. Global and domestic demand for cleaner processes and products will increase, given trends in pollution and environmental degradation, and clean companies will have more opportunities open to them.[3]

Formulation and Enactment

From the perspective of the political process, the evolution of the Clean Air Act Amendments is instructive. The time seemed ripe to debate new environmental legislation in 1988. Candidate George Bush had discovered the political potential of environmental policy, having served as chairman of the Reagan administration's Presidential Task Force on Regulatory Relief (1981-1983 and 1986-1988). Considerable progress had been made in scientific research on the health effects of air pollution. Environmental protection was increasingly viewed as a public health issue, rather than as the conservation of ecological systems. Concern about global air pollution had been intensified by research findings on the destruction of the stratospheric ozone layer and theories of global warming. The opening of Eastern Europe revealed to the world what can happen when air pollution problems are ignored. Given this climate, it may seem strange that Congress took so long to revise the 1970 act even though many deadlines and goals had not been met. But there are so many possible veto points in the legislative process that such inaction should not be a surprise. Would there have been a clean air bill in 1990 without the president's active support? Most observers and participants in the debates have said no. The Senate came close to passing a bill in 1988; furthermore, John Dingell would eventually have had to give in to Henry Waxman. The president's involvement meant that the bill was probably passed sooner, and was more stringent, than it would have been if it had been the result of deliberations alone. Perhaps most notable is the importance of personalities and political agendas; the recent history of the Clean Air Act would probably have been much different if individuals other than Henry Waxman, John Dingell, and George Mitchell, representing different geographical regions, had held leadership positions in Congress. The separation of powers has generally been blamed for policy deadlock, but just as important are the regional and ideological divisions in Congress.

House and Senate efforts to amend the 1970 Clean Air Act differed considerably. The Senate Environment and Public Works Committee had reported out legislation several times over the years, but further action was blocked by the majority leader, Robert Byrd, who opposed acid rain controls because of their consequences for West Virginia coal miners. The election of George Mitchell as majority leader in 1989 was important because he was successful in dealing with opposition to the committee's bill by some senators and the White House. When a filibuster seemed imminent, he removed the bill from the floor and held an extraordinary series of meetings for four weeks, beginning on February 2, 1990, with other senators and a few representatives of the administration. The talks sometimes appeared to be on the verge of breaking down, but Mitchell managed to keep them going until a compromise was reached, thus living up to someone who can make deals and patiently work out conflicts. Mitchell's leadership was also instrumental in maintaining the compromise once the bill was presented to the full Senate. A number of amendments designed to strengthen the agreement, generally to replace it with the original committee provisions, were all defeated. Mitchell and minority leader Robert Dole skillfully used the resources of the Senate leadership. Mitchell called for his colleagues' support and explained that the bill was the best that could be done, for to demand more would doom all chances for a clean air bill in this century. His biggest challenge came when Senator Byrd, now chairman of the powerful Appropriations Committee, proposed the creation of a fund to assist coal miners who would lose their jobs as a result of the Clean Air Amendments. Many senators were torn between offending the majority leader and offending the keeper of the purse. The measure failed by a vote of 49-50, giving Mitchell a slim but significant victory in the battle for control of the Senate.

In contrast to the Senate Environment and Public Works Committee, the House Energy and Commerce Committee had not reported out a clean air bill for nearly a decade. John Dingell, chairman of the House committee, thought that new legislation would impose unreasonable burdens on the auto industry, which, in his view, had already done more than its share to reduce air pollution. He also argued that more stringent regulation aimed at other industries would result in widespread unemployment and reduce the competitiveness of American industry in international markets.

House subcommittee politics was also dominated by regional differences. The Subcommittee on Health and the Environment, chaired by Henry Waxman, reported out aggressive clean air legislation in the 1980s, but not without controversy. Dingell was able to pick up a few other Democratic votes and combine them with those of the Republicans to block some of the Waxman proposals. Members were constantly having to choose between supporting the subcommittee chairman and the full committee chairman. Once the Senate had acted on the clean air bill, the House Energy and Commerce Committee was pressured to take action. Dingell continued to play a crucial role. He and the ranking Republican, Norman Lent, who had cosponsored the president's bill in the House, introduced a revision of that bill, but Dingell still sought to distance himself from it; some observers believed that he was content to sit on it and perhaps even sought to kill it. Pressures on the committee to reach an agreement came from a number of sources. Dingell and Waxman caught everyone off guard with a compromise on tailpipe emissions in November 1989. Action was again stalled until late March and early April, when the Dingell-Waxman-Lent troika began their own closed-door negotiating sessions, this time without inviting representatives from the White House, and reached a series of compromises that were accepted by the full committee.

The debates over the 1990 amendments provide a useful case study of congressional politics. Environmental groups, particularly those belonging to the National Clean Air Coalition, coordinated congressional lobbying and grass-roots efforts to mobilize letter-writing and phone campaigns that would put pressure on members of Congress, many of whom were sensitive to charges reported in their districts that they were taking anti-environment positions. The Senate Environment and Public Works Committee passed its version of the bill rather quickly and with little opposition, but a major lobbying and media blitz by the Clean Air Working Group (the industry coalition) and representatives of key industries aroused such concern among senators about the costs of many proposals that the specter of a filibuster appeared. White House lobbying was also effective in raising objections to the Senate committee bill. The administration's proposal, attributed to then Chief of Staff John Sununu, was that a line be drawn at $22 billion, the maximum amount the administration believed the federal government could afford to spend on new clean air efforts at that time.

Policy Implementation

The number of pages required to list the regulations that concern implementation of the 1990 amendments will eventually exceed those of the act itself. Rule making under the Clean Air Act will be one determinant of its success.

In recent years both Congress and the White House have sought to gain control of the rule-making process. The regulatory review process established in the Reagan administration is a powerful tool that allows a president to shape and restrain rule making in ways that many members of Congress believe conflict with their intent in enacting a law. The response of Congress has been to write detailed laws with specific deadlines, and to include citizen suit provisions that permit individuals and groups to obtain a court order compelling an agency to take action. In the first year and a half, Congress and the White House have been embroiled in disputes over what kinds of regulatory provisions are required and permitted under the law.[4]

Rule making is an extension of the policy-making process and the critical step in moving from legislative action to administrative action. The pressures and conflicts that members of Congress must deal with are similar to those that arise in the administrative setting. Rule makers face a number of challenges, ranging from procedural constraints and delays to the difficulties of accommodating competing values and demands in the setting of priorities, and of managing intra-agency conflicts over what constitutes adequate information and how rules are to be worded.

The economists who dominate the EPA Office of Policy Evaluation, for example, favor marketlike approaches to regulation and have clashed with officials from the Office of Toxic Substances, the Office of Drinking Water, and other offices who are skeptical of untested approaches. There are often also significant differences between the positions taken by the political appointees and those taken by career employees. Bureaucratic, ideological, and political factors can account for these differences.

The EPA must publish proposed regulations and allow the public to submit comments before the regulations can be legally binding. Public participation can be problematic, even though it orients the agency toward interest group bargaining and political compromise. It may generate information useful to agency analysts, but it may also complicate the task of analysis. The courts that review EPA actions sometimes favor adherence to procedural provisions and at other times require scientific justification.

The Clean Air Act and many other environmental laws that concern rule making by administrative agencies do not reflect sufficient consideration of the actual implementation process and the kinds of provisions that are most likely to be readily implemented by regulatory agencies. The rule-making task requires the making of difficult choices. Rules are expected to be clear and specific in order to define administrative duties and limit administrative discretion, yet they must also facilitate administrative flexibility and meet managerial needs. They can state goals and performance standards, and they can specify the control equipment to be used and the other means by which the goals are to be achieved. All rules should provide the basis for compliance by regulated parties—effective incentives and sanctions. They should also specify important procedural guidelines, particularly concerning public participation in agency deliberations. Finally, they must be clearly stated and should constitute, over time, an integrated and consistent regulatory program. The innovations in terms of flexibility and incentives included in the 1990 amendments are significant and make political sense. An important test of the Clean Air Act will be the extent to which it facilitates innovative policy making by states as they grapple with their own air pollution problems.

In drafting the 1990 amendment, members of Congress did not adequately consider how state officials would balance regulatory mandates and local economic pressures or how agency officials would deal with the competing pressures of White House review and congressional oversight. The actions taken by the EPA in implementing the 1990 amendments are subject to the regulatory review process centered in the executive branch.

White House Oversight

Although the Bush Administration rightly claims much of the credit for gaining enactment of the 1990 amendments, doubts have been expressed concerning the commitment of many top administration officials to environmental quality.[5] The 1988 Bush presidential campaign was widely criticized as a cynical attempt to manipulate and downgrade certain issues for political advantage.[6] Environmental issues that were raised in the campaign were no different. Nevertheless, the Bush administration did move in 1989 to prepare clean air legislation as promised in the campaign, a somewhat rare occurrence. The president's speech announcing the proposed clean air legislation was widely heralded as a strong statement in favor of protection of public health and environmental quality. But when the text of the bill was made public, praise turned to criticism, for many groups saw in the details a retreat from the broad claims made earlier. The administration was ever responsive to business demands to soften the impact of provisions on that sector. Furthermore, effective lobbying by the auto industry caused the White House to strike the provision requiring production of clean-fuel vehicles in its original bill when it was being considered by the House Energy and Commerce Committee.

When the Senate was debating the bill in February and March 1990, there was little evidence that the administration cared about the content of the provisions and their consequences for air quality; its only concern was that the president's cost ceiling not be breached. Nor was there a hint of cost-benefit analysis, of a willingness to consider more stringent regulatory controls if they promised a wide range of significant health benefits. Cost is hardly the sole consideration in formulating an appropriate environmental policy, and the exclusion of other factors is really rather hypocritical, given the Reagan-Bush rhetoric promising cost-benefit analysis in the review of all regulations issued by federal agencies.[7] This narrow focus led administration officials to make arbitrary and sometimes unrealistic estimates of compliance costs. The costs of complying with provisions that will almost certainly have to go into effect, such as those requiring use of alternative fuels in the dirtiest cities, were not counted because the requirements were not expressly stated. Administration officials even appeared to be just as ignorant as industry executives of the tremendous economic benefits to be gained from more efficient, less polluting industrial operations.

The threat of a presidential veto throughout congressional consideration of the bills also aroused a sense of cynicism about the Bush administration's interest in effective environmental protection. These threats were widely discounted as a response to industry complaints. How could the environmental president veto the most important piece of environmental legislation in the past ten years, which was such an important part of his domestic agenda?

The Regulatory Review Process

The regulatory review process was instituted by the Reagan administration in response to criticisms of government regulation in the 1960s and 1970s.[8] The effort was initially directed by the Presidential Task Force on Regulatory Relief, established on January 22, 1981, and chaired by the vice president. The Office of Management and Budget's Office of Information and Regulatory Affairs was authorized to review major regulations and to assess their compatibility with the administration's guidelines for regulation. On March 31, 1989, President Bush established the Council on Competitiveness as part of the review process. The Council is headed by the vice president and includes the secretaries of the Treasury and Commerce, the attorney general, the director of the Office of Management and Budget, the chairman of the Council of Economic Advisers, and the chief of staff to the president. It oversees the regulatory review process by the Office of Management and Budget, serves as an appeals board for disputes between agencies over regulations, provides a forum where parties can air their concerns about regulations with which they are expected to comply, and identifies areas where it believes major changes can be made to enhance competitiveness. The council has stated that its primary goals are: (1) to reduce regulatory burdens on the economy; (2) to develop strategies to improve the human resources required for an effective work force; (3) to eliminate government-imposed burdens on scientific and technological progress that threaten the competitiveness of U.S. businesses; and (4) to facilitate the free flow of investment capital necessary for economic growth. During its first year it focused on streamlining federal regulation of energy production, reforming products liability laws, ensuring that the costs of clean air regulations did not exceed the ceiling imposed by the president, organizing the drug approval process, and reducing the costs of and delays in federal courts. It did not really become actively involved in reviewing agency regulations until 1991.

Democratic members of Congress and public interest groups have attacked the council for encouraging agencies to pursue regulatory options that are inconsistent with congressional intent, usurping agencies' authority to determine the content of regulations, and arranging secret meetings with industry officials at which arguments and complaints are raised, thus contravening the procedural protections provided for in administrative law and failing to give others the opportunity to rebut the contentions. It is frequently noted that the Council on Competitiveness operates under no procedural constraints and keeps no record; no explanation is required for rejection of agency proposals. (In contrast, rule making by the EPA has two procedural requirements: The rule-making group must keep a log of all meetings; and documentation concerning the provisions of the regulations must be included in a formal rule-making record open to public scrutiny. There are three restrictions on OMB intervention in rule making: Only one person is authorized to discuss the review with outside parties; comments are to be made on the record; and any communication submitted to the OMB is to be placed in the agency's rule-making record.) Defenders of the council argue that the president is constitutionally and politically responsible for the regulatory process and that proposed regulations must be coordinated to eliminate duplication and integrated with other policies such as economic growth and competitiveness.[9] The debate ultimately arises from differences over whether more regulation is needed to protect the environment, public health, and the consumer, or whether more emphasis should be placed on economic growth.

Opinions differ as to whether the formulation of regulations is an executive branch function, ultimately accountable to the president, or whether congressional committees should guide the development of regulatory policy to ensure consistency with legislative intent. Some argue that the process should be insulated from politics altogether. (They point, for example, to the competition between Congress and the Office of Management and Budget for control of important regulatory initiatives.)

Advocates of White House involvement in rule making argue that the president has the prerogative to give priority to his concerns because he is the only participant in the review process who was elected. The problem with that argument is that the president was elected to ensure that the laws are faithfully executed. Constitutionally, that is a relatively limited mandate. The administrative process consists of rule making and implementing the laws enacted by Congress. It also involves political decision making, an area where the president, because he was elected, can claim some special legitimacy. A process that permits executive branch bureaucrats to revise decisions made by Congress challenges the rule of law—which itself is sometimes problematic. Some laws and regulations are vague (in part the result of White House rewriting) and give little direction to administrators.

Defenders of the presidential prerogative in regulatory review also base their argument on constitutional theory, asserting that the Framers recognized the importance of a unified executive. A unified executive branch must have a mechanism for setting priorities and coordinating the policy-making process, thus reducing or eliminating conflicting efforts. It is hard to argue that such a mechanism is unnecessary. But a decade after its establishment, there is still no evidence that the regulatory review process has improved coordination of regulatory agencies, eliminated duplicative and contradictory programs, or increased administrative efficiency through the sharing of information as it was originally designed to do. The review process has clearly reduced the number and stringency of new regulations and has heightened concern over the costs of compliance with regulatory programs. The secrecy surrounding OMB review of regulations has inhibited improvements in agency analyses of the regulations they issue, however. If the real purpose of regulatory review was to improve the analytic basis of regulations, then the review process would be formalized and interactions among the parties would be made public.

The real motivation behind regulatory review, as participants in the process themselves have admitted, is a reduction in regulatory costs and burdens. This may be an important goal, but the architects of the review process have not been able to establish with certainty that the problem is too much regulation; a better case might be made that there is not enough regulation. In any event, many statutes simply call for more regulation, and it is hard, from a constitutional standpoint, to justify a process that seeks to avoid faithful implementation of the laws. The review process is not neutral. It is not aimed at making a balanced assessment of costs and benefits. Nor does it address the costs to society of pollution and other problems; it is concerned only with reducing the costs to industry of compliance with legally imposed responsibilities. It provides a forum where industry interests may gain concessions that they were unable to get in public settings, in Congress and in agency hearings, comment periods, and negotiations.

The regulatory review process is not a systematic approach to regulatory coordination and improvement. Critics argue that the process is weak and aimless, and subject to haphazard intervention by White House staffers. Defenders of regulation point to the expressed purpose of the council: "reducing regulatory burdens on the free enterprise system." [10]

Some of the problems with the regulatory review process became clear with the first rule proposed by the EPA under the 1990 amendments, which dealt with municipal incinerators. The agency included in its draft a requirement for 25 percent recycling and the separation of lead batteries before incineration, but those provisions were deleted by the Council on Competitiveness in December 1990—despite a statement made by President Bush in a 1988 campaign speech that "some feel the EPA's national goal of a 25 percent reduction in waste is excessive. I'd like to see us exceed that goal in my first term." The contradiction was explained away by a council staff member who said that the administration favored "voluntary recycling and market-based recycling programs." [11]

A lobbyist for local government groups explained how the regulatory review process works. The groups had failed to convince Congress to delete the recycling provision from the 1990 amendments. "We began to think we had done everything we could do," she remarked, "when we were heartened to find the regulation was stuck—as it were—in [the Office of Management and Budget]. So we began to concentrate our efforts in the White House and OMB." An industry lobbyist complained that people at the EPA were not inclined to "focus the issue on the merits." As a result, the issue was taken to the Council on Competitiveness, which "has the unfortunate, and I think unwarranted, appearance of trying to address politically what one can't address on the merits." [12]

The experience with the first major rule passed under the 1990 amendments, intended to provide the basis for state permit programs, is another example of the administration's willingness to weaken provisions of the law. The permit program is an important innovation in the 1990 Clean Air Act and the key to effective enforcement of regulations concerning stationary sources in nonattainment areas (even though the permit provisions are technical and detailed and may lack the visibility of the provisions concerning smog, air toxics, acid rain, and mobile sources). The EPA submitted draft regulations to the Office of Management and Budget, as required by the regulatory review process.[13] On March 22, 1991, Vice President Quayle announced that the Council on Competitiveness would assume responsibility for the review of federal agency regulations, congressional testimony, policy statements, and even press releases.[14] On April 6 the council issued a memo that described more than 100 changes it was making in the EPA's proposed permit rule. The staff of the House Energy and Commerce Committee's Subcommittee on Health and the Environment analyzed the changes and concluded that none of them "would serve to strengthen the permit program. . . . In most instances these changes are in conflict with the statute, and are therefore illegal." Its analysis focused on the advantages to industry of the Council on Competitiveness review process:

The Vice President has prevailed on EPA to propose regulations substantially weaker than those mandated by Congress. The [regulatory review] process is apparently now one where polluting industries, which failed in their efforts to weaken the [Clean Air] Act as it passed the Congress, are now succeeding in undermining the law through the Vice President's Council on Competitiveness.[15]

The changes made by the council were substantial. With regard to a provision entitled "minor permit allowances," for example, the council would allow a source operating under a permit that did not establish "emission limitations" to unilaterally rewrite it, and even increase the level of allowed emissions. (Requirements for monitoring and inspection, since they do not directly impose emission limits, could thus be changed at will, making it difficult to determine whether sources really are complying with their emission limits.) The changes would simply be submitted to the state regulatory agency and would go into effect unless the agency rejected them within seven days. The 1990 amendments give sources no such authority to make these kinds of changes. The council also deleted from the original EPA proposal a provision requiring public notice of permit revisions and restricting the amount of increased emissions. The 1990 amendments were clear in requiring public notice (including an opportunity for public comment), EPA review, and an opportunity for judicial review of all permit revisions.[16] The council's revised regulation would not only circumvent the law but would weaken enforcement of the law. Any source that became the subject of a citizen suit or state enforcement action could simply file for a revised permit, and if the state regulatory agency failed to respond within seven days, the source would escape legal action. The 1990 amendments also require all sources to include in their permit application a compliance plan and a schedule that is enforceable by the EPA and can be the subject of a citizen suit while the permit application is pending. The council's revised regulation would require a schedule only from facilities that were shown to be in violation of the law at the time the permit was requested, and the schedule would be enforceable only after the permit was approved.[17]

The final permit regulation was required to be issued by November 1991, but the dispute dragged on until May 1992, when the president ordered the EPA to propose the version of the regulation favored by the Council on Competitiveness.[18] The issue will eventually be addressed by the courts; Rep. Henry Waxman notified the EPA in 1992 of his intention to sue the agency for missing this and other deadlines. The matter will not likely be resolved until well after this book is published. The way it is resolved will determine whether the regulatory review process will be used to weaken the Clean Air Act and facilitate industry efforts to obtain changes they were not able to gain through the legislative process, or whether Congress and the reviewing courts will insist on a faithful implementation of statutory provisions.

But the problem extends beyond the permit provisions. The House Energy and Commerce Committee's Subcommittee on Health and the Environment held a hearing one year after passage of the 1990 Clean Air Act and found that the EPA had missed most of the rule-making deadlines, that the Council on Competitiveness had undermined a number of key regulations, and that the White House had directed the EPA to propose regulatory provisions that had been specifically rejected by Congress during its consideration of the Clean Air Act Amendments.[19] These kinds of actions raise fundamental questions about the extent to which the goals of the Clean Air Act will be achieved.

The EPA has experimented with negotiated rule making in an attempt to prevent judicial challenges to regulations. In the past, the agency has prepared a draft regulation, released it for public comment, gained the approval of the OMB and other executive branch officials, and was then usually sued by groups unhappy with the result. Instead, the EPA now tries to bring in relevant parties from the beginning to hammer out compromises and formulate a regulation that all parties will accept and agree not to challenge in court. Three "reg negs" were initiated soon after passage of the 1990 amendments. The most important regulation was that concerning alternative fuels, which was accepted by representatives of some forty groups. The rule will have a tremendous impact on the domestic oil industry, and the completion of the negotiations in 1991 is a hopeful sign that the new regulation will be implemented.[20] But this experiment is also threatened by the regulatory review process. Many OMB officials are wary of the negotiations, since the result may be insulated from their control. Moreover, participants are hesitant to invest time in the process when they know the product of their efforts may be rejected by OMB overseers. Until the conflict between the White House and Congress over the control of rule making is resolved, the implementation of the Clean Air Act will continue to face obstacles.

Impact and Evaluation

Although the overall impact of the 1990 amendments will not be clear for many decades, a preliminary evaluation is possible, given the timetable that was included for achieving the goals. In many ways, the Clean Air Act of 1990 reinforces a prevailing approach to environmental law that has been widely criticized for its reliance on centralized, bureaucratic controls. Both Congress and the executive branch were content to expand some provisions of the 1970 law such as those specifying deadlines and technological standards, and giving mandates to states. But they also launched some important new initiatives, and those are the developments to watch. The idea of harnessing marketlike incentives for regulatory purposes—relying on economic means to achieve environmental goals—is so powerful as a basis for political compromise that framers of future regulatory statutes will probably explore the applicability of such incentives to every practical situation. And the permit program promises to make environmental law and regulations more effective. Increased flexibility for regulated sources also makes political sense. How well these innovations work will be one of the ultimate tests of whether Congress and the executive branch have achieved any gains in their decade-long effort to revise the Clean Air Act.

Ideally, Congress and the executive branch should regularly conduct an assessment of how well the act is working and make statutory changes as they are needed. Too little emphasis has been given in both branches of government to the evaluation of existing laws, to determine whether their purposes are still relevant and whether their provisions are well suited to the problems they are expected to remedy.

Policy evaluation is especially important in environmental policy in general, and clean air policy in particular, given the uncertainty over the causes and consequences of ecological problems (due in part to the long lag between exposure and evidence of a problem), the problem of ensuring that pollution is reduced rather than simply transferred to another medium, the difficulty of changing human behavior (discussed in Chapter 1), and the requirement that clean air policies provide for learning from experience and facilitate flexibility. In a complex, rapidly changing world, in which control technologies are constantly improving and health researchers are identifying new pollution-related problems, congressional oversight provides an opportunity for frequent review.[21]

The Importance of Congressional Oversight

The separation of powers is the constitutional basis for oversight, but interpretations differ concerning the principle's application. According to one view, the separation of powers is inherently adversarial and intended to check action, particularly when different political parties control the two branches. Another view is that the separation of powers is intended to achieve a balance of frequently competing and conflicting interests and to bring different perspectives to bear on the solution of common problems. Improved management of the separation of powers—increased communication between the executive and legislative branches—is in the interests of both branches, and in the public interest. Both the legislative and executive branches are involved in making and implementing policy. A basic equality between them is acknowledged; they should be willing to share power rather than attempt to divide it, for the implementation of complex policies cannot easily be divided.

Relations between Congress and the EPA have been strained over the past decade, however. Members of Congress distrust the agency and doubt its commitment to implementing legislation in a manner consistent with their intent. Agency officials have chafed at intrusive congressional oversight hearings. But members of Congress and officials of the executive branch should perceive oversight not as a peripheral activity, not as a means of second-guessing agencies, but as the foundation of good legislation and of virtually everything else that Congress does, including the making of difficult choices. Oversight relations between the two branches will be productive only to the extent that the executive branch accepts congressional oversight of its activities.

Even legislators who are sympathetic to the claims that industry makes ought also to be concerned about protecting the institutional prerogatives of Congress. There is a clear assumption that presidential powers in domestic affairs are largely delegated. Unless they do not really care how the statutes they enact are implemented, members of Congress ought to set the parameters of the regulatory review process, to ensure that regulations are coordinated, thus avoiding duplication and conflict, and to improve regulatory analysis by facilitating interagency communication and sharing of information. To be effective overseers, they should be willing to invest the time and resources required to develop expertise in the areas under their jurisdiction, and to pursue thorough, systematic investigations and studies that may take months and even years. They also have to attract able professional staff members and keep them long enough to provide continuity and perspective in oversight.

If the agencies of the executive branch are willing to implement the laws in a way consistent with congressional intent, then congressional oversight can focus on broader issues and facilitate a cooperative effort by the two branches to improve statutes, their implementation by the states, and the level of compliance by regulated sources. The more trust is fostered between them, the more Congress will be willing to allow agencies some discretion and flexibility. The perception of secrecy in the regulatory review process is a major problem. The more Congress knows about the oversight activities of the OMB and the Council on Competitiveness, the more likely that it will be willing to work with the president to pursue common goals. The longer statutes have been in place, and the more agreement there is concerning what they mean and how they are to be implemented, the more likely it will be that the two branches can work reasonably well together.

Oversight may improve decision making by allowing a second (or third) look at agency actions, but it may also cause unnecessary delays. Oversight activity that focuses on individual regulations and agency decisions may provide an opportunity for the individuals and groups affected (or expected to be affected) to have the action reversed or made less severe. Although such demands may deserve sympathetic consideration, they may also weaken the consistency and fairness of the laws' application, result in less effective policies, and deflect the policy-making process from more important concerns. The key here is to attempt to balance oversight efforts so that congressional purposes (including the search for information) can be pursued and administrative excesses remedied without permitting interests that should comply with appropriate policy requirements to avoid doing so. No formula or structure guarantees that such a balance can be achieved; an open process and the continued examination of its likelihood are all that may be possible. Political differences do not have to be eliminated for oversight to work. The vigorous debate over the direction of public policy that is essential must be combined with a recognition that a minimum level of cooperation is necessary if government is to function.[22]

Oversight is most likely to contribute to the achievement of statutory purposes by regulatory agencies if its objectives are clearly defined by law. Authorization and appropriations legislation and processes should be coordinated to ensure consistency and eliminate duplication. Much of the contentiousness that characterizes oversight relations can be traced to the gap between statutory mandates (which are sometimes vague) and the resources available to agencies. The two branches disagree over the priorities to be followed by the agency, and the amount of discretion it should have, in using its scarce resources. Not only must regulatory agencies compete with one another (and with other agencies) for funds, but Congress may further limit their appropriations because of uncertainty concerning the costs and benefits of regulatory tasks, particularly when the tasks are first assigned. The EPA is continually receiving additional regulatory responsibilities, as new enabling statutes are added and existing ones amended and as technologies change. Although it is in the interest of Congress to make political judgments in setting agency priorities, legislators should give more attention to how the limited resources they allocate are to be used. Their clear expression of agency priorities, combined with some administrative flexibility and discretion, can provide a firm basis for careful oversight.

The kind of oversight the Clean Air Act needs is comprehensive and systematic, not only examining specific instances of implementation, but also evaluating the statutory framework. The oversight hearings and studies of airline regulation and the Civil Aeronautics Board conducted by the Administrative Practice and Procedure Subcommittee of the Senate Judiciary Committee in the mid-1970s are a good example of systematic oversight. The subcommittee reviewed the problems that initially led to government intervention, considered whether the existing laws still provided the appropriate remedy and whether the specific mechanisms of intervention were accomplishing their purposes, and examined implementation by the executive branch. Its findings largely provided the basis for the subsequent deregulation statute.

A New Phase of Policy Making

The enactment of the 1990 Clean Air Act is only the beginning of a new phase of policy making. The debate over the act will, of course, continue. In the two decades that will be required to implement it, there will be continual pressure to weaken its provisions by means of the regulatory review process. States will feel pressure to proceed gingerly with enforcement efforts to avoid harming industry. The EPA will be pressured to ease up on imposing sanctions for noncompliance. The public will lose track of what is happening, particularly when decisions are made by the OMB and the Council on Competitiveness. The grass-roots interest in aggressive legislation will be hard to maintain throughout twenty years of the hard, less glamorous work of developing and implementing regulations. Politicians will continue to make grand speeches promising their commitment to environmental protection, but will lend a sympathetic ear to industry lobbyists who seek to minimize their compliance costs.

The extent to which the 1990 Clean Air Act achieves its goals depends on whether the provisions are stringent enough to reduce or eliminate the regulatory problems at which they are aimed, whether they include sufficient incentives to ensure maximum compliance by state and local governments and regulated industries, and whether state and local governments have the political will to enforce the provisions and to go beyond what is required of them when necessary to achieve the act's goals. Congress can only do so much in writing legislation; it must use its oversight powers and apply continual pressure to make sure that actions taken accord with its intent. The extent to which the EPA and the White House are able to resolve their differences in formulating regulations will also contribute to ensuring effective implementation by the states and compliance by industries and individuals.

One potential cause of concern is that Congress will feel that there is no need to review the Clean Air Act of 1990 and will forget about it and move on to other pressing legislative matters. But the law is complex and detailed, and because it will likely fall short of achieving its goals in several areas, it will need to be amended or to be strengthened by state laws. Its provisions only begin to recognize the potential for reduced motor vehicle emissions. They will need to be reduced further through transportation control measures and increased use of alternative fuels. Congress needs to be thinking now about what to look for in assessing implementation. It needs to go beyond a simple check to ensure that deadlines have been met to a much broader examination to determine whether the main provisions of the Clean Air Act continue to make sense, given the nature and the causes of air pollution.

Detailed statutes have many disadvantages in a situation marked by considerable uncertainty. For example, companies have little incentive to go beyond the minimum required in statutory mandates even though greater pollution reductions may be technically possible. Congress should be realistic in its expectations regarding implementation of the laws and take into account the problems that can result when an agency's mandate exceeds its resources. Ideally, Congress should give the EPA discretion to make adjustments. But because members of Congress distrust the agency, they write increasingly detailed laws. To the EPA's credit, it seems serious about implementing every provision, has outlined its schedule in detail, and seems committed to meeting it.[23]

A Final Note

From a political perspective, the Clean Air Act of 1990 is a success—evidence that divided government can work. The lesson to be learned is that breakthroughs require concentrated effort; they were achieved because the White House gave priority to the issue; Congress held exhaustive, time-consuming congressional negotiations and attended to delicate brokering of interests. But the good will engendered by passage of the legislation will dissipate if the implementation process is complicated by White House attempts to unravel the agreement. The success of this kind of legislative effort may ultimately lie in the ability of Congress and the executive branch to address more effectively the imperatives of implementation and the politics of administration. From a policy perspective, the success is ambiguous. The Clean Air Act of 1990 relies largely on the traditional (command-and-control) approach to regulation, which will probably continue to come under attack. Congress and the executive branch should explore how the weaknesses of this approach can be overcome and whether there is a more effective strategy. Some provisions will become technologically obsolete and will need to be revised. It is not evident that policy makers have the political will to revisit such contentious questions. To a large extent, the future of clean air lies in the hands of state officials. Innovative states will find ways to go beyond the Clean Air Act in devising effective air pollution programs. The impact of the Clean Air Act of 1990 may extend beyond air pollution. Environmental legislation, and clean air laws in particular, have aroused high expectations about the capacity of government to solve pressing problems. When such legislation is not aggressively implemented, because of underfunding, policy disputes, and partisan posturing, the public becomes more cynical about law, politics, and government in general. Members of Congress and the president, in weakening the integrity of law, ultimately reduce its power as a tool for collective problem solving in the common interest.

Notes

1. Philip A. Davis, with Mike Mills and Holly Idelson, "Outcry Greets Bush's Plan To Delay New Rules," *Congressional Quarterly Weekly Report*, January 25, 1992, 164-165.
2. See, generally, Ira C. Magaziner and Robert B. Reich, *Minding America's Business: The Decline and Rise of the American Economy* (New York: Vintage, 1982); and Avinash Dixit and Barry Nalebuff, *Thinking Strategically: The Competitive Edge in Business, Politics, and Everyday Life* (New York: Norton, 1991).
3. Pollution control companies in the United States sold $130 billion worth of equipment in 1991. Worldwide sales reached $370 billion. This country has a positive trade balance with all of its major trading partners for these kinds of products, and the growing awareness of environmental degradation in Eastern Europe and elsewhere will further stimulate demand for pollution control devices. Commerce Department figures cited in Michael Silverstein, "Bush's Polluter Protectionism Isn't Pro-Business," *Wall Street Journal*, May 28, 1992, A19.
4. Keith Schneider, "Bush on the Environment: A Record of Contradictions," *New York Times*, July 4, 1992, A1; Henry A. Waxman, "The Environmental Pollution President," *New York Times*, April 29, 1992, 21.
5. For an interesting critical analysis of the Bush administration in this regard, see "The Cynicism Thing," *The New Republic* 204, no. 25 (June 24, 1991): 9-10.
6. This theme is pursued in many of the essays in Gerald M. Pomper, ed., *The Election of 1988: Reports and Interpretations* (Chatham, N.J.: Chatham House, 1989); see also Michael Nelson, ed., *The Elections of 1988* (Washington, D.C.: CQ Press, 1989).
7. See Executive Order 12291, 46 F.R. 13193 (February 17, 1981); and Office of the Vice President, "Memorandum for Heads of Executive Departments and Agencies," March 22, 1991, from Vice President Quayle reminding agency officials that proposed agency regulations, guidelines, policy manuals, and "press releases and other documents" must satisfy the "benefit-cost requirements of the Executive Order."
8. Executive Order 12291; and Executive Order 12498, 50 F.R. 1036 (January 4, 1985).
9. David Clarke, "Point of Darkness: The White House Council on Competitiveness," *Environmental Forum*, January-February 1992, 31-34; Jonathan Rauch, "The Regulatory President," *National Journal*, November 30, 1991, 2904-2906; Bob Woodward and David S. Broder, "Quayle's Quest: Curb Rules, Leave 'No Fingerprints'," *Washington Post*, January 9, 1992, A1.
10. Marianne Lavelle, "For Bush, A Subtler Approach," *National Law Journal*, May 20, 1991, 32.
11. Ibid., 32-33.
12. Ibid., 33.
13 See, generally, National Academy of Public Administration, *Presidential Management of Rulemaking in Regulatory Agencies* (Washington, D.C.: NAPA, 1987).

14. Office of the Vice President, "Memorandum for Heads of Executive Departments and Agencies."

15. U.S. Congress, House, Committee on Energy and Commerce, Subcommittee on Health and the Environment, *The Vice President's Initiative to Undermine the Clean Air Act,* 102d Cong., 1st sess., May 1, 1991, 2.

16. Clean Air Act Amendments, Pub. L. No. 101-549, 104 Stat. 2399 (November 15, 1990), secs. 502(b)(6) and 505.

17. House Committee on Energy and Commerce, Subcommittee on Health and the Environment, *The Vice President's Initiative,* 2-4.

18. Ann Devroy, "Environmental Presidential Politics," *Washington Post,* national weekly edition, May 4-10, 1992, 14.

19. U.S. Congress, House, Committee on Energy and Commerce, Subcommittee on Health and the Environment, *Inauspicious Beginnings: A Review of the First Year of Implementation of the Clean Air Act of 1990,* 102d Cong., 1st sess., November 14, 1991.

20. With regard to negotiated rule making, see Philip J. Harter, "Negotiating Regulations: A Cure for Malaise," *Georgetown Law Journal* 71 (1982): 1-118; Administrative Dispute Resolution Act of 1990, Pub. L. No. 101-552, 104 Stat. 2736 (November 15, 1990); and Alana S. Knaster and Philip J. Harter, "The Clean Fuels Regulatory Negotiation: Balancing Scientific, Economic, and Political Realities" (unpublished manuscript).

21. For an elaboration of this argument, see National Academy of Public Administration, *Presidential Management* and *Congressional Oversight of Regulatory Agencies* (Washington, D.C.: NAPA, 1988). On the importance of trial-and-error learning in the policy-making process, see Joseph G. Morone and Edward J. Woodhouse, *The Demise of Nuclear Energy? Lessons for Democratic Control of Technology* (New Haven, Conn.: Yale University Press, 1989).

22. It will be interesting to watch the activity of the House Energy and Commerce Committee's Subcommittee on Oversight and Investigations, which is closely controlled by Representative Dingell, an aggressive protector of congressional prerogatives who has, at times, been very critical of the EPA. What will happen when provisions of the Clean Air Act that he cared about during the legislative process are addressed in the making of administrative decisions?

23. Environmental Protection Agency, *Implementation Strategy for the Clean Air Act Amendments of 1990* (Washington, D.C.: EPA, 1991).

Glossary

Some of the key terms used in discussions of air pollution include the following:

ACID DEPOSITION, ACID PRECIPITATION, ACID RAIN. A complex chemical and atmospheric phenomenon that occurs when emissions of sulfur and nitrogen compounds and other substances are transformed by chemical processes in the atmosphere, often far from the original sources, and then deposited on earth in either a wet or a dry form. The wet forms, popularly called "acid rain," can fall as rain, snow, or fog. The dry forms are acidic gases and particulates.

ACUTE. Immediate, brief, and severe—refers to both the duration of exposure to pollutants and the effects of pollutants that follow exposure almost immediately as a direct reaction to it.

AEROSOL. A gas that contains suspended solid particles or droplets of liquid able to stay suspended in air because of their very small size (usually less than 1 micrometer in diameter).

AIR TOXICS. Any air pollutant for which a national ambient air quality standard does not exist (that is, excluding ozone, carbon monoxide, lead, particulate matter, sulfur dioxide, nitrogen dioxide) and that may reasonably be anticipated to cause cancer, developmental effects, reproductive dysfunctions, neurological disorders, heritable gene mutations, or other serious or irreversible chronic or acute health effects in humans.

AROMATICS. A class of high-octane hydrocarbons that currently constitute about 35 percent of gasoline. This percentage has increased in recent years, as refiners have blended more aromatics into gasoline to replace the octane lost as a result of lead reduction. The chief aromatics in gasoline are benzene, toluene, and xylene. The toxicity of benzene has been a cause of concern; in addition, because some aromatics are highly reactive chemically, they are likely to be active in ozone formation.

187

ATTAINMENT AREA.   An area considered to have air quality as good as or better than that required by the national ambient air quality standards as defined in the Clean Air Act. An area may be an attainment area for one pollutant and a nonattainment area for other pollutants.

BENZENE.   A member of the aromatics family that currently constitutes about 1.5 percent of gasoline. The EPA has identified benzene as a carcinogen and has regulated exposure to it in the workplace. The agency is currently considering limitations on the benzene component of motor vehicle emissions.

BEST AVAILABLE CONTROL MEASURE.   As determined by EPA guidelines, the best measures for controlling small or dispersed sources of particulate matter, such as roadway dust, and smoke from woodstoves and open burning.

BUTANE.   A light hydrocarbon added to gasoline to raise octane levels and increase volume. Since butane has high vapor pressure, refiners usually add or remove it to raise or lower the vapor pressure of gasoline. Removal of butane was made necessary by the EPA's imposition of gasoline volatility limits.

CARBON MONOXIDE (CO).   A colorless, odorless gas that is toxic because of its tendency to reduce the oxygen-carrying capacity of the blood.

CHLOROFLUOROCARBONS (CFCs).   A family of inert, nontoxic, and easily-liquefied chemicals used in refrigeration, air conditioning, packaging, and insulation, or as solvents or aerosol propellants. CFCs are not destroyed in the lower atmosphere but drift into the upper atmosphere, where the chlorine is released and destroys ozone. CFC-12 is a chlorofluorocarbon with a trademark name of Freon, commonly used in refrigeration and automobile air-conditioning units.

CHRONIC.   Long-lasting or long-term with reference to either the duration of exposure to a pollutant or the effect of exposure to a pollutant. (Chronic exposure to even low levels of ozone, for example, can result in permanent scarring of the lungs, causing chronic lung disease.)

CLEAN COAL TECHNOLOGY.   Any technology not in widespread use as of the date of enactment of the Clean Air Act Amendments of 1990 that will achieve significant reductions in pollutants emitted in smoke from the burning of coal.

CLEAN FUELS. Mixtures of or substitutes for gasoline fuels; they include compressed natural gas, methanol, and ethanol.

COKE OVEN. An industrial process that converts coal into coke, which is one of the basic materials used in blast furnaces for the conversion of iron ore into iron.

COLD TEMPERATURE CARBON MONOXIDE. A standard for automobile emissions of carbon monoxide to be met at a low temperature (such as 20° F.). Conventional catalytic converters are less efficient when start-up is at low temperatures.

CONTROL TECHNIQUES GUIDELINES. Guidance documents issued by the EPA that define maximum achievable control technology and other technologies to be applied to existing facilities that emit certain threshold quantities of air pollutants. They contain information on the economic and technological feasibility of available techniques.

EMISSION. The discharge of a pollutant from a source into the environment.

EMISSION STANDARD. A legally imposed limit to the amount of a pollutant that can be discharged into the environment from a particular source. Under the Clean Air Act, emissions from existing sources are controlled by the states, which include such provisions in state implementation plans approved by the EPA. The federal government establishes maximum emission standards for new sources of pollution.

ENVIRONMENTAL PROTECTION AGENCY (EPA). The federal agency responsible for issuing and enforcing air quality and emissions regulations and approving state implementation plans. Created by an executive order in 1970, the EPA is also responsible for regulating water pollution, toxic chemical production and use, hazardous waste disposal, solid waste disposal, pesticides, radiation, and noise pollution.

EPIDEMIOLOGY. An investigative approach to disease that seeks to determine the factors that account for its frequency and patterns within defined populations.

ETHANOL. An alcohol produced from starch or sugar crops such as corn and sugar cane. Ethanol can be used as a fuel, as is done in Brazil, or blended into gasoline to boost octane levels and increase volume. In the United States, ethanol is usually blended with gasoline in a 10 percent mixture to form gasohol. As an oxygenate, ethanol supplies oxygen to gasoline, thus reducing motor vehicle carbon monoxide emissions. Ethanol cannot be transported in the same pipelines as gasoline, however, so it must be blended into gasoline outside the refinery. Another problem is that ethanol increases the volatility of gasoline. These drawbacks can be overcome if ethanol is converted to its ether form, ethyl tertiary butyl ether.

ETHYL TERTIARY BUTYL ETHER.   An ether compound formed from ethanol. Although it is not yet produced in commercial quantities, it could be used as a gasoline additive to boost octane levels and provide oxygen. Since it has a low vapor pressure, it would be useful in achieving compliance with volatility controls on gasoline. Unlike alcohols, the compound could be produced and blended with gasoline at the refinery and shipped in gasoline pipelines.

FEDERAL IMPLEMENTATION PLAN.   Under the Clean Air Act of 1990, a federally implemented plan to achieve a national ambient air quality standard, used when a state is unable to develop an adequate plan. A partial federal plan containing control measures developed and promulgated by the EPA may also be issued in order to fill gaps in a state implementation plan.

FLY ASH.   Gas-borne solid particles resulting from the combustion of fuel and other materials.

GASOLINE VOLATILITY.   The property of gasoline that causes it to evaporate into a vapor. It is measured in pounds per square inch, a higher number indicating more gasoline evaporation. Gasoline vapor is a volatile organic compound.

HALONS.   A family of compounds containing bromine that are used in fighting fires whose breakdown in the atmosphere depletes stratospheric ozone.

HCFCs   Chlorofluorocarbons that have been chemically altered by the addition of hydrogen. They are significantly less damaging to stratospheric ozone than other CFCs.

HYDROCARBONS WITH HIGH BOILING POINTS.   Hydrocarbons are compounds of hydrogen and carbon. Many of the hydrocarbons with high boiling points contained in gasoline are very reactive chemically and are thought to contribute to ozone formation. These hydrocarbons are the last to boil away when gasoline is subjected to high temperatures. The group of hydrocarbons being tested by the joint research project of the auto and oil industries is referred to as the "T_{90} Boiling Point Group"; it consists of the 10 percent of hydrocarbons that remain after 90 percent of the gasoline has vaporized.

INSPECTION AND MAINTENANCE. A program for periodic inspections of motor vehicles to ensure that emissions of specified pollutants are not exceeding established limitations. Enhanced inspection and maintenance is an improved program that includes, as a minimum, coverage by vehicle type and model year, more stringent inspections, and improved management practices to ensure effectiveness. It may also include annual, computerized, or centralized inspections; under-the-hood inspections to detect tampering with pollution control equipment; and increased repair waiver cost.

LOW NITROGEN OXIDE BURNERS. One of several combustion technologies used to reduce emissions of nitrogen oxides.

LOWEST ACHIEVABLE EMISSIONS REDUCTION. The most stringent standard for emission control, reflecting the highest degree of control attained by any relevant source, required of new sources built in areas that have not yet met national ambient air quality standards.

MAXIMUM ACHIEVABLE CONTROL TECHNOLOGY (MACT). Emissions limitations based on the best demonstrated control technology or practices used by similar pollution sources to be applied to major sources emitting one or more of the toxic pollutants listed in Title III of the 1990 amendments.

METHANOL. An alcohol made primarily from natural gas. Methanol may be used as a pure (or neat) fuel, in which case it is called M100 (100 percent methanol). Because M100 vehicles are hard to start and are still in the developmental stage, some gasoline is usually added to methanol to form M85 (85 percent methanol and 15 percent gasoline), used in M85 vehicles. Methanol is not currently used as a gasoline additive for several reasons, including its adverse effects on the fuel system components of conventional vehicles. It is widely used as a gasoline additive in its ether form, methyl tertiary butyl ether.

METHYL TERTIARY BUTYL ETHER. An ether compound formed from methanol. It has been widely accepted by refiners as a gasoline additive, and its use has steadily increased in the past several years. As an oxygenate, it supplies oxygen to help reduce carbon monoxide emissions. The compound boosts octane levels but has little effect on vapor pressure. Unlike alcohols, it can be produced and blended with gasoline at the refinery and shipped in gasoline pipelines.

MONTREAL PROTOCOL.   An international environmental agreement, signed by thirty-one nations on September 16, 1987, to control chemicals that deplete the ozone layer. The protocol, which was renegotiated in June 1990, calls for a phase-out of CFCs, halons, and carbon tetrachloride by the year 2000, and a phase-out of chloroform by 2005. It includes provision of financial assistance to developing countries to enable them to make the transition away from use of ozone-depleting substances.

NATIONAL AMBIENT AIR QUALITY STANDARDS.   Limits established by the EPA for a pollutant in ambient (outside) air that are the target in local air quality improvement or protection programs. The primary standard protects public health; the secondary standard protects public welfare. Stricter standards may be established by state governments.

NITROGEN OXIDES (NO_x).   Chemical compounds containing nitrogen and oxygen; in the presence of heat and sunlight, they react with volatile organic compounds to form ozone. They are also a major precursor of acid rain. Nationwide, approximately 45 percent of NO_x emissions come from mobile sources, 35 percent are discharged by electric utilities, and 15 percent are a result of industrial fuel combustion.

OLEFINS.   A group of highly reactive and volatile hydrocarbons that currently constitute about 12 percent of gasoline. Olefins are considered to be likely contributors to ozone formation.

ON-BOARD CONTROLS.   Devices placed on vehicles that capture gasoline vapor during refueling and route it to the engine after the vehicle is started so that it can be efficiently burned.

OXYGENATE.   Any gasoline additive containing oxygen. Oxygen in gasoline tends to reduce motor vehicle carbon monoxide emissions. For this reason, four states (Arizona, Colorado, Nevada, and New Mexico) require the use of oxygenated gasoline during winter months in areas with high levels of carbon monoxide emissions. Oxygenates include the alcohols, such as ethanol and methanol, and the ethers, such as methyl tertiary butyl ether and ethyl tertiary butyl ether. These compounds also boost the octane of gasoline, but their effects on volatility vary.

OXYGENATED FUELS. Gasoline that has been blended with alcohols or ethers that contain oxygen in order to reduce carbon monoxide and other emissions.

OZONE. A compound consisting of three oxygen atoms that is the primary constituent of smog. It is formed as a result of chemical reactions in the atmosphere involving volatile organic compounds, nitrogen oxides, and sunlight. Ozone can cause damage to the lungs as well as to trees, crops, and materials. There is a natural layer of ozone in the upper atmosphere (or stratosphere) that shields the earth from harmful ultraviolet radiation.

PARTICULATE MATTER (PM_{10}). Solid or liquid matter suspended in the atmosphere that is more than 10 micrometers in diameter—a standard of measurement. The smaller particles penetrate to the deeper portions of the lung, affecting sensitive population groups such as children and those suffering from respiratory diseases.

PARTS PER MILLION (ppm). The number of parts of a given substance in one million parts of a mixture by volume.

REASONABLY AVAILABLE CONTROL MEASURES. Technologies (such as reasonably available control technology) and other measures that can be used to control pollution. The term is broadly defined; in the case of particulate matter, it refers to approaches for controlling small or dispersed source categories such as road dust, and smoke from woodstoves and open burning.

REASONABLY AVAILABLE CONTROL TECHNOLOGY. An emissions limitation on existing sources in nonattainment areas, defined by the EPA in a *Control Techniques Guideline* and implemented by the states.

REFORMULATED GASOLINE. Gasoline whose composition differs from that of conventional gasoline (for example, lower aromatics content); it results in the production of lower levels of air pollutants.

REPOWERING. The replacement of an existing coal-fired boiler with one or more clean coal technologies to achieve an emission reduction significantly greater than that produced by technology in widespread use as of the enactment of the Clean Air Act Amendments (November 1990).

RESIDUAL RISK. The threat to health remaining after application of the maximum achievable control technology.

SANCTIONS.   Actions taken by the federal government against a state or local government for failure to formulate or implement a state implementation plan. Examples include withholding of highway funds and a ban on construction of new sources.

SMOG.   A visible combination of smoke and fog (hence the term, coined in Los Angeles). Photochemical smog is the result of the chemical reaction of nitrogen oxides, hydrocarbons, and sunlight.

STAGE II CONTROLS.   Equipment placed on service station gasoline pumps to capture and control gasoline vapors released during automobile refueling.

STATE IMPLEMENTATION PLAN.   A document prepared by each state, and submitted to EPA for approval, which identifies actions and programs to be undertaken by the state and its subdivisions to implement its responsibilities under the Clean Air Act.

SULFUR.   A contaminant found to varying degrees in crude oil. Most of it is removed during refinery processing; the amount remaining in gasoline averages only about 300 parts per million. Industry researchers believe that even this amount may adversely affect the durability of catalyst material in catalytic converters, however.

SULFUR OXIDES (SO_x).   Heavy, pungent, colorless air pollutants made up of sulfur and oxygen that are formed primarily by the combustion of fossil fuels. They are a respiratory irritant, especially for asthmatics, and are a major precursor of acid rain.

SYNERGISM.   A phenomenon in which the effect of a combination of materials is different from (usually greater than) the sum of the separate effects of the individual substances.

THERMAL INVERSION.   An atmospheric meteorological condition in which a layer of warm air acts like a lid and traps a layer of cold air beneath it. This frustrates the normal convection of air upward that occurs when the surface of the earth is heated; the air and any pollutants vented into it are trapped.

TRANSPORTATION CONTROL MEASURES.   Steps taken by a locality to adjust traffic patterns (bus lanes, allowing right turn on red traffic light) or to reduce vehicle use (ride sharing, high-occupancy vehicle lanes) to reduce vehicular emissions of air pollutants.

VARIANCE.   Permission by a legal body for a company or an individual to operate outside the limits prescribed by a law or standard. Industries often apply for and are granted variances to exceed air quality regulations.

VEHICLE MILES TRAVELED.   A measure of both the volume and extent (within a specified geographical area during a given period) of motor vehicle operation.

VOLATILE ORGANIC COMPOUNDS (VOCs).   A group of chemicals that react with nitrogen oxides in the atmosphere in the presence of heat and sunlight to form ozone; includes gasoline fumes and oil-based paints but does not include methane and other compounds determined by the EPA to have negligible photochemical reactivity.

Source: Environmental Protection Agency, *The Clean Air Act Amendments of 1990: Summary Materials* (Washington, D.C.: EPA, November 15, 1990); Charles E. Kupchella and Margaret C. Hyland, *Environmental Science: Living within the System of Nature* (Boston: Allyn & Bacon, 1989); and General Accounting Office, *Gasoline Marketing: Uncertainties Surround Reformulated Gasoline as a Motor Fuel*, RCED-90-153 (Washington, D.C.: GAO, June 1990), 17-19.

Index

Methyl chloroform, 127
Methyl tertiary butyl ether, 191-192
Mitchell, George, 80, 92, 94, 100-106, 109, 143, 169
Mobile sources, 125-126
Molina, Mario J., 71
Monitoring, costs of, 12-13
Monsanto, 15, 151
Montreal Protocol on Substances That Deplete the Ozone
    Layer, 74-75, 111-112, 127, 148, 192
Motor vehicle emissions, 81-85, 96, 112, 125, 149-150
Mulroney, Brian, 95
Muskie, Edmund S., 83

NAAQS. *See* National ambient air quality standards
NASA (National Aeronautics and Space Administration), 74
National Academy of Sciences, 152
National ambient air quality standards (NAAQS), 42, 44, 103, 150-154, 192. *See also* Ambient air pollutants
National Association of Manufacturers, 147, 154-159
National Clean Air Coalition, 87, 95, 103-105, 146, 170
National Commission on Air Quality, 86
National parks, 114
National Wildlife Federation, 87
Natural Resources Defense Council, 87
New Source Performance Standards, 122-123
New York Times, 30
Nitrogen dioxide, 42, 59
Nitrogen oxides, 45, 69, 127, 192
Nitrous oxides, 71
Nixon, Richard, 82-83, 84
Nonattainment provisions, 103, 123-125
Nuclear Regulatory Commission, 87

Occupational Safety and Health Administration (OSHA), 65
Office of Drinking Water, 171
Office of Information and Regulatory Affairs, 173

Office of Management and Budget (OMB), 25-27, 30-31, 87, 95, 134, 173-174, 178
Office of Policy Analysis, 30
Office of Policy Evaluation, 171
Office of Technology Assessment, 30, 52, 68, 100
Office of Toxic Substances, 171
Olefins, 192
OMB. *See* Office of Management and Budget
Omenn, Gilbert, 28
On-board controls, 192
Oxygenated fuels, 193
Oxygenates, 192
Ozone, 42-43, 45, 51-53, 59, 125, 193. *See also* Stratospheric ozone layer

PACs (political action committees), 93
Particulate matter, 42-43, 53-56, 193
Parts per million (ppm), 193
PCB (polychlorinated biphenyl), 10-11
Penalties, 156-158
Permit system, 21-22, 103, 127, 154-159, 176-178
Photochemical oxidants, 52
Photochemical smog, 42
Policy-making process, 3-5, 182-183. *See also* Environmental policy making
Political action committees (PACs), 93
Political coalitions, 137-144
Pollutants, 42-43. *See also* Ambient air pollutants; Toxic air pollutants
Pollution control costs, 9-10, 12-13
Pollution fees, 22
Pollution Prevention Act of 1990, 14
Pollution taxes, 22
Polychlorinated biphenyl (PCB), 10-11
Polystyrene foam products, 149
Porter, Roger, 111
Portney, Paul, 28
Powell, Jimmie, 99
PPM (parts per million), 193
Presidential Task Force on Regulatory Relief, 25, 168, 173
Prevention of significant deterioration, 85-86
Primary standards, 121
Public health, 6-8
Public Health Service, 30, 81